Get the Edge at Craps

A Scoblete Get-the-Edge Guide

Get the Edge at Craps

How to Control the Dice!

by Sharpshooter

Foreword by Frank Scoblete

bonus books

Chicago and Los Angeles

06 05 04 03   5 4 3 2

Library of Congress Control Number: 2002112239
ISBN: 1-56625-173-7

Bonus Books
160 East Illinois Street
Chicago, Illinois 60611

Printed in the United States of America

To the other members of the original "Rosebud" dice team: Long Arm, Guardian, High-5, and 007. They studied, practiced, excelled, and pushed this Sharpshooter to perform at his peak, nearly all the time!

Table of Contents

Foreword

by Frank Scoblete

Roll this idea over in your mind: Craps can be beaten! It can be beaten legally and within the established rules of the game as set down by the casinos.

When I started flirting with that idea in the 1980s, I felt like a lone voice crying in the wilderness. I knew I was taking a dangerous plunge into uncharted waters as no credible gaming writer ever seriously entertained the notion that craps was a beatable game. After all, I was writing about concepts of play, developed by the Captain (see my books *Beat the Craps Out of the Casinos, The Captain's Craps Revolution!,* and *Forever Craps*), that had never been seriously discussed before and that had, as their underpinnings, the very radical concept that some players could physically alter the game of craps to favor them by the nature of their rolls. The Captain referred to these players as "rhythmic rollers."

The Captain came upon his ideas from direct observation over a career that has spanned the life of Atlantic City as a gaming town. As someone who played several days a week, every week, and for substantial sums, and as someone who was keenly aware of his surroundings, the Captain slowly began to realize that the shooters who tended to have the better rolls were those who did two things:

1. set the dice in a certain, predetermined way before rolling, and
2. delivered the dice very softly so that they just touched the back wall and died without much hopping, skipping, and bounding all over the table.

The Captain, to my knowledge, was the first to coin the phrase "rhythmic roller," the first to understand that some rhythmic rollers were conscious of what they were doing and had deliberately, through trial and error and practice, developed a shooting style that changed a game with a small house edge on some bets to a game that could slightly favor the player. He also articulated the idea that other rhythmic rollers were "unconscious rhythmic rollers," that is, they too had developed a set and delivery, again through trial and error, but were not fully cognizant that they had altered the game, but shot as they did because they had gotten "pretty good results."

I became increasingly more interested in rhythmic rolling in the late 1980s and early 1990s. I had developed my own set in 1990, the 3V, sometimes called the "Flying V," (one craps player referred to me as "the Father of the Flying V"— hey, it's not like being the "father of our country" but I'll take it!), and I shot a soft, underhand shot. I had decent results with this technique, although I never really kept track of the actual numbers I was hitting, just the money I made (or lost) on my rolls. By the mid-1990s, I flirted with an even better way to roll the dice using an overhand method, the method the Captain used. My preferred position was immediate stick right. I would switch back and forth between the underhand roll and the overhand roll, depending on which was serving me the best at any particular time, but gradually I made the switch to overhand—I just had better rolls overall with that method.

My dice set remained the 3V and with this I gradually realized that I had certain "signature" numbers: 4, 6, and 8. With great confidence in my rolling ability, I would go right up on these numbers, not use the 5-Count to "qualify" myself. The results have been good.

Although my craps books have sold an impressive number of copies over the years, countless legions of craps players playing in American casinos are hardly aware that a new and potent weapon has been introduced into the players' arsenal; that this weapon and the theory behind this weapon have existed for over a decade now. And that's a good thing for those of you reading this book. Very few players are "deliberate" rhythmic rollers so learning to utilize this skill will not, as of now, make you a pariah in the casinos the way learning how to expertly count cards will.

It's a Physical Ability, Stupid!

Critics of rhythmic rolling or rhythm rolling or precision shooting or controlled shooting or dice influencing (it goes by a host of names) contend that the casinos have set into place measures that make it impossible for players to affect the outcome of their own rolls. The shooter must roll the dice so that they hit the back wall, where foam-rubber pyramids deflect the dice, effectively randomizing them. In addition, all the bets at the game have a long-run negative expectation when the game is random. These two factors make the game unbeatable.

The critics observations sound good, but upon closer observation, their arguments are specious. First, the foam-rubber pyramids, while formidable (or is that "foam-idable"?), do not preclude a successful rhythmic roll. When we say the dice "must hit the back wall," there is no rule as to how hard they must do so. A soft delivery system will often see the dice barely touching those pyramids, making the randomizing effect much less potent. By setting the dice in certain ways and making such a soft delivery, a player can indeed affect the outcome of his or her rolls.

A critic might just jump in here now and say: "Is this just Scoblete's opinion or is it a fact? Scoblete's ideas are just wishful thinking."

It's a fact. It's not a fact because I want to believe it is a fact; it is a fact because enough players have now documented their rolls based on something called an SSR (Seven-to-

Rolls-Ratio) during thousands and even tens of thousands of casino and practice sessions to show us clearly that, with the proper sets and deliveries, they are able to play with a 1:6.5, 1:7, 1:7.5, and 1:8 (and higher) Seven-to-Rolls Ratio. A random game, where the casino has the edge on every bet, is 1:6!

Rhythmic rolling is a fact.

Enter Sharpshooter

Although the Captain was the first to talk about rhythmic rolling, he is not the one who developed the teachable art and science of it. All great discoveries start with a visionary (in this case, the Captain), but it takes the practical genius who can see the worth of a vision to figure out how to make that vision workable for the rest of us. That practical genius is Sharpshooter.

One glaring thing I noticed playing with the Captain and his crew for many years was this: Only one crew member, Jimmy P., now deceased, ever fully played as the Captain did. The rest never bothered to employ the 5-Count, and never bothered to work on their sets and deliveries, despite being with the Captain and seeing him win for all those years. I'd always ask myself why? Why don't these guys see what's right in front of their faces?

Now, I think I finally know why. Two reasons, really. The first is simply that most craps players are not aware of what is happening right in front of their faces. They don't notice what the other players are doing all that much. Most craps players are watching out for their own bets and looking to see what number was just rolled—not how the shooter was delivering it. The Captain never really bothered to impose his views on his crew and he would discuss dice only if asked (needless to say I asked and kept on asking).

The second reason is also pretty obvious to me now. Most people do not learn by observation, since most people are bad observers. They learn through rote, that is, physical and/or mental memorization. In short, they have to be taught. They can be taught by a book, by a demonstration, by a teacher—but they rarely can learn things that have not been discovered previously. In short, very few of us can figure out something new. The Captain did. But he was not able to get his closest friends to see craps the same way because he never bothered to take them by the hand and lead them.

But somewhere in the mid-1990s, a young man named Sharpshooter, through reading and his own keen observations, developed his own methods for setting and delivering the dice (one of the dice sets he recommends is my own 3V). Unlike me, who used the casino environment as my learning landscape and money won/lost as my ledger, the brilliant Sharpshooter took a trained engineer's mind and applied it to what he calls "a problem in physics" before he started to put his money on the line. He studied all the possible "presets" of the dice; the various permutations the dice could go through when heading from point A to point B in the air; how the dice could bounce, and so forth. After this exhaustive study, he came up with his best methods of setting and delivering the dice to get an edge for the player—and documented them! These methods he teaches in his and Jerry Patterson's PARR classes.

These methods work. They are the practical application of a physical theory. Learn the application as Sharpshooter teaches it, and you'll be able to beat the game of craps—at least when you roll.

The Fatigue Factor

Those pesky critics will say: "Okay, I can do a billion simulations on my computer to show that card counting works and prove it beyond a shadow of a doubt. Can you do that with craps?"

Well, to be cute, you could. Just program in a SRR of 1:8 and see what happens in a billion decisions. But that still doesn't tell you if someone can do it in the real, physical world of casino play. Instead, to prove rhythmic rolling, you have to have a human being set and deliver the dice over and over again—until he gets tired. And he will get tired. Roger Clemens and Randy Johnson are great pitchers, with outstanding control, but after 1,000 pitches in a row, both of these guys will be in deep trouble. There's a good chance that on the next ten throws, I'd be able to throw more strikes than they. Does that mean they are just ordinary? Obviously not. They merely overextended themselves.

So "proving" rhythmic rolling is not as simple as a blackjack computer simulation. But it is not impossible. I find that I can do approximately 160 rolls in a row before the fatigue factor settles in and I get sloppy—sloppy enough to not have any more control over the dice than a random roller. Most of the documentation of craps rolls that I previously mentioned were not done in one orgy of rolling, but over extended sessions, each lasting from 30 to 300 rolls. In fact, practicing in short sessions is a very good strategy, as casino craps will often see you at the table with other shooters. Like a pitcher, you aren't playing every half of an inning and like a batter, you aren't continuously at bat for nine innings. There's a lot of wait-time in craps.

Over time those 30 to 300 roll sessions will add up to tens of thousands of rolls and you'll be able to clearly see whether your dice set and delivery are indeed changing the nature of the edge in your favor.

What About Those Other Shooters?

The biggest problem that all craps players face is—other craps players! As facetious as this sounds, other craps players are the reason why even some of the best rhythmic rollers will end up in the red when they play. As a good shooter, you might be rolling with a 1:7 SRR, but you'll be facing all those random rollers—at a full table maybe 12 to 14 of them. You can't really hope to win playing such a game. Take this to the bank (for a withdrawal): If you bet on every shooter, even if you have a slight advantage when you roll, you will ultimately lose.

My recommendation is to use the 5-Count on those other players. It will eliminate approximately 50 percent of the other shooters, those who are not going to have good rolls by definition, and only risk money on the remaining shooters, among whom will be all those few-and-far-between great rolls. In that way, at a crowded table, you will be able to have a rhythmic roller (you!) being one of every six or seven shooters who rolls. That definitely increases your chances to get away with the money!

Better still, I would recommend that you use my Five-Step Method from *Forever Craps* to determine on whom to bet.

The Bottom Line

The book you hold in your hands is the definitive book on rhythmic rolling. It is a breakthrough book. The remarkable Sharpshooter has sifted and refined all the physical elements of advantage-play craps—the set, the grip, and the delivery—and all the elements of the mental game—the proper bets and mind set—to give you the most powerful weapon for beating the casinos at their own game.

To conclude: Craps can be beaten! It can be beaten legally and within the established rules of the game as set down by the casinos. Read this book carefully. It is a road map to victory!

Introduction

Imagine walking up to a craps table and knowing that you have a good shot at creating a "hot table." By using your skill, you can expect to generate a 15- or 20-minute roll most times you touch the dice. It's a great feeling. At one instance at Bally's in Vegas, I was laying the foundation for a monster roll. After keenly grooving in, I began to accurately predict what I would throw next. After successfully calling the second hop bet for my throw, one stickman off-handedly remarked, "You must have ESPN." However, after watching my routine, it became apparent that skill and coordination were responsible, not my ability to forecast. After accurately calling four hop bets, no less, I had the boxman across from me intently looking on. One supervisor was stationed where the dice were landing near the back wall. A second was about five feet away, to my right, probably making sure that I wasn't switching dice. The pit boss and some 80-year-old in a suit were standing behind the boxman and conversing. The old guy was waving his pen in the air and explaining something to the pit boss as I was shooting. . The dice went through identical motions when I threw them. The right die was the perfect mirror image of the left die as they arced and rotated in perfect synchronicity. It took me years of development and practice to fine-tune my throw to this point.

The pit did not try to break my rhythm or directly speak to me. They were more intrigued with my ritual of dice setting and my well-practiced delivery. After making my fifth point pass, I felt supreme confidence. I was able to tune out all distractions and focus purely on my dice delivery. At one point, I awoke from my trance when people were pushing to squeeze in at the table and jostled me a bit, but I very quickly recaptured my hypnotic state. As I announced my next hop bet to the stick, scores of red and green chips appeared in front of the boxman, all wanting the same bet. The other more conservative players would place the same numbers that I had placed . . .the 5, 6, 8, and 9. The pit looked apprehensive and many bystanders were watching. After calling another hard 8, and making my point, all bets were paid and then something happened that I never saw before. *The pit actually closed down the table!* The resentful and indignant players were instructed to play at the other tables (all full) across the pit.

After this little stunt, I ceased advertising to the rest of the table what I intended to throw next. There is no sense in calling unnecessary attention to yourself, even if it is just by calling hop bets. This is just one of countless experiences I have enjoyed after perfecting my throw. It is wonderful to say the least and makes you feel like some kind of a folk hero. How do I do it? The quick answer is *consistency* based on the laws of rigid body mechanics. It involves controlling certain degrees of freedom and eliminating others from the motion of the dice. A well-practiced delivery along with the appropriate dice set can tilt the game in the shooter's favor. In this book, I will share with you all of the secrets for developing your own controlled throw.

Let me introduce myself. My teammates know me as "Sharpshooter" and I have been beating the casinos for close to a decade on a regular basis. I've trained and assembled a dice team along with someone I'll call "Long Arm" and we've been averaging over 62 percent return on bankroll per trip. I realize that some players may not believe that this is possible, but that is fine. The more people who believe and become proficient at doing this, the more countermeasures the casinos will employ. Permit me to share with you a little bit regarding what I do to win consistently. I am what some might call a *rhythm roller* or *controlled thrower*. The casino personnel often refer to me as a dice mechanic. Some of the grizzled craps veterans have discovered, over years of play, that the right dice set coupled with a consistent delivery can tilt the edge in the player's favor. Many of these old timers do not understand the mechanics behind what they are doing; they only know (through trial and error) that they have found a means to garner an edge by playing this way. My background, both academically and professionally, is grounded in two of the engineering disciplines. I can tell you that there is a scientific basis for what is happening.

The game of craps cannot be beaten mathematically of course. Any system that has you size your next wager based upon whether you lost or won the previous bet, or has you believing in "The Law of Large Numbers" or "Due Theory" in a game of independent trials (like craps or roulette) is a mathematical system. Save your time and, more importantly, your bankroll. The way to attack the game of craps is by altering the physical phenomena of the event when you shoot the dice. By applying the laws that govern rigid body mechanics (found in any Newtonian physics or engineering dynamics handbook), you can eliminate certain degrees of freedom from the parabolic trajectory of the dice and affect some positive amount of control over the remaining degrees of freedom that the cubes experience. The cubes can possibly traverse three translational and three rotational degrees of freedom.

I will show you how to eliminate some of these ranges of motion and synchronize the remaining ones. Both dice will exit from your hand at precisely the same time. They will simultaneously travel the same parabolic trajectory and experience the same gyrations, side-by-side. The dice will land, bounce and come to rest together. Utilizing the grip and delivery that I will share with you, you will be surprised at the level of influence you will impart upon the dice. My personal delivery eliminates three degrees of freedom (DOFs) and greatly influences the remaining three. In addition, other issues regarding conservation of momentum, elastic collisions, angles of reflectance, and other mechanical details are accounted for. My controlled throw does an excellent job of factoring in all of these phenomena; however, it must be exercised in the proper manner.

I believe that every craps player, sufficiently motivated, can develop the skill necessary to attain an advantage over the casino. That advantage may be small or moderate, depending upon the level of skill acquired through study, practice, and discipline. This skill can be measured by your ability to avoid the dreaded 7 during the point cycle. If one 7 occurs every six throws on average, then you are shooting random and the house will enjoy its customary mathematical edge. Even if you can average one 7 every six-and-a-half throws, you will enjoy a large advantage on the Pass Line and 6, 8 Place bets. I will show you how you calculate your Sevens-to-Rolls Ratio (or SRR for shorthand notation) and then calculate your edge for some of the more popular wagers. How many rolls you average before throwing a 7 will depend on your efforts and level of mastery. Before we begin our journey, let's briefly examine the basic elements you will learn about in this book.

The foundation for your craps delivery mechanics is based on three elements:

The Dice Sets—These are your consistent starting points and will vary depending upon your objective for that throw (i.e. coming out vs. making the point).

The Dice Grip—It is important that you pick up and grip the dice such that they do not move or shift in your hand, yet easily and comfortably will exit your hand when you go to release them.

The Controlled Throw—An easy, consistent delivery system that maintains relationship between the dice when you set them. The dice should travel together, land together, and bounce together.

Other elements that you should address after mastering the controlled throw are:

Betting Strategies and Money Management—You can wrestle a subtle edge away from the casino through physical means, but you must stick to the lower house edge bets. In addition, your method of betting will be ultra-conservative when random throwers have the dice.

A Sense of Confidence and the Ability to Keenly Focus— Being tense or anxious causes involuntary muscle movements that will disrupt your consistency. You should remain calm, comfortable, and confident when shooting the dice.

All five elements are necessary to fully exploit your sharpshooter craps advantage. You will learn how each of these fits into to your craps arsenal and how to develop these tools for a comprehensive attack on the game.

I visit the casinos some 40 to 50 times a year, and I have documented much of my play in my "pro-play journal." I have enough statistical proof to put me over three standard deviations to the right of the mean (99.85 percent confidence range). I also have slow motion videos of my throw where you can see exactly how the dice are reacting in unison. I have half a craps table set up in my dinning room where I practice about 45 minutes a day. What do I practice? . . . a consistent delivery system. You can liken it to playing just about any sport. Much like the pro-athlete who works on his delivery system for his particular sport, I practice my dice sets, my carefully balanced grip, and soft release. After I release the dice, they travel side-by-side and go through identical motions. They land together, hitting the table flat, then taking what I call a "dead cat bounce" up just grazing the rubber pyramidal backing and quickly coming to rest. In fact, as the dice travel and land side-by-side, it looks as though only one die was thrown along the length of a mirror, and the second die is just its reflection. The key is to get both dice going through the same gyrations. You are developing and using what pro athletes refer to as your "muscle memory" to breed consistency in your throw. Each time you grip and throw the dice, your brain will remember exactly every movement that your muscles should be making. As your brain processes that information, your muscles are instructed to execute the precise and intricate maneuvers needed to duplicate the delivery.

How you are able to handle the casino environment is also important. Playing in the casinos is analogous to always playing "away games." You are the visiting team and will have to develop a thick skin. There is a mental aspect to the game that is critical and the casinos are pros at knocking a skilled thrower "off his game." Like the athlete, you have to work on staying in the zone once you've found it, and maintaining a keen focus when you are shooting. I will give you the lecture about not playing while feeling tired, sick, hungry, depressed, or under the influence. We will discuss proper money management and the importance of documentation as well. We will look at calculating our edge for various bets based on our Sevens-to-Rolls Ratio and selecting the betting tactics that make the most sense for our bankroll and objectives.

I would like to acknowledge a few individuals who helped shape the scope of this book. Several years ago, I had been working quietly on my dice control skills, privately enjoying my spoils. I did not intend to share my techniques. My good friend Jerry P., also known as "Long Arm," a major gaming author and instructor, encouraged me to compare notes, organize them and work with him to teach this methodology to clients in his network. I had also been corresponding quite frequently with Frank Scoblete, who is arguably the most prolific gaming writer today. Frank was able to convince me to write the very book you are holding. Without these two gentlemen, you would not be reading these words right now! I also would like to acknowledge Eric N., or the "Guardian," who worked together with me to develop the "perfect pitch" delivery system. This is a basic component in our approach to controlled throwing. Robin F. (High-5) and Donnie B. (007) round out the rest of my posse.

Their dedication to being the best shooters, beta testing most of the new concepts and eventually assisting me as instructors, is greatly appreciated. You will read more about Donnie's dinosaur rolls a little later. I'd also like to thank Christopher Pawlicki, a fellow author and a real math wizard, who completed all the calculations for this book.

Can you control the bones 100 percent? . . . No, but with the proper methodology and a fair amount of practice, you certainly can *influence* the dice 10 or 12 percent! If you stick with the more intelligent wagers on the table, you can easily overcome the thin house edge in this game. Do the casinos let you shuffle and deal your own blackjack hand? No way! How about kicking up the rotor to some practiced speed and sniping out your heavily bet sector on the roulette wheel? Hell no! Craps is the only game where you, as the shooter, deal your own fate. *You* directly determine the results and that is why I feel it is the best game offered in the casino. Some folks may believe that I'm just circulating the air with this talk, but tell that to the many casinos who show me the door whenever I walk in. Folks, my days of strolling right to any open table I fancy and having a roll are numbered. Using the concepts and techniques I will now share with you, your years are just beginning. This is your book. Read, study, practice, and enjoy your advantage!

Part One
Getting Started

Chapter 1

A Cast of Characters and Their Props

Craps is the most exciting of any game in the casino. No other game offers the same dynamics and exhilaration. It is fast and furious, but it can also be intimidating for the novice. For one thing, the betting layout is a hodge-podge of different bets, with various payouts and different rules applying. Some of these bets are placed by the players and others are positioned by one of the three dealers at the table. Then there is the strange vernacular all these people speak. Some guy in the middle, sporting a flexible stick, starts barking something about Hard Ways, Any Craps, and C and Es and the players start screaming and throwing chips at the guy. Then the dice are pushed over to some quiet-looking player in the corner who snatches them up in his hand and starts shaking them as if his life depended on it. As he lets them fly, he belts out a loud, "Y-O-O-O-LEVEN!!" A 5 and 6 both appear and the table erupts into a frenzy! You hear frantic instructions like, "Press my yo," "Make my eleven look like a quarter," and bettors wanting the Horn-High yo or World bets. It's enough to scare the be-Jesus out of any newbie. The action is wild, but it's also addictive. Once our novice tiptoes in and gets his feet a little wet, he will probably be hooked for life. Let's talk about those two cubes and how they determine the fate of our wagers.

The Dice

Dice, or some form of them, have been around for thousands of years. I'm not going into an extended version of their history, but a very quick discussion might be helpful. Early dice were fashioned from sticks, clay, ivory, and the ankle bones of sheep. They were used for fortune telling. Tribal leaders cast dice to determine when to plant crops, war with neighboring tribes, or relocate. Later in history, dice were used in Greece, Rome, and ancient Egypt. Some types of dice were discovered in Asia and even in the Americas. Rolling them bones is probably the oldest form of gambling. The dice game of "Hazard" emerged in England around the 1100s and was popular until the 1800s. Private craps evolved in the 1800s with rules very similar to today's game. In modern times (last 75 years or so), manufacturing of precision die-cast dice that were finished to extremely fine tolerances became possible. The dimensions, squareness of faces and corners, proper balance, and consistent finishes are all very important in creating a "fair" pair of dice.

The game seemed to enjoy a high degree of popularity around the time leading up to the Second World War. Illegal casinos, many with mob influences, were in their heyday. Even in the streets and back alleys of big eastern cities, wise guys and hustlers set up and ran illegal dice games—and usually with crooked dice. Those that couldn't make money fast enough with the mathematical edge inserted *shapes* or *loads* into the game. Shapes are dice that are not true cubes. Sometimes called *flats* or *bricks*, these dice have faces that are trimmed down to resemble a brick. The two faces on the ends are less likely to result because they have less surface area to land on and a higher relative center of gravity. Try tossing a brick down the sidewalk to see how many times you can get it to land standing up. Loads are exactly what the name implies, certain combinations of faces are cleverly weighted down, causing the other faces to have a higher relative center of gravity and a better chance of turning over. The faces that are opposite the loaded faces will have a higher percentage of resulting, or ending up on top.

Some old-timers from WWII and Korean War days talk of running private games on ship decks and behind mess halls. I first became interested in casino craps in the early 1990s when I was a serious blackjack player. I heard stories of guys pulling down figures from one craps session that were equivalent to a month's worth of my laborious efforts at card counting. One colorful WWII veteran that I met, relayed stories of banking such games behind the army barracks. The games he ran were simple. You either bet with or against the shooter. There were no odds, Come bets or Place bets . . . not even a table or betting layout. In many cases an old army blanket was laid out to serve as a playing surface. This particular vet, who became a minor celebrity, made enough money from his dice games to buy and manage his own Harlem nightclub after the war. Although most of the money was made by banking these games, a select few were able to beat the game by influencing the dice as they cast them. These skilled shooters would preset the dice and carefully let them roll out of their open hand. The dice would hit the blanket at the same time and roll together like cartwheels, end-over-end, down the blanket. Certain numbers would remain on the "hubs" of the wheels while the "tread" numbers would stay aligned to each other. When executed properly, the roll was fairly affective at diminishing or even removing certain possibilities from the outcome. These types of shooters were often referred to as "blanket rollers."

Eventually, the game made its way out of the back rooms of illegal gambling joints and on to the main floor of the casino. Dice tables were set up and the cubes had to be thrown to the far end where they interacted with the back wall. Other types of shots were developed and the casinos initiated counter measures. One such shot, mastered by some well-practiced shooters, was called the *spinshot* or the *helicopter shot*. The skilled thrower would set his number on top, and slide the dice in such a way that they spun about a vertical axis. Their set number would stay on top and the side numbers would rotate around without the dice actually turning over. It sounds like it would be easy to spot, but I witnessed one individual who could whip and spin them fast enough to make it look convincing. This guy could throw the dice onto a low coefficient of friction surface, like a Formica countertop, with padded walls and the dice would slide and rebound off at least three walls very quickly without ever turning over. This skilled individual could call and throw his number better than 90 percent of the time on his special table. The dice seemed so lively; it was very difficult to tell that they were sliding the whole time.

Casino tables were modified over 25 years ago to thwart the slider. Thicker wool layouts with hard rubber tabletop coatings underneath, instead of just very hard wood under a thin layer of wool, all work to cause the dice to turn over. Another innovation is the use of heavy strings embedded under the wool layout, running across the width of the table near the proposition bets. These strings act like speed bumps, blocking the bottom of each die while forcing the top to roll over them, hence the slide is broken and the dice tumble. A little later I'll share my controlled technique that I've specially developed for the modern dice table. It employs the same basic idea as the blanket roll, but the dice need not roll or slide all the way from your hand down the table to the back wall. The dice will be thrown through the air and upon landing, will tumble end-over-end to the back wall, thus qualifying as a legal shot. You do not need to have the coordination of a professional athlete or the accuracy of a diamond cutter to be successful. What's necessary is maybe 10 percent influence on the result, not 90 percent control. This level of control does not take years to master. It will enhance your craps enjoyment, add several percentage points to your game, and if you stick to the more intelligent wagers (lower house edge bets), you can actually make money on a regular basis. I have been doing this and so too have many of the students that I have personally trained.

The Tables

Unfortunately, the casinos would rather have two jam-packed tables, instead of four half-filled tables in operation. I can't argue with their reasoning—why pay four crews of dealers when two are able to handle all the action. Your typical craps player loves camaraderie and will look for loud, full tables where people seem to be winning. As a "skilled thrower," your mindset will be different. You will find yourself looking for sparse or even empty tables where you will get more opportunities to shoot. We'll discuss some techniques for playing empty tables in Chapter 10's "Playing Variations." Generally, the tables are eight to 14 feet long and 42" wide. The table surface is 28" high with another 12" to the chip rail. The surface or playing area is covered with a wool fabric, usually green in color. The green layout is soothing to the eye and provides a subtle contrast so that bets placed can be easily seen. The betting layout has a side-to-side symmetry so that any player can view and access all possible bets. A typical table will comfortably accommodate 12 to 16 players. There are over 30 different bets that can be made, but only four combinations of bets will yield less than a one percent edge for the house. It's amazing how many people will drive across town to save five cents a gallon on gas and then belly up to a craps table and routinely make the most horrendous wagers on the table; wagers with 13.889 percent or even 16.667 percent casino advantage.

When you first approach the tables, you will notice different colored placards mounted on the opposite inside walls near the dealers. These cards state the minimum betting requirements (minimum unit size) for that table at that particular time. Tables may have limits as low as $1 or $2 betting units usually shown on white placards (downtown Vegas). The red cards denote $5 minimums, with blue sometimes indicating $10 and orange for $15 table minimums. Green is displayed to show $25, brown for $50, and black for $100 minimum bet sizes. Anything over $100 minimums for each bet is usually by special request and reserved for mega-rollers. The game is played with casino checks (called chips by the players). These checks are typical house chips that come in $1 whites, or "dollars," $5 reds (often called "nickels"), green $25 chips (referred to as "quarters"), $100 blacks called "checks," purple $500, orange $1,000, and the sometimes seen gray $5,000 denominations.

Just after the bets from the last roll are paid, you can buy in. Place your cash down in the Come box and announce, "Change only please" to obtain chips with which to bet. Do not attempt to hand money directly to the dealer. The first chance the dealer has, he will slide the currency over to the boxman who spreads it out as he counts it, announces the amount, and pushes it through a slot in the table with a plastic or acrylic paddle. The dealer will count out an equivalent amount of chips and slide them over to you. Pick up your chips and place them in the arm rail down in front of you. Just as a side note, always keep an eye on your chips. There are rail thieves who make their living stealing chips off the ends of their neighbor's stacks! If you saw the movie *Casino* you will recall Sharon Stone's character stealing $500 chips in this manner from her high roller escort. By the way, if you like Vegas or mob movies and have not seen it, clear off a three-hour block one evening and rent it. It's a true story based on the mob's "Lefty" Rosenthal who ran the Stardust Casino back in the '70s and early '80s.

When I place my chips in the rack, I like to organize them into similar colors, or denominations and break them down into stacks of five. I alternate them with one stack standing and the next one laying, or on its side. That way I'll notice right away if some chips are missing and I can quickly and easily take inventory of how well I am doing at that table. If you wish to buy in and place a wager at the same time, then place your cash in the Come box and announce which bet and the amount you wish to stake. For example, if you wish to bet on the Pass Line, drop your money and announce, "Ten dollars on the Pass." The dealer will reply something like, "Ten dollars say they do. That's a bet sir," and you know you are in the action. The dealer should acknowledge your bet in some manner. After the dice are thrown, the bet will be settled and the remainder of your buy in will be placed in front of you.

Try to buy in before the dice are passed back to the shooter for his next throw. If the shooter should throw the dice and hit your hand as you are buying in, you will very quickly feel the heat from the rest of the players. Most craps players are superstitious; they believe that a 7 will appear if the dice strike someone's hand after they are thrown. A 7 during the point cycle, will wipe out everyone's Pass Line, Come, Place bets, etc. Sticking your hand out in the impending path of the dice *will* alter their outcome. If the dice hit your hand and a 7 shows up, you would probably want to leave that table; unless you welcome the icy stares, the negative pub, and even the blatant threats thrown your way. There is another element to consider. The shooter may be a controlled thrower and anything that destroys the dice set, or relationship established between the two dice, will be detrimental to the outcome. Whether the dice hit someone's hand or the chips that are positioned out on the table, chances are great that they will be knocked off their axis of rotation and out of synch with each other. Hence, if you hear the dealers or other players yelling, "hands high," you should immediately (if not sooner) withdraw your hand from the playing area.

If you have established credit with the casino, you can request a marker or IOU for any amount up to your credit limit. A floorman with a pen and small clipboard will come over so you can sign your marker. You will get a copy for your personal records. If you wish to establish credit with a casino, talk to a casino host before you play. Be prepared to disclose pertinent financial information about yourself. At the very minimum, they will require a checking account number that contains a balance equal to or exceeding the credit amount you are requesting. Having casino credit can be convenient. You will not have to worry about carrying large amounts of money around and you will be better able to get the comps, or complimentary services, you deserve. However, with that privilege comes the responsibility of betting with your brain and not your emotions. If you are not a disciplined gambler, then forego the credit and don't worry so much about comps. I could tell you dozens of stories where rated players blew an extra $800 or $1000, waiting for the boss to write up their "free" buffet.

The Bosses

The pit boss is in charge of a whole *pit*, or group of tables. These may consist of eight or ten tables with various games being played. The *floormen*, or supervisors, report to him. The *floorman* stands behind the tables in the pit and may supervise two or three tables at a time. He is usually wearing a suit. He brings over the markers and okays credit. He can hook you up with a casino-rating card and dispense comps. The floorman will keep an eye on high rollers or junket members for their level of betting activity. He will watch for any cheating. The boxman reports to the floorman. If there is a discrepancy that the boxman cannot handle, the floorman will step in and settle it. Usually if a problem reaches the floorman, there is a good chance he will lean in favor of the customer.

      The boxman (or woman) is the overseer of that craps table game. He is wearing a suit or sports coat and is seated at the center, directly behind the table. If the table is large and crowded, there may be two boxmen seated side by side, each observing his end of the table. When you first buy in, the box-man will count out your cash in front of him, announce the amount and stuff it down a slot in the table just in front of him, where it collects in the table drop box. The boxman is the table authority. He will watch both players and dealers to ensure against any cheating and that proper payouts are made. He will examine the dice just before the shooter gets them or may closely inspect them if one die was thrown off the table. An old ploy used by early cheaters was to throw the dice so hard they flew off the table. A seemingly innocent and helpful passerby would stop to retrieve them. This passerby was actually an accomplice who will quickly switch the casino's dice as he is picking them off the carpet with loaded dice. The weighted or loaded dice would then be introduced into the game. The boxman watches the overall operation of the game and usually handles any disputes.

The Crew

The crew consists of four *dealers* who team up to handle one craps table. They are dressed in the uniform of the casino. At any given time, three will be working and one will be on a 20-minute break. They will be working one of three eight-hour shifts: the day shift, the swing shift, or the graveyard shift. The two dealers on either side of the boxman are said to be working the bases. The third is situated on the same side of the table as the players and will stand directly across from the boxman. This dealer, who uses a hooked stick to retrieve the dice after they are thrown, is referred to as the *stickman*. When the fourth dealer comes back from his break, he will tap the stickman on the shoulder, signifying that he is back. The current stickman will pass any pertinent betting information on to the new stickman, including who the shooter is. The old stickman will rotate over to the base, a few feet right of the boxman and that dealer will move over to the position just left of the boxman. The dealer working that base will in turn take his break.

The dealers "on base" will help you cash in to get chips. They will collect your cash from the Come box and push it over to the boxman. After the boxman announces the amount, the dealer will count out an equal amount of value in chips and slide them over to you. These dealers will assist you if you wish to change up to higher value chips before leaving the table. Just count out your chips (so you know exactly how much you have) and place them in stacks of like colors. Before the shooter throws, slide them in the Come box and announce, "Color coming, no action." The dealer may nod yes to signify it's okay to slide the chips toward him or he may ask you to hold up for a minute if he is busy. When the dealer does get around to bringing in your chips, he will slide them over to the boxman who will color them up for you to higher denominations. He will announce the amount, and your dealer will slide them over to you. After each throw, these dealers will collect the losing bets and pay the winners. Right after the shooter either makes his point or sevens out is when these guys are the busiest. You will make your own Pass Line, Don't Pass and Field bets as well as taking the odds behind your Pass Line bet. The base dealers will assist you when making Come, Don't Come, Place, Buy, or Lay bets (we'll cover all these types of bets shortly).

The base dealers will operate the On/Off puck on their prospective side of the table. If the shooter is in the initial stage of his cycle, called the *come-out* roll, then the puck will be in the *Don't Come box*, next to the 4 point box (left side) or the 10 point box (right side). The black side will be up with the word *off* displayed. After the shooter establishes a point, the dealer will flip the puck over to the white side labeled *on*, and place it in the appropriate point box so everyone knows which number the shooter is trying to repeat. These dealers can be very helpful if you have questions about how to make a particular bet or which bets belong to you. Many times they will observe each player's betting style and will anticipate which bets you will make and how often you will press up your winnings. After a while, they may know your staking style better than you do. I've seen countless times where the base dealer has to remind a player that he forgot to make one of his favorite bets, or that he didn't take odds behind his Pass Line wager. Dealers are well trained at watching the action and making fast, accurate payouts. They will notice any minor change in betting from one throw to the next.

The stickman is usually a loud, colorful character. A good stickman can "talk up" the game and increase the number of bets, especially the higher casino percentage ones. He is stationed in the middle of the table, on the same side as the players. The stickman controls the pace of the game. As a new shooter is about to throw, he will offer the shooter two of five dice with which to throw. After the shooter has made his selection, the stickman will announce, "New shooter coming out," or, "Dice are coming out. Bet the yos, Any Craps or C and Es!" After each throw, the stickman will call out the result generated by totaling the two top faces and retrieve the dice with his hooked stick. The bets that are affected by that throw are dealt with accordingly and the pair of cubes is brought in front of the boxman for a quick visual inspection. The boxman will use the mirrors along the flat walls, just under the player's chip racks, to see the backside of the dice. The stickman may turn the dice over once or twice for the boxman. After the boxman nods okay, or says to "send 'em," the stickman will then slide the dice over to the shooter for his next throw. The stickman will make sure that a 7 is not showing when the shooter is trying to make his point and may even preset the dice if the shooter is tipping well and likes to set the dice before he throws.

The stickman may encourage the shooter by saying something like, "Point is 5, make that point shooter!" as he slides the dice over. If the shooter has been trying for a while to make a point, he may encourage the bettors with something like, "The point is 8, bring it out with a hard ways bet!" or after the shooter makes his point, "Same good shooter, press them [your bets] up folks." Either way, a good stick will keep the banter flowing. After the shooter ends his hand, or series of rolls, by sevening out, the stick may say, "Seven . . . line away, Don'ts to pay," or, "Seven-out, take the Dos, pay the Don'ts." He will then offer two of five dice to the next shooter, further left, as the dice travel in a clockwise direction from one shooter to the next. The stickman places all bets in the center of the table, between him and the boxman. These include the *Hard Ways* combinations and the one-roll or *Proposition* bets. These wagers yield the house the greatest advantage and should probably be minimized or avoided altogether . . . more on these bets a little later.

The Shooter

As the dice move clockwise to the next prospective shooter, he must have a line bet out (Pass Line or Don't Pass) to be eligible to roll the dice. You can refuse to throw the dice if you are not so inclined, or have your lovely female consort do it for you. The shooter may place other bets in addition to the required line bet. Ninety percent of all craps players are optimistic about the shooter repeating the point before hitting a 7, so they tend to play the Pass Line. In fact, many Don't Pass players will change their betting over to the Pass Line when it is their turn to throw. Other Don't players will pass the dice, refusing to throw, and a scarce few may throw from the Don't. After the dice are brought over to the shooter by the stickman, the shooter will pick them up and throw them to the far end of the table. You are supposed to hit the back wall containing a grid-work of rubber pyramids with both dice to qualify. However, many times the roll will count if only one die reaches the wall. If the shooter does not hit the back wall in successive throws, the stickman will admonish the shooter to do so or the roll will not count. I have seen situations where the shooter repeatedly ignored the stickman and an angry boxman not only disallowed the roll, but also instructed the stickman to pass the dice to the next shooter. We'll talk more about *getting the dice to the back wall without hitting it very hard*.

Another situation that arises is that the shooter throws the dice too hard and one or both dice fly off the betting surface. If they end up in the player's chip racks, you may hear the stickman bark out, "Too tall to call," or "In the wood, no good." Also, one die may leave the table altogether, in which case you might hear, "Man overboard!" I observed one situation, where the shooter bounced both dice completely out of the table and down the isle two or three tables away. Everyone tried to see where the dice landed. The stickman paused for moment, and then burst out with a, "In the lobby, Kemosobie!" The table erupted into laughter and the shooter turned about as red as the dice. Anytime the dice leave the table, the boxman will physically inspect them and mix the dice back in with the others residing in the bowl. Many shooters, out of superstition, will request that the same two dice be returned to them for the next throw. The shooter will continue to throw, cycling through come-out rolls and point rolls, until a 7 results during the point roll part of the cycle. At that moment, the shooter has sevened out and will relinquish the dice to the player on his left.

Chapter 2

Dice Combinations and the Basic Game

Craps probably offers a player the best chance to make the most money in the shortest amount of time. My good friend and teammate Eric N., "Guardian," personally witnessed a mega-win at the Caesar's Casino in A.C. one Saturday night at a $100 minimum bet table. Some high roller strolled up and bought in for $15,000. There were two other players at the table, one of which was about to shoot the dice for his come-out roll. The high roller started with $500 on the Pass Line, taking full odds and placing across the board. The shooter continued to make point after point and our high roller pressed heavily. Forty minutes later, the shooter finally sevened out. All of the players were enjoying a huge score. Circles where the felt looked a little newer and more brightly colored were left from the high denominational chips that were paid out during the hand! A case of chips was brought in by security to replenish the depleted table bank.

The dice passed on to the next shooter. By now the table had attracted a few more players. Not to be out done by the first shooter, the second guy begins establishing and making a series of eight or nine points. He too holds the cubes for over 40 minutes before sevening out, creating back-to-back monster rolls! The high roller leaves some $12,000 to $14,000 up on the betting layout, but his racks and the racks on both sides of him are spilling over with thousand-dollar chips. The high roller leans over to his friend and declares, "That was a hell-of-a run. I think I'll just lay back for a while and savor the victory!" He throws a few of the purple chips out to the dealers as one of the floormen brings several acrylic racks over and accompanies this guy to the cage. My friend Eric tags along to overhear the final tally: $255,000+ in chips, making a net win of over $240,000! I think, "hell-of-a run" was a huge understatement! How did he do it so fast? Well, it helps to understand the various bets available and their payoffs, but first we must look at the different dice combinations and their odds of being made.

Different Dice Combinations

Let us look at all the possible dice combinations, with two regulation dice. Figure 2-1 depicts all of the possible outcomes present with two six-sided dice. Because of the way that the dice are configured, certain totals have more ways to appear than others do. For example, if one die results with a 2 on top, then there is no way to make 2, 9, 10, 11, or 12 come up. Only a total of 3 through 8 is possible. How about if one die is a 4? Then only a total of 5 through 10 can occur. As you begin to examine more possibilities, you will see that the midrange numbers occur more often than the outside numbers. In fact, the number situated right in the center, the 7, has the highest frequency of occurrence with six ways to be made. The 7 can occur no matter what combination the first die ends up with: 1 matches up with 6; 2 with 5; and 3, 4, 5, 6 with 4, 3, 2, 1 respectively. For this reason, the 7 total has the greatest chance of being thrown, six ways out of 36 possibilities. As you move outward from the center, the frequency of occurrence steadily drops off. The 6 and 8, on either side of the 7, can each be made one of five ways. The 5 and 9 can result in one of four ways, the 4 and 10, three ways; two ways for the 3 or 11 and only one way to make a 2 or a 12.

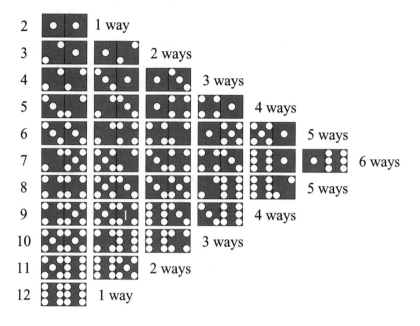

Figure 2-1
Master Dice Combinations

When we discuss the probability of an event occurring or the odds against such an event, we should be speaking the same language. Taking any six-sided cube that is marked with from one to six pips, or spots, on each face, you can easily see that one of six outcomes is possible when you cast the die out onto a surface. The *probability* of an event measures the ways to succeed out of the total sample size. If the die is a fair die, then the probability of throwing any specific number is 1/6, or one face in six faces. When you throw a die, you will affect a result that is mutually exclusive to the others. That is, only one face can result, or be on top after the die is thrown, for a decision to be rendered. For mutually exclusive events, all of the possible probabilities will total up to 1.0. Six possible outcomes times a probability of 1/6 equals 1.0, or 6 x 16.67

percent = 100 percent. When you throw the die, one of six sides will appear 100 percent of the time to affect a decision; each side has a 1/6, or 16.67 percent chance of occurring. Also, when considering a series of throws, each result is independent of the previous or any future trials. Craps is a game of replacements. Just because a shooter has thrown three 12s in a row does not change the fact that on the very next trial, or toss of the dice, there is still a 1 in 36 chance of throwing another 12.

The term *odds* describes something a little different. The odds of an event occurring are the ways of succeeding versus the ways against succeeding. For example, the odds against throwing a specific number when casting a single die are five to one. That is, one way to throw the number you desire and five ways not to throw the number. You'll notice that the word "to" is inserted between the numbers. If a game is fair, the winning payoffs are calculated from the odds of an event occurring. The correct payout for successfully wagering on the resulting face of a single die occurring should be 5 to 1. Every $1 wagered should win $5 in profits (plus the return of the original $1 bet). However, the casino will alter the payout schedule slightly so it is in their favor. That is why the casino is said to have a mathematical edge. For example, the odds against throwing a total of 6 before throwing a 7 are 6 to 5. As depicted in Table 1-1, there are six ways to throw a losing 7 and five ways to throw a total of 6 with a regulation pair of casino dice. If you "Place" the 6, or wager on it to appear before the 7, the casino will pay you $7 in winnings for every $6 wagered. The correct odds say that you should be paid $6 for every $5 wagered. Therefore, your $6 bet should return you $7.20 in winnings, or 6/5 x $6. The 20¢ that they short you on a winning bet is what pays for the construction, operation and profits of all these elaborate structures.

Twenty cents does not seem like that much of a price to pay, you think. However, it does add up quickly when you figure you've got four or five other bets (or more) out on the layout for each roll of the dice. Then multiply that by 50 to 75 rolls per hour over the course of a playing session and it adds up quickly! Another thing that the player should be aware of is the use of the word "for" to describe the payoff. The use of the word "for," indicates a payoff, plus the return of the original wager. For example, "8 for 1" means that you wager one unit, win seven units and are returned a total of eight units. This is exactly the same as winning 7 to 1, where you win seven units and still retain your original one-unit bet. Another example is the Any Seven wager. The true odds against throwing a 7 are 5 to 1, but the casinos pay 4 to 1. Some casinos, thinking that they're clever, will mark the betting area "5 for 1," but they are only paying you four net units.

The Game

When asked how the game of craps is played, an inveterate gambler once replied, "7 you win, 7 you lose." While the statement is confusing, it also happens to be true. Craps is really a dichotomy of two different games with two different objectives. A 7 thrown at the beginning of the game, or during the come-out roll, is a winner for the Pass Line bettors. However, a 7 rolled later, when the shooter is trying to repeat the point, loses the Pass Line wager and ends the shooter's hand. The first part of the game, as we mentioned, is the *come-out roll*. The new shooter selects two dice and tosses them down the table. If the come-out roll is 7 or 11, often referred to as a *natural*, the game is over. Any bets on the Pass Line win 1:1, or even money. Bets on the Don't Pass line lose. If the shooter tosses a 2, 3, or 12 on the come-out roll, he is said to have thrown *craps*. If the come-out roll is craps, the game is also over. Any bets on the Pass Line lose. Bets on the Don't Pass win—unless the result is a 12. In this case the house gains its edge by calling it a push instead of a win. The Don't Pass line bettors neither win nor lose. This is indicated in the Don't Pass betting area with the marking "Bar 12." On some really old tables, you may even see the 2 barred. Be sure to double check which craps number is barred if you are a Don't player.

If either a craps or a natural is thrown on the come-out roll, the shooter continues to come-out until a *point* is established. This happens when the shooter throws a number of 4, 5, 6, 8, 9, or 10 on the come-out roll. Then, the number thrown becomes his point. It is not yet determined if he has won or lost his wager. The shooter now enters the second portion of the game referred to as the *point cycle*. The dealer will turn over the puck to the white side, labeled *On*, and move it to the point box of the number that was just thrown on the last come-out roll. If the shooter wishes to continue throwing the dice, thus extending his game, he must try to avoid the now fatal 7, and attempt to repeat his point number first. If the shooter throws a 7 without repeating his point, he is said to have sevened out and must relinquish the dice to the person on his left. All bets on the Pass Line lose; any wagers on the Don't Pass will win 1:1, or even money. If the shooter successfully repeats his number (making his point), all the Pass Line bets at that table win 1:1 and the Don't Pass bets lose. Now, the shooter has the privilege of rolling the dice for the next game. He will come out again and eventually establish a new point to repeat.

This point cycle portion of the game can be short, or it can last a long time. I've had situations where I came right back on the very next roll and made the point, for three or four successive point cycles. I also had an experience in Tunica, Mississippi, where I established a point of 10 and threw for a half-hour straight without sevening-out or hitting the point 10. Everyone, including myself, made a lot of money on all the other numbers that appeared—everyone, except for the miserable soul standing next to me. He had wagered his last $5 chip on the Pass Line and made sure I was aware of it. I could sense his frustration as everyone else collected multiple times on all the other numbers. The other players were laughing and filling up their racks with chips. My happenstance companion was practically demanding that

I make the 10. "Relax," I assured him. "It will come around eventually," but the 10 never came. Just after I sevened-out, I received a nice round of applause from the table. I could see my unhappy neighbor storm off out of the corner of my eye. You can't always please everyone! Typically, the point cycle portion makes up about 75 to 80 percent of all the shooter's rolls. However, on this particular roll, I came right out with a 10, and then threw some 35 times, trying to repeat it.

Okay, let's summarize the basics:

1. The Come-Out Roll

A new shooter comes out with a roll. A 7 or 11 are instant winners for the Pass Line and losers for the Don't Pass. A 2, 3, or 12 are instant losers for the Pass Line and win for the Don't Pass, except for the 12, which is a push. Irrespective of throwing a craps or a natural, the shooter continues to come out until a point number is thrown.

2. The Point Cycle

Once a point has been established, the same shooter will roll until he sevens-out or repeats his point. A 7 thrown at this time ends the game. Bets on the Pass Line lose and the Don't Pass wins even money. The current shooter loses his turn and the dice are passed over to a new shooter. Making the point results in the Pass Line winning even money and the Don't Pass losing. The same shooter continues to roll for the next game (new come-out roll) and recycles through the process again.

There are many more wagers that can be placed during the course of the game, but the Pass Line wager and its decision, as demonstrated above, determines the pace and the direction of the game. The length of the shooter's turn depends on his ability to make the dice pass, or at least avoid the seven-out. Next, we'll take a more in-depth look at the

Pass Line and Don't Pass line bets. For your reference, Figure 3-6 diagrams the entire betting layout, including where these two wagers are placed.

Chapter 3

They Do, They Don't (Pass, Come, etc.)

"They Do"—the Pass Line Wager

Some say they do, some say they don't . . . some wager they will, and others bet they won't. Most craps players are optimistic, hoping that the shooter will sport a nice, long hand. These 90+ percent of the players are betting that the dice will pass, the shooter will continue to roll and lots of money will be made. These Pass Line players, referred to as *right-way* bettors, seem to enjoy a camaraderie with the other Pass Line players at the table. As points are made, and multitudes of numbers are thrown, they will celebrate with high-fives and shouts of encouragement to the shooter. It becomes an "us against the house" mentality. If the dice continue to pass and the table action heats up, you may see the casino bosses starting to sweat a bit. Although just the Pass Line players appear to be playing against the house, the casino books all bets made at the table. Both the Pass Line and Don't Pass wagers give the house a bona fide mathematical edge, so technically speaking, all the players are betting against the casino.

A bet on either the Pass Line or the Don't Pass is called a *line bet*. These bets are placed at the beginning of the game, before the come-out roll. The shooter is required to make a line bet in order to shoot the dice. The most popular line bet is the *Pass Line* bet. This is a wager that the dice will *pass*. A 7 or 11 on the come-out roll is an instant winner (the dice passed) and the shooter starts a new game by coming out again. A 2, 3, or 12 thrown on the come-out roll is an instant Pass Line loser. The Pass Line bettor has a huge, mathematical edge over the house during the come-out roll. The Pass Line player has eight ways to win (six ways to a 7 and two ways to an 11) versus four ways to lose with one 2, one 12, and two ways to a 3. $(8 - 4)/12 = +33.333$ percent mathematical edge to the right-way bettor. If every roll in the game of craps were a come-out roll with no points to establish or make, then all the Pass Line bettors would be millionaires and the casinos would be out of business. If a 4, 5, 6, 8, 9, or 10 is rolled on the come-out, then that number becomes the point. Once a point is thrown and thus established, the edge swings wildly in favor of the house. This is the reason why the Pass Line bet must remain out on the line until a decision is reached (referred to as a contract bet). The casino, of course, wants to take their best shot at your stake.

If the point is repeated before the 7 appears, the dice have passed and the point is made. The Pass Line bettor may now (before any come-out roll) leave his bet up for the next game, increase it, decrease it, or remove it altogether. Once a point is established the bet cannot be reduced or removed until a decision is rendered. If a 7 is rolled while a point is set to be made, the shooter has sevened-out and the Pass Line wagers lose. The dice move along to the next shooter. When the 4 or 10 becomes the point, the house edge skyrockets to 33.333 percent for the remainder of the point cycle. Three ways to make the 4 or 10 versus six ways to seven-out, $(3 - 6)/9 = -1/3$. The 5 or 9 gives the casino an even 20 percent edge, four ways minus six ways divided by ten equals $-1/5$. A point of 6 or 8 yields the house a 9.091 percent edge for the rest of the game, $(5 - 6)/11 = -1/11$. This would be okay, except that 75+ percent of the time the shooter is in the point cycle. When you *blend*, or take the weighted average of the house's edge over the entire game, you come up with the –1.414 percent edge that you read about in most books. In the final section of this book, I have several sets of calculations, including how this –1.414 percent figure is computed. Just remember that this is an average figure, calculated over the entire life of one game.

The edge is heavily in favor of the Pass Line player on the come-out roll and swings violently over in the house's favor once a point is established. The casinos, in all their benevolence, allow the Pass Line player to soften the blow. The Pass Line player is allowed to make a supplemental wager that does not yield the casino any long-term profit. The player is permitted to take *free odds* behind his Pass Line wager. The free, or *true odds*, bet can be an amount equal to the Pass Line bet (called *single odds*) or some multiple times the original Pass Line bet, with correct odds paid if the point is made. Check out Table 3-1 below to see the correct odds and payouts for each possible point number. Different casinos in different areas will permit the Pass Line player to take varying amounts of odds. I've seen anywhere from single odds (small "ma and pa" type operations) up to 20 times odds (downtown Vegas) permitted. The casinos in Atlantic City allow double odds for the most part. Although some A.C. casinos will allow you to take three or even five times odds at their $25 minimum tables. You may take any amount of odds that you wish, up to the house limit.

This is the only wager in the casino that is paid out fairly, the only bet giving the house no mathematical edge. So, at a time when the Pass Line player has his back against the wall, the house allows him to mitigate his circumstance by taking free odds. There is no designated area on the betting layout for the odds bets. The casinos are not going to heavily publicize a wager that gives them no edge. Just place your odds bet directly behind your Pass Line bet after the point is established. If the Pass Line wager wins (it is paid even money) then the odds bet wins and is paid according to the correct odds of making that point. Unlike the Pass Line wager, which is a contract bet, an odds bet can be removed or modified at any time. If you have any questions concerning your odds bet, ask the dealer for clarification.

Table 3-1
Taking Correct Odds for Each Point Number

Point Number	Ways Made	Ways to 7 out	Odds Against	Payoffs
6 or 8	5	6	6 to 5	$5 odds wins $6
5 or 9	4	6	3 to 2	$2 odds wins $3
4 or 10	3	6	2 to 1	$1 odds wins $2

So, for example, you have a $5 Pass Line bet out and the point becomes 6 or 8. The casino allows double odds so you drop $10 behind your Pass Line bet. Your point is made and you are paid as follows:

$5 Pass Line bet wins even money, or $5.
$10 double odds for a 6 or 8 pays $6 for every $5 wagered, so $12 is won.

You will win $17 for your combined bet of $15 (Pass Line plus odds). Let's say that the 4 or 10 becomes your point after you wager $10 on the Pass Line. The house offers triple odds and you wish to take full odds. Your point is made and paid:

$10 Pass Line bet wins even money, $10.
$30 odds (three times) for a 4 or 10 pays $2 for every $1 wagered, so $60 is won.

Your total payout is $70; even money on the Pass Line and two times your odds bet. There are a couple of points to remember. The Pass Line bet is always paid at even money. When the point is either a 6 or 8, take odds in multiples of $5 so you can be paid correctly (6 to 5). If the point is 5 or 9, the dollar amount of odds should be an even number (in multiples of $2) so you can be paid $3 for every $2 wagered. Because the 4 or 10 pays 2 to 1 on the odds portion, you can take any dollar amount of odds up to the table maximum without getting short changed.

Many of the casinos down the Vegas strip are now initiating the 3x, 4x, 5x odds system. They will let you take three times odds for a point of 4 or 10, four times odds behind the 5 or 9, and up to five times odds if the point is 6 or 8. This does three things for the casino and its patrons. First, the casino limits its exposure on the outside numbers that have higher odds, yet offers the players decent multiples of true odds at the same time. Secondly, it makes the payout the same if you take max odds no matter what the point is. This makes the dealer's job easier and speeds up the game. Thirdly, this system helps eliminate payoff mistakes, which can hurt both the casino and the patrons, but at different times. Table 3-2 will show how this system of permissible odds works for a $10 pass line bet. The 3x, 4x, 5x odds payout system works similarly for any unit size.

Table 3-2
$10 Pass Line with 3x, 4x, 5x Odds, Vegas Strip

Point Number	Odds Payout	Odds Allowed	$10 P.L. Odds	Total Payout
4 or 10	2 to 1	3 X	$10 P.L. + $30	$10 + $60 = $70
5 or 9	3 to 2	4 X	$10 P.L. + $40	$10 + $60 = $70
6 or 8	6 to 5	5 X	$10 P.L. + $50	$10 + $60 = $70

As you take more odds with zero percent house edge behind your Pass Line bet, you lower the overall edge against you. Effectively, you are watering down the house edge on your original Pass Line bet. As you add more free odds, the average of your combined bets gets further diluted.

This weakening effect occurs with each additional odds amount that you add. For example, taking single odds is the best thing you can do. The house edge drops from

–1.414 percent to –0.848 percent. Taking double odds is the next best thing you do. It reduces the edge from –0.848 percent down to –0.606 percent. It does not reduce the edge nearly as much as taking single odds, but it does a better job than triple odds, which only cuts the edge down from –0.606 percent to –0.471 percent. Another way to look at it is taking single odds removes 40 percent of the casinos 1.414 percent edge. Taking double odds buys you an additional 17 percent, which is less than half as effective as taking single odds. While taking triple odds trims less than 10 percent more off of the 1.414 percent edge overall. As you progressively increase your odds amount, its effectiveness wears off. In fact, to equal the effect of double to triple odds (or see another 10 percent overall reduction), you will have to jump two odds levels from triple to five times odds. In order to see an additional 10 percent reduction, you must now increase your odds wager five levels, from five to ten times odds. For the next 10 percent, you must employ nearly 100x odds! That's a quantum leap of 90 odds levels for the same effective reduction!

Look at the curve in Graph 3-3. The steeper portion of the curve demonstrates how quickly the house edge drops in the beginning. As you add more odds, the curve (and the rate at which the house edge decreases) starts to flatten out.

Personally, I like the 3x, 4x, 5x odds system. You can see that the "bang for the buck" factor starts to fade fast once you exceed five times odds. That is why I usually take somewhere between three and five times odds. Another point to remember when taking even larger odds is that you will have a greater amount of your bankroll at risk on one decision. It will be of little consolation to you that you minimized the house edge a few additional thousandths of a percentage point if you run into a string of eight or ten straight losses. A fully depleted bankroll, early in the game, will not be too encouraging. Just remember that you never want too large a percentage of your bankroll, or session buy-in for that matter, out on one roll of the dice—unless that is the only bet you plan on making for that trip! Then, technically, you are exposing your

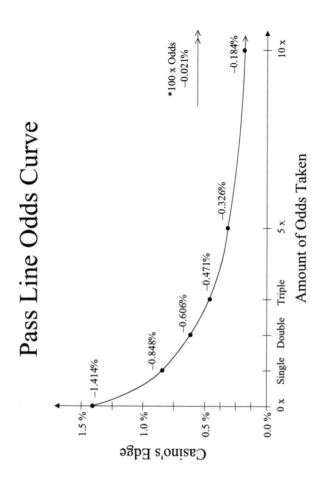

Graph 3-3

bankroll to the casino's edge only one time and there is no compounding effect. But, I do not know of anyone who flies out to Vegas or drives to A.C. just to place one large bet and then leave. With fewer bets of larger size, you will have a higher statistical variance, which means a more unpredictable final outcome.

Most books on the subject simply tell you to take the maximum odds offered. They forget to illustrate the ever-weakening effects of each successive odds amount added.

Depending upon the number of decisions, or games you plan to play, the number of units in your bankroll, and the information herein, you will make an odds decision that is best for you. I know one individual who is a multimillionaire. Anything over a $10 unit size, however, with more than triple odds makes him squeamish. If you are uncomfortable with higher odds, by all means, cut back, but if you want to get more money out on the layout and can afford it, then apply it towards additional odds. Either way, you can now make an informed odds decision that suits your situation.

Another variation on the Pass Line bet that I should mention, but don't necessarily recommend, is the *put bet*. A put bet is a Pass Line bet that is made *after* the point has been established. This is a bet typically made by rank novices. As mentioned earlier, the mathematical edge heavily favors the casino after the point is set. The put bettor never has the benefit of the come-out roll (eight ways to win versus only four to lose). He gives the house a whopping 9.091 percent, 20.0 percent or 33.333 percent edge on his money right off the bat. If the point is made, the put bettor is paid one to one, even though the odds were largely against him. Even if he takes odds behind his put bet, he will not come close to realizing his potential unless he risks an exorbitant amount of odds. For example, if the 4 or 10 becomes the point, our put bettor will need to take in excess of 20 times odds just to pull even with the buy bettor. A $5 put bet on a 4 or 10 plus $100 in odds wins $5 plus $200, total equals $205. The buy bettor who pays a 5 percent commission on winnings can buy a $105, 4 or 10, win $210, and pay $5 in commission for a total of $205. But, it is probably a moot point. Very few casinos allow such large odds and the put bettors that I have witnessed never even took single odds. A more intelligent way to bet on the point after it has been established is to Place it, or Buy it if it is a 4 or 10. We'll cover these bets a little later in this section.

"They Don't"—The Don't Pass Wager

Betting on the Don't Pass, or the *wrong-way* as it is sometimes called, is simply a bet that the dice will not pass. The Don't Pass wager must be placed before the next come-out roll. Working in the opposite manner of the Pass Line wager, Don't Pass bets lose when the come-out roll is 7 or 11, and win when the come-out roll is 2 or 3. Don't bets tie when the come-out roll is 12. If the game were fair, the Don'ts would win even money for a come-out 12. The Bar 12 is indicated on the lay-out area where the Don't players wager. The come-out roll puts the Don't player at a big disadvantage with only three ways to win even money and eight ways to lose (a −45.454 percent edge!). Once a come-out roll of 4, 5, 6, 8, 9, or 10 is thrown and a point is established, the Don't player now has the best of it. If the shooter rolls a 7 (the most frequent number) before he is able to make the point, the Don't bettor wins even money. The dice transfer over to the next shooter and a new game is played. Because most of the table will be betting on the Pass Line, the Don't Pass player must celebrate silently. If the shooter does repeat his point before tossing a 7, the Don't bet is lost.

If the point is 6 or 8, the Don't bettor has six ways to win (seven-out) and five ways to lose (point is made). In this instance he will enjoy a positive 9.091 percent advantage for the rest of the point cycle. Because there are four ways to make a point of 5 or 9 and six ways to seven-out, thus winning, the Don't player will hold a +20.0 percent mathematical edge. Our same Don't player will see a bona fide +33.333 percent advantage if the 4 or 10 is established as the point with six ways to win and only three ways to lose. The edge is hugely against the Don't bettor on the come-out roll but swings well into his favor once the point is set to be repeated. The blended house advantage computes out to be 1.403 percent against the Don't player. If the Don't player did not have to go through the come-out roll in order to establish a point to wager against, he could become wealthy rather fast with even money payouts. In fact, if the Don't bettor simply got paid even money for a come-out 12, instead of a push, he would enjoy the same 1.414 percent advantage that the casino holds over the Pass Line bettor. Because the Don't Pass player holds the mathematical advantage once a point is established, the casino will allow him to decrease or remove his bet at any time, but to do so would be foolish.

The Don't Pass player cannot increase his original Don't Pass wager once a point has been set, but he can get more money out against the point by *laying the odds*. Similar to the way the Pass Line bettor takes free odds behind his Pass Line bet, the Don't Pass player may "lay" the odds on his Don't Pass wager. This bet gives the casino no mathematical advantage. After the point is established, simply place the odds wager on top, but slightly offset from the original Don't Pass bet and announce, "laying the odds." The dealer may adjust your odds bet so it is tilted to one side, or he may "bridge" the odds with your Don't Pass wager. Either way, make a note of how he positions it for next time. If the point becomes 6 or 8, the Don't bettor will lay, or risk, six units to win five units. This is the fair, or correct, odds against a point of 6 or 8. The casino's edge on "laying the odds" is also 0 percent and you won't find this bet heavily publicized either. When the 5 or 9 becomes the point, you will lay multiples of three units, for every two units up to the house limit, that you wish to win. So, for example, you have $25 on the Don't Pass at a table allowing double odds. A 5 is thrown so you lay $75 in odds. If the shooter sevens-out, you will win even money on the $25 Don't Pass bet and $50, or double odds, for your $75 odds bet. Since there are six ways to win (seven-out) and only four ways to lose (the 5 is made), you will risk three $25 units to win two $25 units. In this case $100 total was risked to net $75.

Table 3-4
Laying the Odds Against Each Point Number

Point Number	Ways to Win	Ways to Lose	Odds Against	Payoffs
6 or 8	6	5	5 to 6	$6 odds wins $5
5 or 9	6	4	2 to 3	$3 odds wins $2
4 or 10	6	3	1 to 2	$2 odds wins $1

If the point becomes a 4 or 10, the Don't Pass player wishing to lay odds must lay two units for every one unit win. There are six ways to seven-out and three ways to make the point. See Table 3-4 for a summary of laying the odds against different point numbers. There is one point I should interject here. Like the Pass Line player who may at his option take odds, the Don't bettor has the option of whether or not to lay odds. Unlike the Pass Line bettor who needs to take odds after the point is established to improve his staggering disadvantage, the Don't player actually waters down his positive advantage by laying the odds. Probably half of the Don't players do not lay odds for one or more reasons:

1) Once the point is established and the come-out roll is over, the Don't bettor now has a bona fide mathematical advantage. Placing any additional money out, even laying odds at a 0 percent house edge, *will average his now positive advantage down, closer to 0 percent.* This lower, but still positive advantage, will be spread out over a greater sum of money.

For example, our $25 Don't player with a point of 5, now holds a +20.0 percent edge on his original Don't Pass wager. By introducing $75 at a 0 percent house edge, his overall average is now 5 percent on the entire $100 at risk. This is another decision you will have to come to terms with. Would you prefer a 20 percent advantage on $25 (by not laying odds), or a 5 percent advantage on $100 (laying triple units to win double odds against the 5 or 9)? Or how about just risking the entire $100 on the Don't Pass (through the come-out roll) and hoping for a huge edge on the whole thing? This is a personal decision you and your bankroll will make. The second reason that you may not elect to lay odds follows:

2) Even though there is no casino advantage on the bet, you are laying more money to win a lesser amount. That is because the true odds are mathematically against the point repeating. If you happen to hit a run of nine or ten passes with maximum odds laid, you will get creamed. You will need a very large bankroll to weather the storms if you wish to lay maximum odds.

The Pass Line bettor is in a weakened state once the point is set. Taking odds is just what the doctor ordered to mitigate his situation. The Don't bettor, however, is most vulnerable on the come-out roll. Laying odds after the come-out roll works to water down an already superior position. Personally, I do not lay odds, but I cannot tell you it is the wrong decision if you are inclined to do so and have a sufficient bankroll. During the course of several games, I've wiped out many heavy players who bet the Don't and laid the odds when I was shooting from the Pass Line. Most of the patrons bet that the dice (and the shooter) will pass when I'm throwing, but a few feel compelled to bet against my throw. There was a guy in Tunica who began wagering $1,000 units on the Don't Pass after I made my third point. I guess he thought that I was due to seven-out. I established a point of 4 and he laid $2,000 in odds, attempting to win $1,000 in odds plus even money on his Don't Pass wager. As he turned to drop the cocktail waitress a few bucks for his drink, I promptly set and threw the hard 4, coming right back and making my point. Before he could set his drink down, he was out $3,000! This unfortunate individual went through $15,000 before he realized he was getting the worst of it and needed a break.

Another poor soul went through $25,000 at the Trump Marina after I made seven successive points. As he laid $4,800 in odds along with his $1,000 Don't Pass bet, I could see his hand trembling. Just as I began to throw the dice he banged on the table and yelled, "Seven-out!" at the top of his lungs. The shout startled everyone including me and the resulting throw had no control. I did seven-out, and the Don't player won back $5,000. I thought the table patrons were going to lynch the guy. One of his friends, who came over afterwards to apologize for his behavior, told me he was still down $20,000 for that session. I told his friend to get him some help before he loses the farm. And these are just a couple of experiences I am recalling as I write this section. It mystifies me how some of these guys (a small minority, luckily) see me make point after point with a very consistent throw and still decide to bet against me. I feel bad for them, but I have my own financial affairs to look after.

The Come Bet

If you missed the come-out roll for the Pass Line bet, but still wish to wager on the "do" for the next roll, you can make what is called a *Come bet*. The Come bet works exactly like the Pass Line bet, except it is placed during the point cycle portion for the Pass Line wager. Just place your wager in the boxed area labeled "Come," and tell the dealer, "$10 (or whatever the amount is) coming." The very next roll of the dice is treated as the come-out roll for that particular Come bet. If the next roll is 7 or 11, the Come bet wins even money. Of course, the 7 (a natural winner for the Come bet) will wipe out all of the Pass Line bettors (as a seven-out). The mathematical edge for the Come bettor works exactly the same as it does for the Pass Line bettor. The Come bettor's come-out roll has eight ways to win versus four ways to lose, the same 33.333 percent positive edge. If a 2, 3, or 12 is thrown on the next roll, after the Come bet is placed, the wager is lost.

If a 4, 5, 6, 8, 9, or 10 is tossed, then that number becomes the point number for that Come bet. The dealer will then pick up the Come bet and place it inside of that number's point box. He will position it inside the front part of the box, relative to where the bettor is standing at that half of the table. Think of each point box as a mini-map of that half of the table. The point boxes to the right of the stickman represent the right half of the table, while the boxes on the left side are used for players who are situated around the left half of the table. For example, if the bet belongs to the player standing to the stickman's immediate left, then the dealer will position the wager in the front of the point box and on the right side (relative to the player). If the bettor were stationed at the end of the table to the stickman's right, then the bet would be positioned on the end, or right side of that point box.

Once a point is established for the Come bet, the Come bettor must deal with the same huge disadvantage that the Pass Line bettor faces. The Come bettor may take free odds on his Come bet to help soften the blow. The maximum odds advertised by the casino are the same for Come bet points and should be placed in increments of $5 for the 6 or 8, $2 for the Come point of 5 or 9, and any dollar amount up to the table max for the 4 or 10. If the Come bet wins, these bets are paid correctly with no mathematical edge for the casino. See Table 3-1 for a schedule of payouts. As with taking odds on the Pass Line, the Come bettor will need to decide what level of odds he is comfortable with on his Come bets. Just place the odds wager in the Come box and announce, "Odds please." The dealer will place the odds bet on top of, but offset, from the original Come bet. The Pass Line rules and mathematics work out the same for the Come bet.

Please be aware, the game for a Come bet will continue until the Come point is repeated or a 7 appears. Even if the shooter makes his Pass Line point and begins a new game, the Come bet is still awaiting a repeat or a seven-out. Because Come bets are typically made by Pass Line bettors, the casinos, by default, turn the Come bettor's *odds off* on the Pass Line come-out. That is to say that the odds portion are inactive or not working. After all, a come-out 7 would be bittersweet at best. The Pass Line bet would win even money, but all of the active Come bets would lose. The odds portion of your bet can be increased (up to the house limit), reduced, or removed at any time. You cannot turn your Come bets off because they are a contract bet. Turning a bet off is like removing it temporarily and then placing it back up shortly thereafter. If you wish to keep your odds on during the come-out roll, simply announce, "odds working" to the dealer. He will more than likely place an *On* marker on top of your Come bet odds. If you wish to turn your Come bet odds off during a point cycle, tell the dealer. He will mark them with an *Off* button and wait for you to tell him that they are working again.

I've had a few shooting experiences where I made my Pass Line point and proceeded to set and throw a 7 on the next come-out roll. As I turned to celebrate with some of my companions, I noticed that all of their Come bets and odds were being removed from the betting area. I am typically a Place bettor and did not notice that they established several Come bets. My winning Pass Line 7 was a seven-out for all of their active Come bets including the odds that were working. I now warn my friends ahead of time that I like to set and shoot for the come-out 7 on the Pass Line. If you Come bet, you may be out of synch with the other Pass Line players. In addition, if the shooter is exhibiting any amount of influence on the cubes (a nice consistent delivery) and is setting come-out 7s, then you might consider holding off on the Come bets.

If the shooter makes your Come bet number, the dealer will place it back in the Come box with its corresponding winnings. You must pick up your chips before the next roll or it will all count as a Come bet for the next toss. If you wish to have a Come bet working on the next throw, leave the appropriate amount in the Come box and put the rest of your chips in the rack. Many Come bettors like to have multiple Come bets working simultaneously. Let's say that you have one Come bet established on a number and a second Come bet in the Come box waiting to be established. The first Come bet number is thrown, so you will be paid for that one, but the second Come bet will now move to that same number and replace the first bet. The dealer may ask you if you are "off and on." This means that your second Come bet goes to replace the Come bet that just hit and you wish to keep another bet (same size) in the Come box for the next roll. In that event, the dealer will simply pay you your winnings from the first Come bet (with odds present) and leave the previous Come bet in the point box (with any odds wagered) and a bet sitting in the Come box equal to the last Come bet that you made.

An example here would probably help:

1. You place $10 in the Come box for the next roll and a 6 is thrown.
2. The dealer places your Come bet in the 6 box and you drop him $10 for odds.
3. The shooter repeats the 6.
4. The dealer hands you the old $10 Come bet plus the $10 odds bet along with $10 plus $12 in winnings, for a total of $42 back.
5. He places your next $10 Come bet in the 6 box. Now realizing you need odds for this bet, you give him back $10 for odds. You also realize that you want to establish another Come bet, so you place $10 back in the Come box. You have re-established all your bets and are left with $22.

"Off and on" has the exact same effect without all the bet manipulations. It means that the dealer will leave your Come bet with odds in the point box. He will leave your next Come bet in the Come box and he will simply hand you the $22 that you netted. This has the same result and makes the game proceed more efficiently. If you do not wish to bet in the Come box for the next roll, simply answer, "No bet on the Come," or "No action in the Come," and he'll nudge the Come bet back in your direction. That's your signal to pick it up. If the shooter is letting the dice fly and you haven't had a chance to retrieve your bet, make sure the dealer heard your request. He should repeat, "No action in the Come." He will then return your bet after the dice come to rest.

Don't Come Bet

Similar to the way the Come bet works in relation to the Pass Line bet, the *Don't Come* wager is essentially a Don't Pass bet that can be made in the middle of the point cycle part of the game. As with the Come bet, the very next roll will act as your come-out roll. Place your bet in the Come box and inform the dealer, "Don't Come" or, "D.C. please." The dealer should acknowledge your wager by picking it up and placing it in the Don't Come box immediately next to the 4 point box on the table's left half, or the 10 point box on the table's right-hand side. If the next roll is a 7 or 11, the D.C. bet will be lost. A 2 or 3 results in an instant win and a 12 is a push. If a point number is thrown, the dealer will pick up the wager and place it in the back portion of the point box for the number just thrown. Just a quick note, any bets that are placed "for" a number to repeat (i.e. Come bet or Place bet), end up in the front part of the point box where the number is displayed. Any bets "against" a particular number (such as D.C. or placing, buying against) are set in the back part of the point box (closest to the dealer).

Like the Don't Pass wager, you can lay odds against that number as well. These odds work in the exact same manner as they would for the Don't Pass wager and give the casino no mathematical edge. A point of 6 or 8 has you laying six units to win five. A 5 or 9 requires laying three units for every two that you wish to win and a D.C. point of 4 or 10 has you laying multiples of $2 for every $1 in odds winnings. Just place the odds wager in the Come box and announce, "laying the odds." The dealer should then pick up and place your odds bet on top of, but off center to, your original Don't Come wager. If a 7 is thrown before that number repeats, then the Don't Come bet wins even money and any odds will be paid according to the correct odds of a 7 occurring before that point number. Keep in mind that you may have a D.C. or Don't Come bet active while the shooter makes his point (some other number) and begins a new come-out cycle. You will still be in the point cycle portion of your game. If a 7 is thrown on the Pass Line come-out, it will act as a natural winner for the Pass Line and a seven-out winner for your D.C. bet. The Don't Come odds generally work on the come-out roll.

If I feel that the table is running cold and none of the shooters is showing signs of influencing the dice, then I may place a D.C. bet or two. I like the Don't Come wager because it is a less conspicuous way to play the Don't side. The Don't Pass wager is right out in front of you for everyone else to see and bemoan. The D.C. wager is placed in the rear of the point box near the dealer. It is also less obvious because the bet itself is placed in the middle of the point cycle where it is lost amongst the other payouts and bets being placed. And who knows? You may find yourself cheering with the rest of the table if the shooter throws a come-out 7!

The house advantage for the Pass Line and Come bets are identical. So too is the casino edge for the Don't Pass and Don't Come wagers. Table 3-5, below, is a summary of the Pass Line/ Come bets while taking various odds and the Don't Pass/ Don't Come bets while laying different odds amounts.

Table 3-5
House Advantages for Do and Don't with Various Odds

Odds Amount	Pass Line/ Come Bet	Don't Pass Don't Come
Zero Odds	1.4141%	1.4026%
Single Odds	0.8485%	0.8320%
Double Odds	0.6061%	0.5915%
Triple Odds	0.4714%	0.4588%
4 x Odds	0.3857%	0.3747%
5 x Odds	0.3263%	0.3167%
6 x Odds	0.2828%	0.2743%
7 x Odds	0.2496%	0.2418%
8 x Odds	0.2233%	0.2163%
9 x Odds	0.2020%	0.1956%
10 x Odds	0.1845%	0.1785%

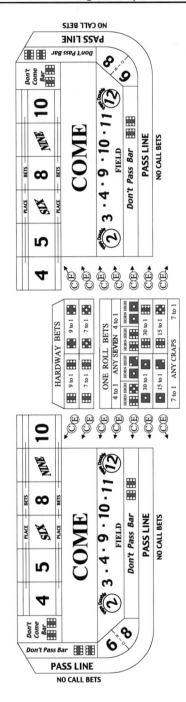

Figure 3-6

Chapter 4

Place, Buy, and Proposition Bets

The Place Bets

Another wager that can be made on one or more of the point numbers is the Place bet to win. Typically, Pass Line bettors who want additional action out on the betting layout make Place bets. They can wager on one or more of the other point numbers by simply placing them to win. Like the Pass Line or Come bet, if the number is thrown—it wins. If the 7 appears, all Place bets lose. If any other number is tossed, there is no decision for that wager. Unlike the Pass Line or Come bets, the Place bettor can place, modify, or remove the Place bets at any time. They are not a contract bet. As soon as the bet is placed on the desired number, the money goes right to work for you. A Place bet to win means that a particular point number will appear before a 7 and you will be paid each time it hits. If the 7 is thrown, all Place bets are wiped out. By default, the Place bets are off on the come-out roll when most Pass Line bettors hope for a 7 or 11. Once a point is established, Place bets are on and are usually rearranged to reflect the current point situation. As different points are made and established, the Pass Line bettors will typically shift their

Place bets off of the new point, covered by the Pass Line wager, and onto the previous point that was just made. Please remember that you can add, modify, remove or turn Place bets on or off at any time.

The casino makes its money on the Place bets by paying out at slightly less than correct odds on winners. Table 4-1 shows the point numbers, their true odds, casino payoffs and the casino's edge. Because of the way these bets are paid, you will have to Place the 6 or 8 in increments of $6 (pays $7 for every $6 wagered). You would Place the 5 or 9 (pays off at seven to five) and the 4 or 10 (pays $9 for every $5 bet) in multiples of $5. Take time to look at the Place bet pay-off odds because they are different than the correct odds paid for "odds" on Pass Line and Come bets.

Table 4-1
Odds Against Placing the Point Numbers to Win

Point Nos.	Ways Made	Ways Lost	True Odds	Payoff Odds	House Edge
6 or 8	5	6	6 to 5	7 to 6	1.515%
5 or 9	4	6	3 to 2	7 to 5	4.000%
4 or 10	3	6	2 to 1	9 to 5	6.667%

The edge is calculated as the actual payoff minus the correct payoff times the probability of the number occurring, all times 100 percent. For illustrative purposes, the edge is calculated thusly for the 5 or 9:

$$(7/5 - 3/2) \times 2/5 \times 100\% = -4.000\%$$
*a negative player's edge

To make a Place bet, you simply place the wager(s) in the Come box and ask the dealer to *Place* the particular numbers that you desire. The dealer will position the Place bets on the outer front border of each point box, relative to where you are standing at that half of the craps table. Clearly state your intended bet to the dealer. Instructions like, "Place the 5 and 9 for $10 each" or "Give me a $12, 8 please." Let's say that you are a Pass Line bettor and like to have all the inside point numbers (5, 6, 8, and 9) covered. It's a $10 table and the point is 5. You would put $34 in the Come box and announce, "$34 inside." The dealer knows to Place $12 on the 6, $12 on the 8 and $10 on the 9; the Pass Line bet already covers the 5. Likewise, "$17 inside" will work for $5 units if the point is 5 or 9. If the point is 6 or 8 and you wish to Place the remaining inside numbers, then $16, or some multiple of "$16 inside" will be the call. Some multiple of $22 inside will work if the point is 4 or 10. Sometimes the player wishes to have all of the point numbers working. If the point, for example, is 9 at a $10 table, then the bettor will throw out $54 and state, "$54 across," or, "Across the board." The dealer will know that you want action on every number. He will place $10 each on the 4, 5, and 10 and $12 each on the 6 and 8.

As with any of your Place bets, if one wins, the dealer may assume no modifications to your bets and place your winnings down in front of you. Sometimes he will inquire, "Same bet?" which means you are not making any modifications to your bets and accept your full winnings. You can plan ahead a little depending on what you want to do. As the dealer pays the player next to you (before he pays you) tell him, "Same bet here," if you wish to keep your bets unchanged. If you tell him, "Press it," he will apply all of your winnings toward increasing the bet on that number. He will put any extra change remaining down in front of you. You can press up matching pairs, like the 6 and the 8 or the 5 and the 9 at once, or you can press up the inside numbers. For example, if you have a $15, 5 and 9 working and the 5 comes in, then say, "Take the 5 and 9 up to green," or, "Make the 5 and 9 look like $25 each." He will take your $21 winnings and press both the 5 and 9 ($10 each) up to $25, or green. He will then place $1 in change on the table in front of you. Let's say that you have a $10, 9 and $12 on the 6 and 8 each. The 8 results winning you $14 and you wish to press all three numbers. Drop $3 on the layout and tell the dealer, "$17 inside press." The 9 will go up to $15 and the 6 and 8 will be increased to $18 each. If you do not wish to press your luck, then instruct the dealer to "turn your bets off" or even, "take them down."

Some craps players have been playing the game for years without even knowing about this next bet. Not all casinos allow this wager. It is called a *Place bet to lose*. Here, the player is wagering that a 7 will be rolled before the indicated number is rolled. The come-out rolls are usually ignored for any Place bet, but the player can request that the bet works on the come-out. You may bet against any or all of the point numbers (4, 5, 6, 8, 9, or 10). The casino requires you to lay slightly more than the correct odds, giving the house its mathematical edge. For example, the correct odds of making a 10 before a 7 are 2 to 1, or 10 to 5 against. If you placed the 10 to lose, the casino requires you to risk (or lay) $11 for every $5 that you wish to win. Refer to Table 4-2.

Table 4-2
Odds Against Placing the Point Numbers to Lose

Point Nos.	Ways Won	Ways Lost	True Odds	Payoff Odds	House Edge
6 or 8	6	5	5 to 6	4 to 5	1.818%
5 or 9	6	4	2 to 3	5 to 8	2.500%
4 or 10	6	3	1 to 2	5 to 11	3.030%

There are six ways to throw the 7 and five ways to make a 6. If it were a fair game, you would lay $6 to win $5. However, the casino has you Place $5 to win $4, so the actual payoff minus the correct payoff times the probability, all times one hundred percent calculates the player's edge:

$$(4/5 - 5/6) \times 6/11 \times 100\% = -1.818$$
*a negative player's edge

The player should win almost $4.17 for every $5 at risk. The edge for the 5 or 9 Place bets to lose, where the player Places $8 to win $5 and 4 or 10 (risking $11 to win $5) are calculated in the same manner.

The Big 6 and 8 Bets

Two bets that are similar to a 6 or 8 Place bet to win are the *Big 6* and *Big 8* bets. They are found at the front corners of some betting layouts, near the line bets. Here, you are wagering that a 6 (Big 6 bet) or an 8 (Big 8 bet) will be rolled before a 7 comes up. Where this bet differs from a Place bet is that it only pays even money and has a whopping house edge of 9.091 percent. A fair payout would be $6 for every $5 wagered. The Place bet on 6 or 8 pays 7 to 6 at least, having a more manageable house edge of 1.515 percent. If you wish to bet the 6 and/or 8 point numbers, the Place bet is highly preferred. Be cognizant of the Big 6 and 8 bets, but don't make them.

Buying and Laying Numbers

Another non-contract option to betting on a number directly and having the ability to turn it off or on at any time, is Buying a point number to win. With a Buy bet, you are paid the correct odds; however, you must pay the house five percent commission on your wager in order to enjoy that privilege. The dealer will put the Buy bets along with the Place bets on the narrow banded areas, just below and atop the point box. The dealer will then place a small blue BUY button on top of the wager. If you wish to take down your Buy bet, the dealer will return your commission as well. The casino edge varies, depending upon the size of the wager. Most books report the house advantage on this bet at 4.762 percent.

That is true for a $20 wager plus $1 commission charged up front (a $21 total bet). The edge, for any other Buy bet, will be higher or lower, based on the wager amount. For example, a $15 (total) Buy bet, for either the 5, 9 or 4, 10 is exactly a –6.667 percent edge. Let's look at the 4, 10 Buy bet. You place $15 in the Come box and tell the dealer that you wish to Buy the 4. He takes $1 commission and places $14 with a BUY button on the 4. The 4 hits and he pays you 2 to 1, or $28.

If you wish to keep the bet working, you will have to pay another $1 commission. Let's say that you take it down after one hit for simplicity's sake. The dealer will give you back $28 plus your $14 Buy bet. Because you started with $15, you actually netted $27. The house edge can be calculated as (casino payoff – correct payoff) x probability = percent advantage.

$$(27/15 - 30/15) \times 1/3 = -6.667\%$$

This is the same edge (and payoff) that you see for a $15, 4 or 10 Place bet. Anything over $15 on the 4 or 10 should be a Buy bet because the house edge is less than 6.667 percent. As you increase the Buy bet relative to the $1 commission, the edge gets smaller. A $20 bet (total bet) gives the casino exactly five percent advantage. A $25 Buy bet ($24 bet with $1 commission) returns $48 minus the original $1 commission and works out exactly to a four percent casino edge. Let's say that you increase the bet up to $30, ($29 Buy plus $1 commission). Your $29 returns you $58 minus the $1 for a net of $57. You are shorted $3 on your winnings. $(57/30 - 60/30) \times 1/3 = -3.333$ percent. Look at Graph 4-3 and follow how the house edge decreases for the 4, 10 Buy bet with each increasing wager.

This tactic of placing a larger wager for the same $1 commission is called *pushing the house*. It was first written about in *Beat the Craps out of the Casinos* by Frank Scoblete. My experience is that most casinos will allow you to bet at the $30-unit level (or possibly higher) for a buck commission.

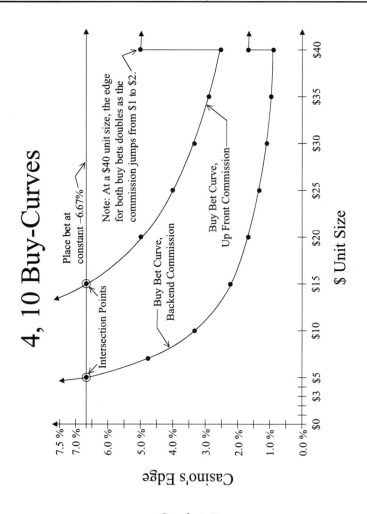

4, 10 Buy-Curves

Place bet at constant –6.67%

Note: At a $40 unit size, the edge for both buy bets doubles as the commission jumps from $1 to $2.

Intersection Points

Buy Bet Curve, Backend Commission

Buy Bet Curve, Up Front Commission

Casino's Edge

7.5 %
7.0 %
6.0 %
5.0 %
4.0 %
3.0 %
2.0 %
1.0 %
0.0 %

$0 $3 $5 $10 $15 $20 $25 $30 $35 $40

$ Unit Size

Graph 4-3

Another situation you should be aware of is this: while most casinos collect the commission up front when the bet is first made, some casinos (a select few) collect the commission only on winning bets. That's right; they collect the commission on the back end. This doesn't sound like such a big deal, except when you realize, that dollar goes from being worth zero to two dollars if a 4 or 10 hits! Instead of being shorted $3 you are only shorted $1. The casino's edge is reduced by a whopping two-thirds! Let's look at that same $30 bet. Now, the whole $30 works, winning you $60. Then the $1 commission is subtracted leaving you $59 net. $(59/30 - 60/30) \times 1/3 = -1.111$ percent. This is a huge concession and the casinos allowing this practice should be commended. Maybe if more players asked for the commission on the back end, more casinos would oblige.

Buying the 5 or 9 may also be advantageous, but at a much higher unit size. The casino advantage for Placing a 5 or 9 is 4.000 percent as compared to 6.667 percent for Placing a 4 or 10. As a result, you will need to get a larger amount of money out for the same $1 commission. This is necessary to lower the edge below 4.000 percent, making the Buy bet worthwhile. This is a concept first mentioned in Frank Scoblete's book *The Captain's Craps Revolution*. A $20 Buy plus $1 commission ($21 total) gives the house a 4.762 percent advantage. It turns out that at a $25 total bet ($24 Buy plus $1 commission) breaks even with the 5, 9 Place bet. The $24 Buy wins 3 to 2 or $36. Then the $1 commission is subtracted leaving you with $35 net.

If you had Placed the 5 or 9 for $25, you would have also won $35. $(35/25 - 3/2) \times 2/5 = -4.000$ percent. If you can Buy a $25 or higher, 5 or 9 for a buck, then the house edge is equal to or lower than the 4.000 percent Place bet edge. Look at this example. Place a 5 for $35 and you win 7 to 5, or $49. However, Buy a $34, 5 for a buck ($35 total) and win $51 minus the $1 commission to net $50. $(50/35 - 3/2) \times 2/5 = -2.857$ percent house advantage. Once you reach a $40 unit size, the casino will require $2 commission. As with the 4 or 10, the ability to pay the commission on the back end is a huge benefit. For the 5 or 9 Buy bet, the casino's edge is reduced by 60 percent, or 1.0 minus two-fifths. The same $25 Buy bet, at -4.000 percent, now looks like only -1.600 percent. Graph 4-4 below portrays the decreasing house edges for the 5, 9 Buy bets. Just a quick note regarding the 6, 8—it never pays to Buy these numbers. You cannot do better than the -1.515 percent edge experienced when Placing the 6 or 8.

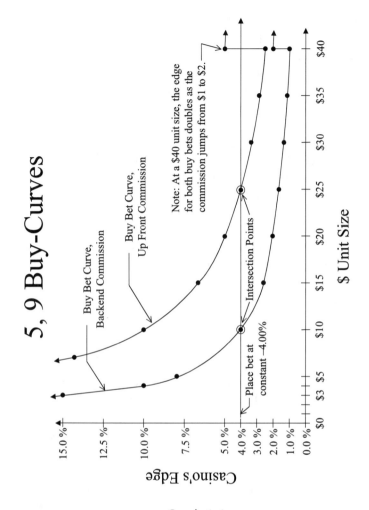

Graph 4-4

The *Lay* bet or *Laying* a point number to lose is a bet that a 7 will appear before a particular number does. You are betting that a specific point number (4, 5, 6, 8, 9, or 10) will *not* be rolled before a 7 comes up. The casino takes 5 percent of the winnings on these bets. If you Lay $40 plus $1 commission against a 10, you will win $20 if the 7 appears first. If the number comes in before the 7, you will lose the full $41. Most bettors do not like to risk $41 to win $20 (actually netting $19), but the odds are 2 to 1 in your favor. Likewise when Laying against the 5 or 9, you will Lay $30 plus $1 to win $20 (netting $19). The odds are 3 to 2 in your favor, so you must Lay more to win less. The 5 percent commission is usually taken up front, but some casinos will take the commission after the bet wins. Again, the house edge is considerably less when the commission is taken off the back end. Table 4-5 shows the house advantage for each point number. In reality, the edge follows a curve like it does for the Buy bets (or any bets involving commissions). Winning payoffs of $10, $20 and $30 are shown in this table. Keep in mind, for example, that winning $20 actually means netting $19 when you factor back in the $1 commission charge. The edge on the 4 or 10 when Laying $41 to win $20, and net $19, is –2.439 percent as shown in the table. As you increase the wager for the same $1 commission, the house edge decreases. Laying $61 to win $30 (netting $29) for a 4 or 10 further lowers the advantage to –1.639 percent.

Table 4-5
Laying to Lose Odds, $1 Commission

Point No.	Odds	To Win $10 (net $9)	To Win $20 (net $19)	To Win $30 (net $29)
6 or 8	5 to 6	9 to 13, –7.692%	19 to 25, –4.000%	29 to 37, –2.703%
5 or 9	2 to 3	9 to 16, –6.250%	19 to 31, –3.226%	29 to 46, –2.174%
4 or 10	1 to 2	9 to 21, –4.762%	19 to 41, –2.439%	29 to 61, –1.639%

If you wish to Lay against (or Buy to lose) any of the point numbers, place your wager in the Come box and tell the dealer which number(s) you are Laying against. The dealer will place your wager behind the point number, in the rear of the point box with the Don't Come wagers. He will place a yellow LAY button on top. The Lay bet is not a contract bet and can be modified or removed at any time. The commission is usually paid up front, but will be returned if the bet is taken down. Generally, Buy or Lay bets do not work on the come-out unless you instruct the dealers to "make them work." Just ask the dealer if you have any questions.

In summary, a rule of thumb would be to *Place* the 6, 8 or 5, 9 because the house edge is generally lower. If you are working with $30 or $35 units, you might consider *Buying* the 5 or 9 for a buck each. Some casinos don't bother with the Place bet to lose wager. If you cannot Place the 6, 8 or 5, 9 to lose, then try *pushing the house* with a larger *Lay* bet or just use the *Don't Come* wager. When dealing with the 4 or 10, you will pay the commission. That is, you will *Buy* the 4 or 10 to win or *Lay* them to lose for a buck.

Playing the "Field" and Handling "Propositions"

Usually on the come-out rolls, you will hear the stickman hawking these bets, "Horn High yos?, C and Es?, Any Craps or World bets?" and for good reason. They have the worst payoffs on the table with some as high as –16.667 percent. In addition to this fact, there is another dark secret that these bets hold. The proposition, or *prop*, bets are exactly that, one-roll propositions. That is, you are betting that a certain pair of dice faces will appear on the very next roll. This is doubly bad, because you are exposing your money to a much higher edge at a much higher frequency! *Each* roll is a win/lose decision, so you are cycling your bankroll (which experiences a negative compounding effect) through the game and high house edge at a more furious pace. The Pass Line bettor's wager, if the point were 10 for example, will last five and a half times longer on average than a one-roll prop bet. There are three ways to make a 10 and six ways to seven-out, for a total of nine decisions out of 36 possible dice outcomes. That means it will take four throws, on average, during the point cycle to affect a decision. Couple that with the average number of come-out rolls (1.5 rolls) it takes before a point is established and you have 5.5 total rolls from come-out to a decision. The prop bettor only gets one roll to a decision; hence he gets a lot less mileage out of his bets in addition to the high tax that he pays on winnings. I'll spend a little time covering these bets so you'll recognize them, but also recognize the very real danger these bets pose to your bankroll. All of these wagers, with the exception of the Field bet, are located right smack in the center of the table, just in front of the stickman. If you do venture forth with one or more of these wagers, you will address him when making these bets.

The Field Bet—The *Field bet* is a one-roll wager that the next number will be a Field number. The Field numbers include the 2, 3, 4, 9, 10, 11, and 12. You have seven out of 11 possible numbers working for you, so it looks enticing, but beware. The most frequent numbers: 7, 6, 8, and 5 are omitted, giving the house more ways to win (20 vs. 16). The Field bet is the only prop bet not found in the center, between the stickman and boxman. It is located on each table half, between the Don't Pass and Come box betting areas. You can place these bets for yourself, just before the next toss of the dice. The 3, 4, 9, 10, or 11 pay even money if rolled. The 2 and 12 typically pay 2 to 1. Some casinos pay triple, or 3 to 1, for the 12. Let's see what happens, on average, with a one unit bet over the course of 36 rolls:

Outcome	Frequency	Decision	Net Units
2	1 x	Win 2 units	+2 units
3	2 x	Win 1 unit	+2 unit
4	3 x	Win 1 unit	+3 unit
5	4 x	Lose 1 unit	–4 unit
6	5 x	Lose 1 unit	–5 unit
7	6 x	Lose 1 unit	–6 unit
8	5 x	Lose 1unit	–5 unit
9	4 x	Win 1 unit	+4 unit
10	3 x	Win 1 unit	+3 unit
11	2 x	Win 1unit	+2 unit
12	1 x	Win 2 units	+2 unit
Totals:	**36 rolls**		**–2 units**

Therefore, for every 36 rolls, or units wagered, you will lose two units on average for a double-pay 2 and 12, Field wager. Two units (lost) divided 36 units (wagered), yields the house a 5.556 percent edge on this bet. If the table has a triple-pay 12 (or 2 sometimes, but not both) then the edge is reduced to one unit (lost) divided by 36 units, or 2.778 percent. Either way, it has the lowest edge of all the prop bets. If you do play on a "triple-pay 12" table and wish to bet the Field, I'll share some special dice sets with you in Chapter 12 that will give you a fighting chance. It is rare, but some of the older casinos may make the 5 a Field roll instead of the 9. Both numbers have four ways to be made so the math doesn't change.

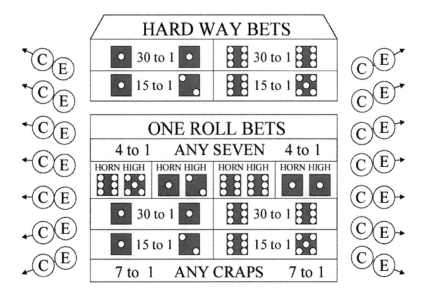

Figure 4-6
Hard Way and Proposition Bets

Any Seven or "Big Red"—The *Any Seven* wager is a one-roll proposition that can be made before any roll of the dice. Being superstitious about uttering the number "7" at the table, the bet is often called big red. This is simply a bet that the next roll will be a 7. If it is, you win 4 to 1. If it is not, then you lose. Because one combination in six, with two regulation dice, produces a 7, the correct payoff would be 5 to 1.

However, at the casino's 4 to 1 payout schedule, you will lose one unit for every six attempts. This means you are bucking a 16.667 percent house edge—enough said!

Any Craps—The *Any Craps* bet is a wager that the next roll will be 2, 3, or 12. Because there are four ways to throw these numbers out of 36 outcomes, the probability of hitting is 1 in 9. Hence, the correct payoff should be 8 to 1. The casino offers 7 to 1, giving them a healthy 11.111 percent advantage. The stickman will place your wager in the circle marked with a "C" that points to your position at the table. This bet is primarily used as a hedge bet, to protect a larger Pass Line wager. Aside from having a high house edge, it misses the mark in two other regards. First, the Pass Line bettor already has a bona fide mathematical edge for the come-out roll, with eight ways to win versus four ways to lose, and doesn't need help at this juncture. Secondly, two-thirds of the time, a point will be established, putting the Pass Line bettor's back against the wall. The Any Craps bet loses immediately and offers no further help during this perilous period. The best advice would be to save your Any Craps wager and apply it to the odds bet after the point is established.

Three-Way Craps—This is another way to bet on craps for the next roll of the dice. This wager is made in units of three, with one unit effectively on the 2, one on the 3, and a final unit on the 12. This is like making three separate wagers. If a 2 or 12 appear (one shot in 36), two units are lost and the winning bet pays 30 to 1. The correct odds are 35 to 1. If the 3 is hit (two ways in 36), then two units are lost and a payoff of 15 to 1 is realized instead of 17 to 1. All in all, you will net 28 units two times and 13 units two times (two ways to make a 3). The other 32 times you will lose three units. (82 – 96) units / (3 x 36) units wagered = –12.963 percent overall player's edge.

Horn Bet—The *Horn* bet is basically just betting on the 2, 3, 11, and 12 at once. It is like the Three-way Craps bet, except you are picking up a fourth number—the 11. This bet covers the smaller frequency numbers on the ends, or the "horn." This wager is made in increments of four, with one unit on each Horn number for the next roll. If one of the four numbers wins, the other three effectively lose. A winning result of 2 or 12 pays 30 to 1 (minus three), while a winner of 3 or 11 pays 15 to 1 (minus three). Thirty-six bets of four units each (or 144 units) will win 27 units each for the 2 and 12 and 12 units *each* for a 3 or 11. That's a total win of 102 units (two ways each to a 3 or 11). There are 30 other numbers that will lose four units each for a total loss of –120 units. (102 – 120) units divided by 144 wagered equals –12.500 percent average edge against the player.

Horn High Bet—The *Horn High* bet is similar to the Horn bet, except you are placing two units on your designated "high" number. This bet is made in multiples of five with one unit on three of the Horn numbers, and two units on the high number. The "Horn High yo," for example, means one unit each on the 2, 3, and 12 with two units on the "yo," or 11. The payouts are 15 to 1 or 30 to 1 for each unit, depending on the winning Horn number. You must subtract three units if the high number wins and four units if a non-high number wins for your total net.

World Bet—The *World* bet is like the Horn bet, except you are wagering a fifth unit on the 7. The 2 or 12 pays 30 to 1, minus four units. The 3 or 11 pays 15 to 1, less four and the 7, at 4 to 1 minus four units, breaks even. It's sort of a Horn bet with insurance against the 7. For every 36 sets of five units that you wager (or 180 total units), you will lose 24. This is a combined 13.333 percent casino advantage!

Single Horn Number Bet—If you like, you can bet just one unit on any of the Horn numbers. A winning bet on the 2 or 12 pays 30 to 1 with a 13.889 percent casino edge. An individual bet on the 3 or 11 pays 15 to 1 with an 11.111 percent house advantage. Of the single Horn numbers, the 11 is most popular. There is a special circle labeled with an "E" on the betting layout for everyone standing at the table. Both the circled "C" and "E" betting areas are lined up in columns, just to the right or left of the proposition box with arrows pointing to each table position. See diagram 3-6 or 4-6 for clarification.

Hard Way Bets—The *Hard Way* bets are located in a separate boxed area above the proposition bets, in front of the boxman. The hard way combinations are point numbers that are made in like dice pairs. You can bet on any of four hard way combinations. The hard 4 (2-2), 6 (3-3), 8 (4-4), and 10 (5-5) appear in pairs and can only be made one way (the hard way). The 2 and 12 are "only" way combinations and are not considered. When you bet on a specific hard way combination, you are betting against both the 7 and the "easy ways." For example, if you wager on the hard 6, you are betting that a 3-3 combination will appear before any 7 or an easy 6 does. A 6 the easy way would include 1-5, 2-4, 4-2, or 5-1. You have ten total ways to lose and only one way (3-3) to win. These bets are not necessarily one-roll propositions. The other 25 dice outcomes will not affect your wager, one way or the other. The odds of making a hard 6 or hard 8 are 10 to 1 against, but the casino pays 9 to 1. This gives them a 9.091 percent advantage on these bets. The hard 4 or 10 can each be made one way hard and two ways easy. Factor in six ways to a 7 and you have eight total ways to lose. The odds are then 8 to 1, but the casino only offers 7 to 1, giving them an 11.111 percent edge on the hard 4 or hard 10 bets.

A phrase that craps players use to place a hard way or prop bet for themselves and the dealers at the same time is *two ways*. If you throw $2 out to the stickman and announce, "Two-way hard 8," he will place a buck for you and one for the crew. If the 4-4 comes in, you will both win $9. The crew will immediately take $9 plus the original $1 bet and put it in the toke box. Your $1 wager will remain on the hard 8. If you threw $6 to the "stick" and called it a two-way, then he assumes $5 for you and $1 for the boys. A $10, two-way would be $5 each. I've even seen players throw $7 out and ask for a *three-way* bet. This would be $5 for the bettor, $1 for the crew and $1 for the *shooter*. In almost all casinos, hard way bets are "off" on the come-out unless you request that they work. hard way bets can be placed, modified, or removed before any roll. I know these bets can add a little more color to the game and are fun to hit, but if you are going to make some of these center-table wagers (against my advice), then keep it relatively small (fractional units) and stick with the hard 6 or hard 8. At –9.091 percent, it is still expensive, but at least it will last about 3.3 rolls to a decision.

Hop Bet—In Vegas, the casinos will book a one-roll bet called the *hop* bet. This is a proposition bet that the next roll will result in one particular combination of the dice. For example, "Fifty-four hopping (or Forty-five for that matter)," would be a bet that the next roll produces a 9 made up of 5-4 or 4-5 dice combinations. As long as one die is a 4 and the other is a 5, this bet would win. There are always two ways to make totals with unlike numbers and 34 ways not to make them. A "Fifty-three" call can only be made with a 5-3 or 3-5. "Thirty-one hopping" would win with a 3-1 or a 1-3. These bets pay 15 to 1 instead of 17 to 1 and give the house an 11.111 percent advantage. Another variation to this bet, is the *hopping hard way* bet. Here, you are wagering that the next roll will be a particular hard way number. Because there is only one way to throw a like dice pair and 35 ways not to, the correct odds are 35 to 1 against. However, the casino treats these bets like a single-roll 2 or 12 bet and pays only 30 to 1 (giving themselves a hefty 13.889 percent edge).

As I write this section on hard ways and hop bets, I'm coming off a great weekend I had with 42 students in Vegas. I showed off with a 45-minute roll (nine point passes) at the Golden Nugget downtown, a 20-minute+ roll at the Treasure Island, and a 30-minute game at the new Aladdin. During my roll at the Aladdin, I became very sensitive to how the dice were coming out of my hand and began making and hitting hard way bets for the crew. I figured it's only a buck per point cycle and it's a 100 percent disadvantage anyway (toke for the dealers), so why not have some fun with it. Just as I set the 5-5 on top in an attempt to make my Pass Line point and a hard 10 for the crew, Dominick, one of my instructing assistants, challenged me by calling a $25, sixty-four hop bet. I set the dice back down and looked over at him. He had a big grin on his face, and so too did about six students who were standing at that end of the table. "Alright," I thought, "I'm gonna make you wish you had a $100 bet up there!" Everyone had multiple odds on the Pass Line 10 and became very quiet as I returned my attention to the dice. I reset the dice so that 6 and 4 were now on top (left to right), and then carefully griped the dice so they stayed square to each other. As I lightly released them, both dice came off perfectly together. They arced and rotated side-by-side, bouncing and landing on axis together, just touching the bottom back wall. The result . . . a 6-4 of course! That was the table's cue to celebrate wildly. The bosses, who were watching me already, just looked at each other. Dominick sprung over like a human pogo stick and shouted a very spirited, "Holy Christmas!" and gave me a pair of high-fives.

Part Two

Mastering the Mechanics

Chapter 5

Element One: Setting for Success

What you have read in Part One alone contains more information then you will find in many of the other books devoted to craps. We are just getting warmed up here, though. We will begin our advanced studies by discussing the pre-arranging or positioning of the dice. Arranging, or *setting*, the dice after the stickman slides them over to you, is the process of positioning the dice with a particular top and front combination before you pick them up and throw them. This is your "ground zero" and everything that happens from here is directly linked to your initial dice set. Some of the veteran craps players have discovered, over years of play, that the right pre-arrangement, or *dice set*, coupled with a consistent delivery can tilt the edge in the player's favor. Many of these seasoned players do not understand the mechanics behind what they are doing; they only know that through trial and error they have discovered a means to garner an edge by playing this way. However, I can tell you that there is a *scientific basis* for what is happening here. Without fully realizing it, many of these players are establishing an initial set relationship, then controlling the components of motion with their smooth, consistent deliveries.

Importance of Setting the Dice

The game of craps cannot be beaten mathematically of course. Any system that has you sizing your next wager based upon whether you lost or won the previous bet, or some other convoluted method of tracking wins or losses is a mathematical system. Save your time and your bankroll. You must attack the game of craps by understanding the physical phenomena of the game and by controlling the rigid body mechanics of the dice. To achieve this you will need a consistent delivery system like a well-practiced golfer or bowler, and a specific starting point. This starting point is very important because you need a common place to begin each throw if you ever hope to see consistent results. Everything else that you do from here directly depends on this point of commencement. Most casinos will allow you to pre-set the dice with a particular combination of spots, on top and on front before you pick them up and toss them. This will be your starting point.

If you look at a single die, you will see that it has six faces, each containing one through six numbers of pips, or spots. Any one of these faces could be set on top for six different top combinations. Once you have selected a top number, you are locked into one of four possibilities for the front position. Applying the Multiplicative Rule of probability for two independent events, we have 6 x 4 = 24 ways to set a single die. Looking at the second die the same way, we have 24 ways to set it individually. Placing the first die on the right with one of 24 possible set positions and the second die on the left (also with one of 24 possible sets), we have 24 x 24, or 576 total combined possibilities for these dice together. If that weren't enough, you can exchange the right die for the left die and produce 576 redundant sets. With two six-sided cuboids (or a pair of regulation dice), there are exactly 1,152 different dice arrangements possible. I have studied each one of them, and some work much better than others do! The dice set that you employ will depend on two things:

1) Your objective for that throw (i.e. you are coming out and wish to throw a 7 for a Pass Line win, or you are in the point cycle and desire to avoid the seven-out).

2) What degrees of freedom the dice go through when you throw them (or how the dice move and rotate through space).

The first item is easy enough to understand. What is it that you wish to achieve on that roll? We will show you which sets make the most sense, depending on your immediate objective. The second item may take some explaining. By developing a consistent delivery system in which the dice act and react in unison, you can eliminate certain degrees of freedom (or elements of motion) from the parabolic trajectory of the dice and affect some positive amount of control over the remaining degrees of freedom that the cubes experience. The main idea is to set the dice a certain way, then carefully throw them so that the set relationship is maintained during the throw.

Degrees of Freedom

We live in a three-dimensional world of height, width, and depth. The dice can move, or *translate*, in any or all of these three directions at the same time. For our discussion, these three translational degrees of freedom are:

1) Front-to-back, or forward motion.
2) Side-to-side, or lateral motion.
3) Up and down, or vertical motion.

Now imagine a line with an arrowhead, or an *axis*, pointing in each of these three perpendicular directions. The dice can also *rotate* about any or all of these axes at the same time. There are three translational and three rotational degrees of freedom (or DOFs) in which the cubes can possibly traverse through space. Think of it this way, if you could simply set the dice directly on the desired result without having to throw them, the dice will have gone through zero DOF from the set to the end result. Congratulations, you have controlled the dice 100 percent. If you could set the dice and just slide them a few feet carefully down a Teflon surface, you could maintain the desired result, maybe 90 percent of the time. If you accomplish this carefully, the dice are undergoing one translational DOF (forward motion) as they slide down a straight line from point A to point B.

Now envision the dice being lightly tossed through the air and landing in a sandbox with no spin. As they land, they sink into the sand slightly and do not bounce. In this case, the dice are only using two translational DOFs (a vertical and horizontal component). Under these circumstances, I can personally demonstrate control over the results a solid 75 percent of the time. Take into account the table surface that the dice must bounce and tumble over and you add at least one rotational DOF and will have maybe 40 percent control if the throw is executed properly. As you add in the back wall and other obstacles (casino chips wagered, the On/Off puck, people's hands, etc.), you very quickly introduce factors that can add more degrees of freedom to the problem. You also increase the likelihood of knocking the dice out of synch with each other. Each DOF, up to a maximum of six, will quickly devour your percent control over the dice. Even if your delivery is near perfect (which is not a bad objective to shoot for), you will still need to keep the dice from colliding or interacting with other objects that can knock them into different directions.

Almost every shooter that I observe just picks up the dice, rattles them around and lets them fly. I refer to these guys as "chicken feeders." There is no control to speak of and the dice are haphazardly flung through space. Not only are they using all six DOFs, but also the left die is doing something totally different than the right die. My specially developed delivery system keeps both dice perfectly synchronized and uses only two translational and one rotational DOF. Hence, three DOFs are eliminated and the remaining three are heavily influenced by my controlled delivery. I also throw in a manner that best avoids obstacles and has minimal interaction with the back wall. My delivery method takes into account things like the conservation of momentum, elastic collisions, angles of incidence and reflectance, and other sorted laws of Newtonian physics. To have any chance of being successful, you must deliver the dice so that they leave your hand at the same time and perform identical gyrations through the air, landing and bouncing together. I will reveal details on my delivery throughout this and the next two chapters, with a primary focus in Chapter 6.

The Hard Ways Set

The dice set I am about to share with you is the most universally powerful set available for avoiding the 7. This set gives you maximum protection against the dreaded 7 when taking *all six degrees of freedom* into account, but still relies on a consistent method of throwing the dice. This set is suitable for an intermediate level dice shooter with a smooth and consistent delivery. The rank novice would also use this set, but should not expect any kind of an edge until he is able to further develop his throw. Because I can successfully reduce the various motions of the dice down to three kinematic DOFs, I optimize my rolls by using a slightly different dice set that is tailored to this level of control. You will read about this and some other specialized dice sets in Chapter 12. Sometimes, if I am lacking the necessary influence, I will fall back to the more universally secure Hard Ways Dice Set described on the following page in Figure 5-1.

Hard Ways Set
with 4-4 Top

Hard Ways Set
with 2-2 Top

Hard Ways Set
with 3-3 Top

Hard Ways Set
with 5-5 Top

Figure 5-1

Just as the name would imply, you will set hard ways combinations all around the dice. For example, you could set 5-5, or the hard 10, on top with either 3-3 (hard 6) or 4-4 (the hard 8) on the front. The 2-2, or hard 4, would then be at the bottom. If you prefer, you can position the hard eight, hard six or hard four on top. What matters most is that hard ways combinations (2-2, 3-3, 4-4, and 5-5) are found all around the dice before you pick them up. There are 16 different ways out of 1,152 that the Hard Ways Set can be formed. Eight of these are redundant because you can exchange the right die with the left die and accomplish the same exact set. Refer to Figure 5-1 for four examples of this powerful set. Because this set involves pairing of like numbers, it is visibly easy to recognize and verify for correctness. As with any dice set that you endeavor to use, you must learn to execute the set in two seconds or less. Otherwise, you will draw undue attention to yourself at the table. Purchase a set of regulation casino dice and practice setting, first for accuracy and then for speed.

In the casino, the stickman will bring the dice in front of the boxman for visual inspection. This is done just before he slides them over to you when you are about to shoot. At that time notice which faces are on top and which faces are on front. You can plan exactly which motions you need to quickly create your dice set. After the stickman slides the dice over to you to throw, place them side-by-side and form hard ways combinations on top and front. A good point to remember— opposite parallel faces of each die will add up to 7. Grab a die and look at it. If a 3 is on top, then a 4 has to be on the bottom face and likewise with the 5-2 and 6-1. This fact will help you to position the dice more efficiently. Another interesting and useful occurrence that develops from this situation happens when you pair up two dice. Whatever number you have on top, its "mate" can be found on the bottom. For example, 6s and 8s can both be made one of five ways. They have the highest frequency of occurrence for the point numbers and are mates. Set a 3-3 (hard 6) on top. Because opposite faces of each die add up to 7, there must be a 4-4, or hard 8, on the bottom. A 5-3 (or 8) on top means that a 2-4 (or 6) is underneath.

If you examine the master dice combination, Figure 5-3, you will see that 5 and 9 are mates (four ways each), as well as 4 and 10 (three ways), all the way out to 2 and 12. The lonely 7 is its own mate, i.e. a 5-2 on top means that a 2-5 is at the bottom. This condition, of course, also works from front to back. If a 2-2 is on the front, for example, then a 5-5 is on the back. That is why we are concerned with the top *and* front formations when we pre-arrange the dice into an exact setting. While we are talking about how the dice are configured, another item worth mentioning is that dice are manufactured in one of two possible configurations. To see this, place a single die down in front of you with the 6 on top. Now, rotate the die around (like a top) until you can see both the 2 and 3 faces at the same time on the sides. If you were to connect the diagonal dots on both of these faces, they would form an arrowhead that points up either to the 6-face or down to the 1-face. The die you are looking at will do one or the other. Different dice manufacturers will create their dice in one of these two configurations, but not both.

If you walk into one casino, you may see the first type that points up to the 6, on all their dice. Then you walk next door and observe the second configuration, pointing down to the 1. Not to worry, a specific casino will use one type or the other. They never mix configurations simply because their particular supplier, whoever it may be, will only manufacture one type or the other. You do not have to worry when playing in the actual casinos. All of the dice sets that I give you will work for either spot configuration as long as you have two dice with the same configuration. The only caveat is for home practice, where people inadvertently mix dice types. You do not want to pair up a die with the 2 and 3 pointing to the 6-face, to one that points to the 1-face. Be very careful not to mix and match different dice types in your home practice. These next several sentences are very important regarding practice dice. When you purchase dice with which to practice, make sure that the dice are *from the same casino*. This will ensure that they will be of the same spot configuration.

Buy 3/4" cubed, casino regulation dice only. Also, do not buy dice that have holes drilled through them. A cancelled marking is okay, but not a hole. When possible, make sure that they have the same lot number on them. This will take care of many inconsistencies that can occur. If not, then you must closely compare the dice. Place the dice side by side so they are flush to each other and slide your fingers down around them. Verify that they are the *exact same size*. If one die is so much as the thickness of an index card thicker than the other die you will feel it. Your home practice results will not be consistent or worse yet, you may get good at throwing with mismatched dice! Keep searching. The dice must also have the *exact same finish* on them. Do not mix, for example, a frosted finish with a polished finish. They will have different coefficients of friction and different perspiration retention factors. This will cause the dice to exit your hand at slightly different times with different trajectory angles. Again, the same lot number will solve all these problems. When not in use, store matching pairs together for future practice sessions.

After a few thousand throws, the dice will get a little beat up. Replace them as necessary. This is a small investment.

More on Degrees of Freedom and the Hard Ways Set

To understand exactly how the Hard Ways Set benefits us, we must revisit our discussion concerning dice motion and degrees of freedom (DOF). As mentioned before, to help control the results when we shoot the dice, we must eliminate some DOFs and heavily influence the remaining ones. It becomes necessary to create a standardized reference frame so we are on the same page, so to speak. As the dice shift or move through space, we can observe any or all of three translational DOFs that we will label horizontal, vertical, and side-to-side. The laws of gravity in our atmosphere dictate that a projectile will traverse a two-dimensional parabolic trajectory with a horizontal and vertical component (two translational DOFs). If the dice simultaneously travel side by side in identical but parallel 2-D trajectories, then you have successfully removed the sideways translation and are controlling the horizontal and vertical translations. The dice should land and bounce together. Hitting a chip or other obstacle on the table is undesirable because it will knock one or both dice off their axis and out of plane. As mentioned earlier, the dice may also undergo various rotational DOFs. Here, an example is helpful. Imagine if you will, an airplane flying straight ahead and level with the horizon. As the plane climbs or descends, its nose will rotate upward or downward. In aeronautical terms, this lengthwise plunging either up or down is referred to as *pitching*. As the dice translate through their trajectory, they may also pivot or even rotate end-over-end like cartwheels. This rotation of the dice about a common, side-to-side axis is also referred to as "pitching."

The dice may also rotate side-to-side about a fore/aft axis running front-to-back. Rotation about this axis will cause the dice to *roll* out of their 2-D planes and result in a sideways motion. This DOF is highly undesirable for a controlled throw because it adds one rotational DOF and reintroduces the third translational DOF, or side-to-side motion. The dice may *roll* out to the left or right side together, or roll out to opposing sides. This rolling is analogous to our plane rotating about its fuselage, forcing one wingtip upward while the other banks downward. If the plane completes a revolution in this manner, it is called a *barrel roll*.

The third and final rotational DOF that may occur is when the dice rotate about a vertical line or axis. Imagine an automobile spinning out on a sheet of ice. As the car continues sliding forward, the front of the vehicle may swing around to the rear and continue all the way back to the front, completing a full 360 degree spin. Keeping with our aeronautical notation, this rotating motion is referred to as yaw. Each die may also spin about an imaginary line that starts in the center of the top face and projects down to the center of the bottom face. The same numbered face may stay positioned on top and bottom, but its sides will rotate around like a top. Because four of six faces of one die will lose their relationship relative to the other die, this result becomes undesirable as well.

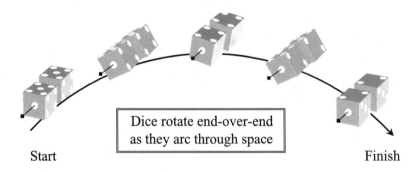

Dice rotate end-over-end
as they arc through space

Start   Finish

Figure 5-2
Pitching About a Lateral Axis with Horizontal and Vertical
Translations

If you can develop a delivery system whereby the dice experience only a horizontal and vertical translational DOF and maybe a pitch-type rotational DOF, you will be well ahead of the game. As you eliminate three degrees of freedom and control these other three, you are greatly reducing the mechanics of the motion and you will exert much influence over the remaining ranges of motion. Now that we understand the rotational degrees of freedom (DOFs) pitch, roll, and yaw, we can better evaluate just how much protection the Hard Ways Set affords us. The following chart shows all 36 results that may occur after the dice come to rest. All of the possible top-face pairings are depicted below in Figure 5-3. As we discussed earlier, at six ways to make a 7, it is the most frequent of all the outcomes.

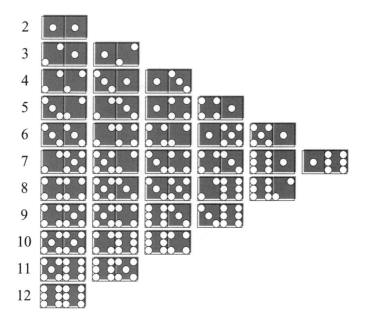

Figure 5-3
Master Dice Combinations

If you deliver the dice such that they perfectly *pitch* together, bounce and land together, then your outcome is what I refer to as a *primary* hit. You have set hard way combinations all around and your controlled throw results in a 2-2, 3-3, 4-4, or 5-5; then you have a primary hit. This relationship between the initial dice set and the final result is meaningful only if you are executing a consistent delivery system. Refer to Figure 5-4 for primary Hard Way Set results undergoing synchronized *pitch*.

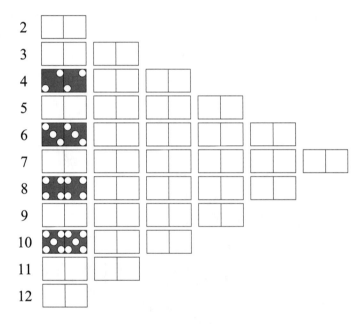

Figure 5-4
Primary Pitch, Both Dice Rotate Together

Another situation where the dice both rotate together in *roll* or *yaw* instead of *pitch* yields slightly different results (shown on the following page in Figure 5-5). All of the possibilities that will occur if both dice *roll* or *yaw* in the same direction are represented. You will note that we retain the four hard way combinations as possibilities, but pick up the 2 and the 12.

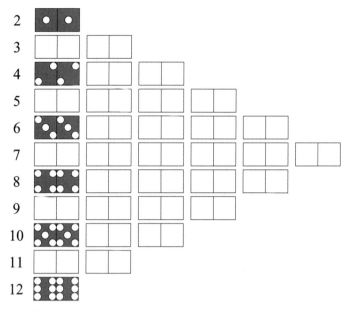

Figure 5-5
Primary Roll or Yaw, Both Dice Same Direction

A *secondary* hit describes a result where one die is one face off in any of the three rotational directions (*pitch, roll,* or *yaw*) from the other die. The next few figures illustrate all of these potential outcomes. A secondary hit is not quite as good as a primary result, but is still plenty good enough to avoid sevening out. Figure 5-6 shows all of the possible combinations that can occur when either die *pitches* plus or minus one face relative to the other die. You can check this out for yourself. Situate two dice side-by-side to form the Hard Way Set. Now, "pitch" the right die forward one face and look at the four resulting combinations around. Okay, reset the hard way combinations. Rotate, or pitch the same right die backward this time and observe the four resulting pairs. Repeat this forward and backward pitch procedure for the left die and note the results. You will see the outcomes for all four scenarios represented in Figure 5-6. Notice that no 7s result with secondary pitch. Upon further inspection, you will see nothing but inside numbers: 5, 6, 8, or 9 will result.

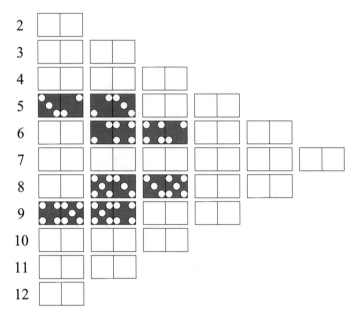

Figure 5-6
Secondary Pitch, + or – Either Die

Figure 5-7 on the following page depicts all of the possibilities when a secondary *roll* occurs. Here, one die has rotated sideways, plus or minus one extra face relative to the other die. This same chart (Figure 5-7) also shows all of the secondary possible outcomes that will occur if one die yaws one extra face in relation to the other die. Again, take out your pair of dice and follow along. "Roll" the right die outward one face, relative to the other die. Note the four resulting combinations. Reset the hard ways and roll the right die inward one face—look at the results. Repeat the entire exercise, using a plus and minus one-face "yaw" rotation for each die. Every possibility that you will encounter is represented in Figure 5-7. Again, there are no 7s present.

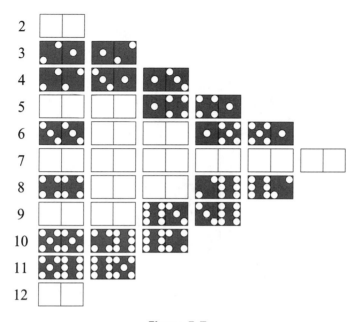

Figure 5-7
Secondary Roll or Yaw, + or – Either Die

A third layer of safety, I call "thirds," represents multi-axial movement, or more than one relative rotation. One die has rotated in two directions relative to the other die. It does not matter which die has rotated, which two extra rotations it has undergone, or in what order they were performed. Either die may rotate plus or minus one face in *pitch with roll, roll with yaw,* or *yaw with pitch.* Any combination of thirds you can create is represented on the next page in Figure 5-8. You are steering clear of 7s, and will notice that almost all of these results (20 out of 24) are point numbers! You can take your pair of dice and run through all of the possible double multi-axial rotations you can conceive of and they will all be depicted in Figure 5-8. Just remember to reset the hard way combinations each time.

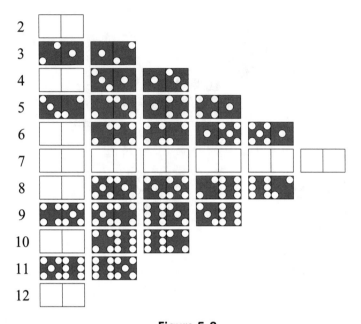

Figure 5-8

Thirds, Roll and Yaw or Roll and Pitch or Pitch and Yaw, + or – Either Die

After the third layer of defense, things start to break down a bit. We cannot avoid the 7 forever, but we have staved it off as long as possible utilizing this dice set. Figure 5-9 shows the *double roll* or *double yaw* possibilities. Here, one die experiences plus or minus two extra faces of *roll* or *yaw* relative to the other die. Half of the results are fatal 7s.

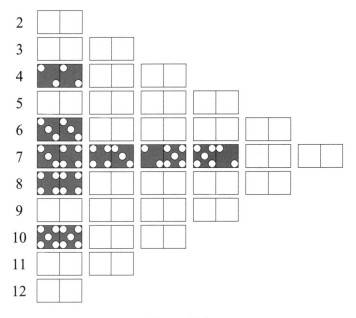

Figure 5-9
Double Roll or Double Yaw, Either Die + or − Two Faces

Figure 5-10 shows the results of a *double pitch*. One die pitches plus or minus two faces relative to the other. Here is where all the 7s are hiding. The 7 is the most common outcome possible of all the combinations with six ways to made. However, by utilizing the Hard Ways Set, we have relegated the 7 to the outer reaches of our result domain.

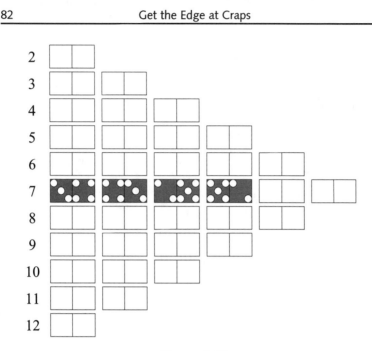

Figure 5-10
Double Pitch, Either Die + or − Two Faces

Now that you understand how the Hard Way Set can give you maximum protection when considering all degrees of freedom, let's walk through the actual setting process. In the casino, you will look at the dice before the stickman is about to pull them over to you. Notice which numbers are on the top and front surfaces and plan out, with the least manipulations, how you will create your initial dice set. Let us say that the stickman has just retrieved the dice and is showing them to the boxman for his inspection. After turning the dice a few times, he will wait for most everyone to get any bets down. During this time, you observe that the 1-3 is on top with the 4-6 on front. To help create the Hard Ways Set, 1s and 6s have to be on the sides. You will want both 6s on either the left or right side of each die. One plan, for this particular example, would be to kick the left die to the left so that the 1-face is on the left side. Now as you grab the right die, rotate the front 6-face over to the right side. At this point both 1s are facing left and both 6s are facing right. Flip the right die until the two top numbers are the same, creating a hard way number. If properly executed, the combinations on the front, bottom, and back will also be hard way numbers.

You should practice moving the dice into the hard ways set position. After you've set them, mix them up and repeat several times. As you become more comfortable and can accurately manipulate the dice, begin to work on speed. Ultimately, you should be able to set the dice in less than two seconds. Otherwise, you will call undo attention to what you're doing and give the boxman an excuse to try and break your focus. Let's review the steps for quickly setting the hard way numbers all around. You should practice setting the dice so it becomes a natural part of your delivery and does not detract from your focus. Grab a pair of dice. Work first on accuracy, and then conquer speed and efficiency.

1. Notice where the 6 or 1 is on either die. If the left or right die has the 6 or 1 already on the side, then that die is set, leave it alone. If no die has a 6 or 1 on the side, then rotate the left die so it has a 6 or 1 on the right side.

2. Pick up the second die and rotate the 6 or 1 outward to match the same side that the first die's 6 or 1 is facing. You should now have both dice with the 1s or 6s on the right side.

3. Without releasing the second die, notice what numbers are on top of both dice. If they already match, then you have hard ways combinations all around. You are done setting the hard ways. If not, you will rotate the second die forward or backward so that they match. Let's say that the first die has a 4 on top. If the second die has a 3 on top, then you know that the 4 is on the bottom. Simply pitch the second die two faces backward so they match. If the 3 is on the front, then flip the 3 to the bottom. This will cause the 4 to appear on top. If the 4 is on the front, simply pitch it up to the top. You will now have hard way combinations all around.

If you would like a certain hard way combination on top and front, then you would operate a little differently. You will need to know the dice faces very well. Let us say that you wish to set 4-4 on top with 2-2 on front. When the stickman goes to pull the dice over, you will need to look at each die and know exactly where the 4s and 2s are and what gyrations you will perform to get them where they belong. I might use my index finger and thumb to set the 4 on the left die while my middle and ring finger set the 4 on the right die at the same time. I can twist the left die with my index finger and thumb to get the 2 on front and use my pinky finger to bat the right die around if needed. The other alternative is to use the index finger and thumb to set the left die and then do the same for the right die. It's a little slower, but can still be done in about two seconds.

There are other good sets out there, but the Hard Way Set gives you the most available layers of protection when considering *all six degrees of freedom*. As you gain more experience and confidence in using the Hard Way Set, you should begin to set the 7 on the come-out roll if you have no previous Come bets working. I will show you how to easily create this Come-Out Set once you become proficient at setting the hard ways!

Come-Out Set

Craps is really two different games with two distinctly different objectives. As discussed in Part One, if we are Pass Line bettors, we want to avoid the 7 during the point cycle. That is where the Hard Ways Dice Set is employed. However, what about the come-out roll, where a 7 is desirable? Well, if we do not have Come bets working, then we may want to consider setting 7s for the come-out roll. After all, the come-out roll is where the Pass Line bettor has a bona fide mathematical edge with eight ways to win versus only four ways to lose. If you are a Come bettor, you will probably want to keep your odds "on" during the come-out roll and continue to use the Hard Ways Set to avoid the 7. If, however, you are a Place bettor and wish to set 7s for the come-out rolls, then you will want to continue reading. The idea is to give the 7 the best chance of occurring by setting 7s all around. If you can throw the dice with perfect pitch, then this Come-Out Set should help. It is important which 7s combination that you set. Some combinations will still give you a chance to hit a 7, even if one die rotates one face relative to the other die. If a 7 is not hit, then there is a greater likelihood at least that an easier to make, inside number will become your point. A point number with a 9.091 percent or maybe a 20.000 percent disadvantage is better than a 33.333 percent disadvantage that you would endure for a point of 4 or 10.

Finally, this particular 7s set also does a very good job of avoiding the come-out craps. The 2, 3 and 12 are removed from any of the primary, single-pitch and double-pitch possibilities. Initially, you can produce the Come-Out Set by creating the Hard Ways Set and simply double pitching the right or left die. Look at Figure 5-11. The upper left picture shows the starting Hard Ways Set with hard 8 on top. For this example, a right-handed shooter will pitch the right die backward or forward (doesn't matter) two faces. The resulting Come-Out Set is portrayed in the lower left picture. A 4-3 is now on top with a 2-5 on the front. The top right picture in Figure 5-11 starts with the hard 4 on top. By pitching the left die backward or forward two faces, you will create the Come-Out Set depicted at the right bottom. Practice this by mixing up the dice, setting the easier to create hard way combination and then pitching one die over two faces. One thing that you may have noticed is all the resulting 7 combinations have a 2-5, 3-4, 4-3, or 5-2 configuration. This is important because a 6-1 or 1-6 can easily double pitch to produce a craps 1-1 or 6-6 result. In addition, a 6-1 coupled with a 5-2 can generate a 1-2 or 2-1 with just a mere single pitch of one die! Hence, using a 1-6 or

6-1 in the mix gives you exposure to all of the craps possibilities, so beware.

Hard 8 Set
on Top

Hard 4Set
on Top

Double Pitch
Right Die

Double Pitch
Left Die

Figure 5-11

A primary hit with the 5-2, 3-4 set will of course produce all 7s. While a secondary pitch knocks off the 7s, it does yield nothing but easier to make, inside point numbers. You can try this for yourself by creating the Come-Out Set we just prescribed and pitching the right or left die forward or backward one face. All of the outcomes will be the inside numbers: 5, 6, 8, or 9. A secondary outward roll of one die keeps two 7s and generates an easy to make 6-2 (or 8) and 5-1 (or 6). A secondary inward roll of one die keeps two 7s also, but produces two 3s. Luckily, the inward roll is rare because the dice are side-by-side and will tend to bank off each other when this starts to happen. A secondary yaw of either die, clockwise or counterclockwise, will retain two 7s for a come-out win and produce two outside numbers. Again, with our delivery method, we will strive to keep the dice pitching end-over-end. If we double pitch one die, then we are back to our Hard

Ways Set and have established a 4, 6, 8, or 10 as our point. One quick word of caution in this last case—if you double pitch the dice on the come-out roll, be careful. Continuing to double pitch, while using the Hard Ways Set to make a point, will produce a fatal seven-out! Find and correct the inconsistency in your grip and/or delivery. As a last resort, use one of the other sets described in Chapter 12. We will cover diagnosing problems with your form a little later.

As you continue to use the 5-2, 3-4 Come-Out Set, you may just find it easier to go right for these set combinations without going through the Hard Ways Set first. That is fine. In fact, that is what I now do. As you get more familiar with the dice and more confident with handling them, you might try going directly to the Come-Out Set.

Chapter 6

Element Two: Delivering the Dice

In the real world, we must pick up the dice and toss them toward the back wall. They must become airborne to qualify. Therefore, we have to use at least two DOFs in going from point A to B: a vertical and horizontal component that will describe a parabolic trajectory. The dice will land on the bed of the craps table where some of their energy will be absorbed. The table exerts an equal but opposite reaction force back onto the dice. Because the table is nearly rigid and quite massive, it remains stationary while the much less massive dice spring back into the air. Some of the dies' energy is converted into thermal energy during the collision. That means that the dice have to burn off the excess energy through multiple reactions with the table, its components and the back wall. The more reactions that the dice undergo, the greater the chance of introducing additional degrees of freedom. It is highly unlikely that we will get from point A to B without some reaction after touchdown. We must, as best as possible, reduce or minimize the amount of dice reaction after touchdown. The best way to accomplish this is to deliver the dice with the least amount of force possible. The less energy to burn off, the less volatile the dice will be. When the dice touch down, we want *minimal* energy left to burn and we want that energy to subside in a *controlled* fashion. The dice land and react with minimal surplus energy and, as a result, will stay better aligned to each other.

Delivery Style

Everyone has the same human form or anatomy, but there are a wide variety of physiques out there at the craps tables. There may be different elements of the delivery that you might have to modify a bit, but try to stay very close to the *perfect pitch* delivery system I will present a little later. The professional athlete learns the optimal delivery system for his sport and then practices tirelessly. I have developed a delivery system that breeds accuracy and consistency. I will show you how to customize this approach to fit your stature. Once you have your optimal delivery system in place, you will use your *muscle memory* to duplicate it from throw to throw. Muscle memory is the term athletes use to describe how they are able to remember exact placements, positioning, movements, accelerations, etc. that the body must go through to properly execute a particular maneuver. The brain precisely controls timing, balance, strength and coordination. It's amazing how much information and how many calculations that gray CPU between your ears can process! Millions of bits of data are stored as you practice and perfect your throw. Your brain can memorize every minute detail of your delivery and help you to duplicate it from trial to trial.

Once you have mastered the delivery, your brain goes into autopilot mode. However, you must retain focus and block out distractions. In addition, stress and anxiety can produce excess adrenaline and causes a person to tighten up on the grip or throw. The movements become forced or contrived. It becomes very difficult, if not impossible, to duplicate your delivery from throw to throw! Physical exercise and relaxation techniques will help improve consistency. We will talk about keeping focus and reducing stress later in Chapter 13, "Regaining the Psychological Edge." You will need a delivery style that helps maintain the relationship that you established when you first set the dice. Unfortunately, you cannot super glue the dice onto the desired combination and then throw them, perfectly maintaining that relationship. So, you will do the best that you can by gently gripping the dice (just firm enough to keep them from shifting) and carefully arcing them down the table without any excess force. If, and this is a big if, the dice can be thrown together, travel and land together, bounce and come to rest together, then you have a good shot at maintaining that *set* relationship. If each die exits your hand at different times and in different directions, then no degree of dice setting will ever help you. I've seen people carefully set the dice, only to snatch them up quickly, rattle them around a bit and fire them off to the opposite side of the table! This totally negates the effect of setting the dice. You will need to employ all the mechanical pieces in the controlled throw puzzle to make it effective.

After you have read Chapters 5, 6, and 7 of this book, you can practice setting the dice and experiment with several different delivery variations and table positions until you find the combination that works best for you. Many of you will find that you need to allow 20 hours or more to develop the muscle memory foundation for a consistent dice delivery. Thereafter, you will need recurring practice to maintain the muscle memory and to "groove in" before a casino session. A few of my students have walked into a casino with just basic instruction and have executed a natural rhythmic delivery. They successfully incorporated all of the elements of the controlled throw into their routine, practically unrehearsed. Admittedly, this is a small percentage. I have also seen the flip side, where students work for three or four months but make only minor progress. These players were practicing hard, but I found basic errors in their delivery. Unfortunately, these flaws were repeated, again and again, in the student's practice and they were getting quite good at doing the wrong things. Muscle memory does not know or care if your execution is wrong—it only knows repetition. You may find it prudent to review this part of the book on the controlled throw mechanics, from time to time. It's possible that you missed or had forgotten some basic aspects of the throw, so treat this book as a reference manual or primer.

General Considerations

When selecting a delivery style, the "Three Cs" should weigh heavily in your consideration: Comfort, Control, and Consistency. You want to strike an optimal balance with all three of these. You may be most comfortable lying on the casino floor and throwing the dice up onto the table, but then your control and consistency will be at its worst! You could insist on using your own practice dice at the craps table for consistency's sake, but your comfort would be compromised when security carries you away. These are, of course, extreme examples, and usually the three Cs complement each other rather well. If you do hit upon a true dilemma with the three, I would lean in favor of *control*. Let's think about what motions are needed to deliver the dice. You will want to minimize the body's kinematic motions to the lowest number practical. The simpler the execution, the fewer things that can go wrong! A simple, but effective delivery is easier to duplicate with less opportunity for error. Another argument for the simpler execution would be the ability to perform it in a more confined space. As the length or your roll increases and the excitement mounts, the table will fill up quickly (if it wasn't full to begin with).

What stance will you use when you throw and how will your body be situated? It is important that your body is comfortable, and balanced. Are you well supported while in your stance? Can your throwing arm swing freely and can you easily see your landing area? Your body should be stable and well supported. Everything should be situated a particular way—from the positioning of your feet and legs right up to your back, neck and head. Your non-throwing, or support arm will be stationary and should provide additional support. Your throwing arm should swing freely (no obstacles) and naturally (without straining). You should have three minimal points of support to form a tripod, or at least one point and one line of contact. No part of your body should be overly strained or become fatigued. You should be holding your breath or exhaling lightly as you throw. Sudden changes in breathing will cause your lungs to contract or expand your ribcage. As your ribcage moves, your posture will be changing during the delivery. This is not conducive to a consistent delivery. If you need to, take a deep breath before you address the dice.

If you are 5'6" to about 6'4", the average craps table will probably suit you fine. Plant both feet firmly on the floor and lean onto the arm rail with your mid-section and support arm, set the dice and go. Sometimes your hip may contact the drink rack if you stand sideways. If you do throw with your body sideways to the table, this extra support will help to stabilize you. If you are taller than 6'4", both of your feet should be flat on the carpet. Your abdomen will contact the arm rail. Reach down with your non-throwing hand and grab the arm rail securely, but not too tightly. This arm will help support your upper body weight as you lean over to grip and throw the dice. Make yourself as comfortable and stable as possible while you execute your throw. Use your height and reach advantage to lean out over the table and cut down the throwing distance. It's fun to watch my 6'7" friend "Long Arm" play on short tables. After he picks up the dice, he seems to just reach out and softly drop them together just in front of the back wall. Needless to say, we bet it up big under these circumstances!

If you are under 5'6", you may have to be satisfied with just one foot on the floor. As you try to gain elevation by pulling yourself up on the arm rail, the other foot will be raised and may kick out a bit. Your stomach or even your lower chest may be up on the arm rail. Use your non-throwing arm to clamp yourself under the inside arm rail edge. This should give you enough support and free up your throwing arm. You may be a little uncomfortable, but at least you can execute a delivery. The wife of one of my clients is a petite 4'6" Asian woman. The first time I played with her and her husband, she asked the boxman for a step stool. I thought, "What's he gonna do—call maintenance and have one brought over?" Surprisingly, the stickman reached down and emerged with a 6" stool. It turns out that as more and more women are playing this game, the casinos are working to accommodate them. If you are vertically challenged, ask for a step stool the next time that you play craps. You may be accommodated as well.

Another important consideration for selecting and practicing your delivery includes which table position(s) you wish to throw from. You should have two or maybe three table positions that you favor. I would recommend the positions just to the left or right of the stickman. These are my personal favorites because they give you the shortest distance over which to throw the dice. If I cannot get the immediate stick-left or stick-right table position, then I will pass the dice. A shorter distance to throw over equates into minimal error potential and minimal energy needed. For instance, twice the throwing distance creates twice the error for the exact same level of shooter. Let's say that our highly skilled thrower can keep the dice in a two-dimensional plane within plus or minus a one-degree tolerance. If he is standing next to the stickman, he will be about four feet away from the die's initial land spot on a ten-foot table. One degree out of plane over a four-foot stretch equals 0.838 inches, or a little less than 7/8" (length of opposite side equals the tangent of one degree times the adjacent side, which is 48 inches). However, our same shooter attempting to throw from the end of the table, perhaps ten feet to his intended landing area, will see two-and-a-half times the error, even though his accuracy is exactly the same one degree out of plane, (the tangent of one degree times 120 inches of distance equals 2.095 inches of error). The greater distance amplifies the error function. As if that weren't enough, the dice were thrown with much more force to cover that greater distance. That means any error is further exaggerated through more and harder reactions with the table, its components or anything else in the path of the dice! This is an important point to remember. Every few inches that you can trim off the range of your throw, leverages your level of control in multiple ways. That is why you should attempt to throw from the immediate stick-left or stick-right table positions.

Projectile Motion

As first determined by Galileo, any projectile that does not possess sufficient velocity to escape the Earth's atmosphere will travel a symmetric two-dimensional parabolic trajectory. Field artillery used this fact during battle to target certain areas when firing cannon balls. Imagine bouncing a rubber ball down the sidewalk. It rises quickly at first then slows down vertically. All the time it continues to move forward. The ball then descends as it continues forward. It contacts the sidewalk where some of its energy is lost due to frictional forces. The forward momentum carries the ball forward and a reaction force from the sidewalk propels the ball upward again. A series of similar shaped, but smaller amplitude parabolas, are scribed by the path of the ball until it completely dampens out. When we throw the dice, we can control the initial velocity and the launch angle. The dice will move forward at a constant velocity during the throw. However, their upward component of motion will immediately begin to slow down because of the acceleration due to gravity. At some point, gravity completely overtakes the dies' upward movement. For an instant, there is no vertical motion, only the constant horizontal component of movement. This is the apex, or top of the parabola.

As the gravitational force continues to take over, the vertical component of motion is now downward and the last half of the object's path will be symmetric, or the mirror image of the upward, first half. The dice come down with the same velocity that they were initially thrown with, only the vertical component has changed directions. A reaction force from the table will cause the dice to bounce upward again and the forward momentum will keep the dice moving forward. Some of the dies' energy will be lost in each collision. The dice will tend to continue traveling in smaller parabolic trajectories until they contact the back wall and their energy is used up. Because the dice are not round, but cubic, their subsequent trajectories may not be exactly parabolic. If the dice can be landed flat or on edge, then the parabolic trajectory and the end-over-end pitching rotation can be maintained. By maintaining the natural trajectory, the dice travel in a predictable and controlled course. If the dice land on a partial edge or worse yet—a corner, then their paths will be altered to varying degrees.

The optimal launch angle is 45 degrees when air resistance is not a factor, otherwise slightly less. The dice should be launched at a 40- to 45-degree angle to maximize the forward range of motion for a given initial velocity. This angle produces the greatest range for the least amount of thrust energy because it lies perfectly between a horizontal path, where the dice will touch down immediately after thrown (0-degree angle), and a vertical path where the dice will go straight up and come straight down (90-degree angle). Both extremes produce no range, or forward motion, whatsoever. The 45-degree angle is the perfect compromise for keeping an object in the air the longest and producing the greatest forward range of motion for the least amount of thrust energy.

Using equations of rigid body projectile motion, found in any Newtonian physics book, and differential calculus, you can solve this classic engineering problem to arrive at this angle. By maximizing the forward range for a given throwing force with this angle, you are minimizing the initial thrust force needed. Minimal projectile force applied means that the dice will react less and be affected less by the table and its components after they touch down. The likelihood of maintaining the initial set relationship is greatly improved. This optimal or ideal angle of launch is not hard to achieve. You will not have to worry about pulling out your protractor and measuring launch angles. With the perfect pitch delivery method and the right arm swing velocity, the 40- to 45-degree launch angle will result. The dice will naturally exit from your hand and create the greatest horizontal range without having to force or measure the launch angle.

Perfect Pitch Delivery System

Work with the immediate stick-left or stick-right table position. Eventually, you should master both throwing positions. That way, you will not only be throwing from the shortest distance possible, but you will give yourself twice as many options. If you are left-handed, then exchange the words "left-handed" for "right-handed," to apply to your situation. At the same time, you must swap out "stick-right" wherever you see the words "stick-left." As a right-handed shooter, throwing from stick-left, you will stand parallel to the table with the arm rail across your front mid-section. The forearm of your non-throwing arm will be flat along the chip rail for support. You will lean out over the table slightly so you can reach down with your throwing hand to set and pick up the dice. Your body will be facing the boxman. You will turn your head to the right (or left if you are left-handed) in order to see your intended landing area near the far wall. You may have to lean out a little when you throw, to clear the stickman and come in to the flat part of the back wall. As you extend your forearm across the stickman's body, it will pivot

about the elbow joint so that just the lower arm is moving. See
Figure 6-1 for clarification. This scenario is identical for left-
handers who are throwing from stick-right; only it will be the
mirror image of the stick-left side.

Figure 6-1

If you are right-handed and throwing from stick-right,
you will stand with your right side up against the arm rail,
perpendicular to the table. You will directly face the stickman
and your targeted area at the far wall. Your non-throwing left
arm will probably be down by your side and out of the way.
If you prefer to, you can bring this arm across your body and
grip the arm rail for added support, or if you feel it is in the
way, then fold your left arm behind your back. Try out all
three and see what is more comfortable for you. With your
right side, you will lean into the arm rail to provide upper
body support. As you lean out to grip the dice with your right
hand, you should be looking at your landing area without
having to turn your head. One thing that you may have
noticed if you tried throwing right-handed from stick-right is
that you may be throwing over a greater distance. This can be
true because you are throwing across the front of your body
plus the stickman's body. You will also discover that you are
using some upper arm motion (pivoting about the shoulder)
in order to deliver the dice. This will hold true. With the right-
handed shooter at stick-left, his right arm is already closest to
the stickman (and the target area) and he is only throwing

across the stickman's body as he extends his arm towards the back wall. His forearm is pivoting about the elbow so he has a little less arm motion and a little less distance to cover. The right-handed, stick-left combination (or left-handed, stick-right combination) described in the last paragraph may be slightly preferred for these reasons, but both positions are excellent. Just realize that the mechanics are a little different.

One caveat here for the stick-right or stick-left position—be careful not to throw the dice at an obtuse angle to the back wall. Your two-dimensional trajectory should be perpendicular to the far wall. In addition, your dice should bounce off the flat portion, not the filleted corners of the back wall. When right-handed throwers shoot from stick-right, they tend to stand straight up, not getting out over the table at all. When this happens, they usually throw the dice in the front far corner (player's side of the table). This rounded portion of the back wall is very undesirable to hit because it acts as a "mixing bowl," thoroughly turning the dice over in multiple directions. The initial set relationship is destroyed. The same thing occurs when a left-handed shooter throws from stick-left. You will have to lean out over the table a bit to avoid the rounded corners, yet come in perpendicular to the back wall. If you cannot meet both conditions, then you will have to be happy hitting the flat section of the back wall on a slightly skewed, or larger than 90-degree angle. You must avoid hitting the rounded corners of the back wall.

If you cannot get the immediate position left or right of the stickman, then you might cautiously try the "one spot out" stick-left or right position. I call these the x-left or x-right table positions because you are *extending* your throwing distance another 18 to 24 inches. It will help if the person standing between you and the stickman will step back while you execute your throw. This will enable you to move in, maybe a foot closer and reduce the distance when you deliver the dice. *Never* attempt a *controlled throw* from the third position out, or at least realize you are playing more for entertainment purposes. I have discussed table positions, body stances and proper support. Let's move on to more of the actual motions that your throwing arm and hand will undergo to create the perfect pitch delivery.

Situate the dice the same way on the table each time relative to your body and intended target. Your hand will come over the dice as you reach down to grab them. The fingers will be on the top front edge that is farthest from you with the thumb on back. Your fingers and thumb should be positioned precisely the same way on the dice when you go to grip them. This is critical because a one-eighth-inch difference here could add up to an eight-inch difference by the time the dice come to rest! After you determine the best type of grip and the exact way to use it, your muscle memory should have you picking up the dice in precisely the same manner each time. Being careful to keep the dice side-by-side and square to each other, you will gently pick them up. With a little bit of experience, you will develop the ability to notice a 1/64" positioning difference. If this happens, set the dice back down and reattempt to pick them up correctly. Once you have gripped the dice, raise your hand up two or three inches so you will have clearance with the table surface at the bottom of your swing.

After you pick the dice up the first few times, turn your wrist over so you can observe how you are holding them. Are your fingers situated around the dice the same way each time you pick them up? Is the holding force you apply comfortable and balanced? You want just enough gripping force to keep the dice steady during the release, but not too excessive. As you go to throw the dice, gently pull your arm back and allow your wrist to break backward somewhat. Let your arm swing forward with a natural pendulum arc. As your forearm points straight down toward the table in the middle of your swing, your wrist should now be straight as well. As your arm continues to move forward, your wrist will now break forward to create a gentle, "whip-like" motion. Your wrist is allowed to break backwards on the back swing and forward on the release. This should be one continuous, fluid motion—not too fast and not too slow. You can almost imagine yourself as an artist, swiping bold brush strokes of paint across the canvas. The forward momentum of this soft backhand release will carry the dice forward. The fingertips will act as a fulcrum and a light backspin is naturally created as the dice pivot around the fingers.

The dice should then float through their 2-D parabolic trajectory with just enough backspin to ward off the other rotational degrees of freedom and provide a light braking force at touch down. Whenever you release the dice, they should exit your hand at the same time and in precisely the same manner. They should travel side-by-side in identical, parallel trajectories. The dice should touch down together in your three-inch diameter target circle, near the end of the Come box. Remember that you are throwing with just enough energy to get to your target area—no more. You want to minimize the number of dice gyrations after they touch down. You will attempt to land the dice side-by-side and somewhat flat or on their edge. With the perfect pitch delivery system, this will be easy to accomplish. Watch to make sure that they continue pitching end-over-end, until they reach the back wall. This will help ensure that the initial set relationship is maintained. They should come into the back wall softly and at a true 90 degrees, or nearly perpendicular. This angle of back wall entry is referred to as the angle of incidence. The angle that the dice exit, or bank, from the back wall is called the angle of reflectance. Ideally, you want the dice to lightly come straight into the back wall and repel straight off of the back wall so the angle of incidence equals the angle of reflectance and the two dimensional plane is undisturbed. Stay away from the fillets or rounded corners on either side and hit the flat portion of the back wall as prescribed earlier.

The ideal throw would see the first bounce in the Come box, with perhaps a second, much dampened bounce between the Pass Line odds bets at the far end of the table. Two bounces may not always be practical depending upon the table's hardness, overall length and location of the far

Pass Line betting area. These factors may also cause you to adjust your initial landing area somewhat. Striking chips on the Pass Line or odds area is undesirable because it will knock one or both dice off their axes. Deliver the dice with just enough energy to reach their intended target. After the dice leave your hand, their motions and paths should be mirror images of each other. Be careful not to slam the dice into the back wall. The more that the dice interact with the back wall, the more baffling effect the pyramids will have on the dice. I have found that if the dice come in lightly, they will instantly repel backward when they encounter any trace of resistance. In other words, as the dice float up and contact the pinnacles of the pyramids, they will immediately reverse their direction. If the dice come in hard, they will wrap around and conform to a triangular face of a pyramid, thus each die may rebound off in any one of four different directions. There is a greater likelihood of reducing the die's alignment with the table bed. When the dice do touch down again, they will land on partial edges or corners. The influence on the dice is greatly compromised.

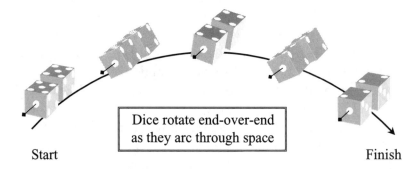

Start   Finish

Dice rotate end-over-end
as they arc through space

Figure 6-2
Pitching About a Lateral Axis with Horizontal and Vertical
Translations

Observe the dice as you throw them. Do they exit your hand together and travel side-by-side? Check out Figure 6-2 to see how the dice should look as they travel through the air. They should land and bounce together, pitching end-over-end to the back wall. How about your body position? As you continue to develop your controlled throw, look at your arm position after following through. Is it consistent from throw to throw? What about the positioning of your hand? Your hand should be flat, with the palm down and parallel with the table surface. Your middle finger will be pointing to the area a couple of feet above your target circle. Make a mental note of where everything is, including your body posture and how you are supported. This will be the basis for developing your muscle memory. Try the above exercises with your eyes closed. Focus on how the dice *feel* as you grip and throw them. After a while you should be able to tell whether the dice are picked up and delivered properly just by feel.

Over the past six years, I have instructed over 600 different dice players at clinics in Vegas, Reno and Atlantic City. One by one, I worked to help them develop and optimize their delivery system. Over that time, I have found that a grip with either three fingers placed side-by-side (index, middle and ring) or one finger (middle) placed across the top, front edge of the dice works best. The thumb would provide opposing force in back, equally split between the left and right die. The dice are carefully picked up off the table and with a gentle swing of the forearm and flick of the wrist; they are propelled on their way. This is done with a backhand motion that unfolds as the arm swings forward. Lateral translation as well as roll and yaw types of rotation are removed. The remaining two translations and pitch-type rotation is heavily influenced. Such a delivery will greatly aid in controlling the dice as they travel and land. This aspect of delivering the dice works hand-in-hand with dice setting and cannot be overlooked. Just remember, whatever delivery style you finally settle upon should, as best as possible, maintain the initial dice set that you created.

Other Considerations

We know that dice propelled over longer distances have to be thrown with more force. To help combat this situation we can throw from the position immediately on either side of the stickman. However, is there something more that we can do? It turns out that we can further cut down on the throwing distance. A shooter throwing from next to the stick position at a 14-foot table may be covering the same distance that a shooter throwing from the end of an eight-foot table is covering. Therefore, to fully minimize the throwing distance, you should not only throw from stick-right or left, but also play at the smallest tables available. It may not be practical to only play at eight-foot tables, but an effort to play at the shortest tables should be made. Please realize that the level of dice influence that you exhibit will be quickly devoured by longer throwing distances.

Another table condition that you must take into account is the hardness of the table surface itself. Typically, an extremely hard or extremely soft (spongy) table surface is bad. You will look for midrange tables that avoid both extremes. Very hard tables, such as those found at the New York, New York casino in Las Vegas, make it more difficult to control the dice. If the dice land slightly off to one corner (even if they touch down on their edge), this slight error is magnified on hard tables. You will hear the dice "clank" as they readily pop up in different directions. Any error is magnified and the predictable parabolic trajectory is altered significantly with one good clank. Soft tables, per se, are fine. The tables that you have to watch out for have a spongy, foam rubber underlay. If you've played at any of the MGM casinos, you know what I mean. MGM actually places a thin layer of foam rubber under the wool betting layout. This sheet of rubber acts like a continuous plane of tiny springs. As the dice touch down, they are suspended for an instant. The tiny springs absorb all of the dice's kinetic energy as they deform around the dice and convert it into potential energy.

The hyper-elastic foam sheet, nearly perfectly conserves all of the impact energy from the dice, and converts it back to kinetic energy when it "springs" into its original, undeformed state. At this time, nearly all the energy is given back to the dice and they jump back to life. In fact, the dice will continue to bounce and spring back into the air at least twice as many times as they would without the rubber underlay. The dice become very "lively" and just won't stop bouncing! Any one bounce will not significantly alter the parabolic trajectory as they will with hard tables, but the cumulative effects of continuous bouncing and reacting with the table is undesirable. Each additional bounce will knock the dice slightly more off kilter with each other and increase the chances of interacting with live bets, the On/Off puck or the back wall. Therefore, avoid both ends of the spectrum—rock hard or spongy soft table surfaces. You can easily check for either situation by simply knocking on the table surface with your knuckles. You will instantly assess the table's hardness by feeling the rock-like surface or spongy soft foam directly underneath the betting layout. As you become an expert level controlled thrower, you may find that you can handle *harder tables* if your *accuracy* is spot on, and *softer tables* if you develop a very *light touch* with the dice.

In addition to the hardness of the table surface, you may have to deal with inconsistent layout thickness at times. This will create an inconsistent bounce from throw to throw and even from one die to the next on the same throw. What happens is the casinos will sometimes place a new craps table layout right over top of the old one. The old layout is unevenly worn out in the heavy traffic, or betting areas. When the new layout is placed directly on top of the old one, *dead spots* on the table result. If one die strikes a dead spot and the other lands on the full double-thick layout, then the first die will tend to lose more energy. The second die will experience a little more bounce and retain more energy on each successive bounce. As a result, the alignment, or initial dice set is disrupted. If you notice, for example, one die hitting the Come box and continuing to bounce, while the other hits the more heavily bet Pass Line area and bounces at a different speed and in a smaller trajectory, then you have probably encountered this situation. If you suspect this, you can rap on the surrounding area with your knuckles to tell. Most casinos will strip off the old layer, but some do not. I have also found inconsistent practices of applying table layouts within the same casino. Be aware of this situation and avoid these tables when you stumble upon them.

Other conditions that you should concern yourself with include the size of the dice. Casino dice are manufactured in three different sizes: 5/8", 11/16", and 3/4" cubed. Are the dice too small? In Reno, Nevada, many casinos use the smaller-sized 5/8" cubed dice. These are harder to handle and control, especially for larger hands. The 3/4" cubed size is much better to grip and throw with. You will be more sensitive to how the larger dice are gripped in your hand. You can also better tell how the dice are coming off your fingertips at the time of release and any adjustments you will need to make. The larger dice will dissipate the energy better after touching down. They also have less of a tendency to pivot about the pyramid's pinnacle and rotate out of our 2-D plane. Generally speaking, the larger the dice, the better the control. While we are talking about dice, be aware if the dice are switched on you during a hot roll. Switching to a different type of dice is a subtle technique that the casino uses to throw off your consistency. For example, dice with a frosted or etched finish will have a higher coefficient of kinetic friction than that of a polished finish. These dice may come out of your hand a little later than the polished ones. Neither dice finish is necessarily bad, but the switching from one to the other may throw off your timing. To a lesser extent, even differently colored dice may feel and react slightly different. The darker dice are cured for a longer period during the manufacturing process and will have slightly different material properties.

As you throw the dice increasingly more, you will begin to develop an overall cadence, or rhythm to your game. You may have heard the phrase "rhythm roller" used to describe this type of shooter. This rhythm will include the actual, systematic execution of each individual throw as well as the flow, or pace of the game. Some players will focus more quickly and have a faster internal pace to their game, while others may be slower. This is okay. The key is to find your own personal timing and *be consistent*. If you tend to be slower, don't rush. If you're quicker, be careful not to hesitate. Some shooters even find a favorite song or tune to mentally hum that fits the pace of their game and helps block outside distractions. You and the stickman will control the flow of the game, although his objectives may be different than yours. The casino is aware of this timing phenomenon and may try to alter your pace. Be aware when the flow of the game changes. The boss may tell you to "speed it along," if you are a little slower. If someone wants to buy in and you're about to throw the dice, the boxman may stop you in mid-swing. This situation gives him the perfect opportunity to "break your rhythm," as they say in the business. Also, multiple payoffs, questions about bets, new people buying in, etc. all work to slow the game down at times. When you finally do get the dice, your first instinct is to jump out and fire the cubes. Before that urge to shoot overwhelms you, step back, take a deep breath and regain your focus.

In Summary

Work with the perfect pitch delivery system. Consider your physique or any personal circumstances you may have. Remember to factor in comfort, control, and consistency with your dice delivery. Develop your optimal delivery and work to get the mechanics down cold in your muscle memory. Once your delivery system is on autopilot, learn to recognize different casino conditions and how they affect your throw. With the proper methodology and a fair amount of practice, you *can* influence the outcome of a dice throw. If you stick with the more intelligent wagers on the table, you can overcome the thin house edge this game has to offer. The Hard Way Dice Set involves setting hard way combinations all around the dice. This set will give you the best possible protection against hitting the sinister 7 when considering all of the possible movements and rotations that the dice may undergo. As a novice, or intermediate level controlled thrower, you will appreciate the better protection of the Hard Way Dice Set. Once you have mastered all the mechanics of your delivery and can demonstrate a high level of consistency, you can experiment with the specialized dice sets described in Chapter 12.

However powerful a set may be, no dice set is useful if the shooter has not yet developed a *consistent method of delivering the dice*. If you teed up the golf ball in a different location relative to your body each time and swung your club in a different fashion each time, then your golf game would be in great trouble. Oh sure, occasionally you might get *lucky* and hit a great shot, but that would be it—pure luck! The same element of success that a practiced athlete develops holds true as you set and deliver the dice with consistency of form. Like the successful athlete, you must learn the mechanics of an optimal delivery system and then practice them until they become second nature. The problem with most craps players is that they hope for the "luck" approach instead of working on the skill necessary to be successful . . . and of course, the casinos foster this idea of "trying your luck." In the next chapter, we'll look at selecting and perfecting your dice grip.

Chapter 7

Element Three: A "Gripping" Issue

Initially, I considered the dice sets and delivery to be the two main components in throwing the dice. These are certainly integral pieces to the mechanics of the controlled throw. However, after conducting ten or 12 weekend clinics and dozens of one-on-one student sessions, I have noticed another element that commands its own special attention. In the past, I have relegated the grip to being part of the delivery, but after careful consideration, I can see that it deserves its own place as one of three elements of the controlled throw. It is separate and distinctly different from the dice sets, which it succeeds chronologically, and the delivery, which it precedes. It is possible to diligently use the same dice sets and delivery each time but have different results because of the grip being used. In fact, 50 percent of all the problems I have corrected during personal tutoring at weekend clinics and dealer school practices are directly attributed to improper dice grip. If you are practicing frequently and taking special pains to adhere to an efficient dice setting routine and a smooth delivery, but the dice just aren't cooperating, then chances are that you need a more consistent way of gripping the dice.

First, there are several different grips that you can try. I have included some of the more common types that are worth looking at. Keep in mind that two different people attempting the same grip may have slightly different results because of different hand sizes, finger widths and lengths, etc. You may have to experiment a little. Several conditions should be met when selecting and working on your grip:

- The dice must remain in equilibrium while you are holding them. That is, they are not shifting or moving while they are in your hand. Any shift, however small, will be greatly amplified by the time the dice travel down the table. This may destroy the initial dice set relationship that you established.
- You should apply just enough holding force to keep the dice in equilibrium and no more. Excessive clamping force will induce shifting and may even cause the dice to "squirt" out of your hand in a less than controlled fashion.
- You will want a grip that has little or no release drag. In other words, the dice are easy "to get out of." Both dice should exit the hand at the same time, with the same rotation and with as little force as possible.
- The grip that you finally settle upon should be comfortable. A comfortable grip will feel natural, and a natural grip will be much easier to duplicate trial after trial. Consistency is very important.

Remember that we want *just enough force* to loft the dice from the starting point to the initial landing point. Also, remember that it is not necessary to put a lot of spin on the dice as they pitch. My experience indicates that a moderate amount of spin is fine, but too much will cause the dice to react more violently once they touch down.

After you select a grip to shoot with, you should become very familiar with how the dice *feel* in your hand when you use that grip. Hopefully, by the time you attack this gripping issue, you will have your dice sets down cold. You are setting quickly and accurately. The dice are set in the same position on the table, relative to your body. When you reach over to pick up the dice, they will be exactly where you expect them to be. This consistency in your routine will help you to grip the dice precisely the same way each time. This is important if you wish to better duplicate your delivery from one throw to the next. When you are setting the dice, you are visually checking them for correctness. However, once you attempt to grip the dice, you should develop a feel for where your fingers and thumb should be. I would recommend that you look away or even close your eyes for a second. The reason for this is that your fingers are right on the dice; your eyes are some three feet away. In addition, your tactile sense of feel is very sensitive and much more accurate than your vision at this point. You can sense if your fingers are very slightly off from where they were on the previous toss. Looking down at the dice as you grip them only causes a distraction.

You are relying on what athletes refer to as *muscle memory* and you will feel exactly how to contact and balance the dice in your throwing hand. As you gain more experience with your chosen grip, you will be able to make very slight adjustments that will create the desired effect you are looking for. Whether it is keeping the dice in a tighter formation, adding more backspin, removing some backspin or whatever the case may be, you will be able to make corrections right at the table. I will discuss my specially developed Three-Fingered Front grip and the adjustments that I make. I will then go on to describe some of the other grips that I have observed, used by other veteran shooters. You can try out all of the grips if you like, but I highly recommend learning the Three-Fingered Front or the One-Fingered Front. Both of these grips do an excellent job of meeting all the conditions mentioned earlier in the chapter.

Sharpshooter's Grip

I have medium sized hands with slender, medium length fingers—average. The grip that works best for me (and probably most of you out there) is a grip that I call the Three-Fingered Front. The index, middle and ring fingers are placed across the far upper edge of the dice as they sit side-by-side on the table. The pinky finger is kicked out to the side and out of the way. My thumb is situated about halfway down across the two near faces, pressing about 50/50 on each die and directly opposed to my middle finger (see Figure 7-1 below). The arrow shows how my wrist bends from the start of my delivery to the point of release.

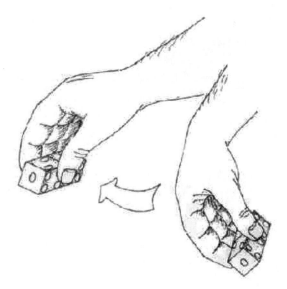

Figure 7-1
The Three-Fingered Front

My grip is light, but not loose. I have minimal contact area between my fingers and the dice. Minimal contact area equates into minimal release drag. My three fingers are evenly situated across the front of the dice. If you were to draw a line connecting the tips of my fingers, this tangent line would be parallel to the table surface (see Figure 7-2). The fingertips should be parallel because the dice will wrap around them when they are released. The fingertips will act as a fulcrum, which imparts a slight backspin to the dice. This is how the pitch rotation originates. If the fingertips are not aligned, then the dice will not come out of the hand together and in parallel trajectories. You may have to rock your hand slightly to the right or left to create this situation.

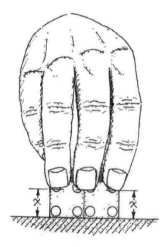

Figure 7-2
Parallel Fingertips

This particular grip is more difficult to master because there is an issue of timing and balance, just at the moment that you grip the dice. If your timing is off slightly, the dice will tend to splay apart in front, as they press against the thumb. If you encounter this situation, practice placing your thumb and fingers down at exactly the same time when you grip the dice. If you still have trouble with this, use the One-Fingered Front for the next ten or 12 hours of play or practice. It is much easier to balance one finger and the thumb. Once you have become accustomed to this grip, you can try gently lowering down the index and ring fingers. When they contact the dice, on either side of the middle finger, you will have created the Three-Fingered Front grip. After a while, this grip will become second nature.

Different Grip Adjustments

I tend to grab the dice higher with the fingers on the top front edge, resulting in less surface contact with the dice. That way drag is minimized and any perspiration would have a negligible effect on the cubes. My thumb is usually about halfway down the back. I grip the dice as high as possible while preventing them from shifting or moving. If the dice are slipping when you cock your wrist back or at any time before you throw them, then you will need slightly more contact area or different positioning to hold the dice stable.

- First, I will try just sliding the thumb down about 1/32 of an inch or so. If this doesn't provide enough contact area . . .
- Then I will slide the fingers down 1/32 of an inch. Usually these adjustments will solve the problem, but if necessary repeat these steps one at a time until you are able to steadily handle the dice.

Remember that the more contact area that you employ, the more release drag that you will create, so be careful.

If the *dice are coming out flat*, with no spin, then lower the thumb slightly down the back. By having the thumb lower than the fingers, you will create a rotational moment of inertia about the dies' centers of gravity, which both lie on the lateral axis of rotation. As you slide your thumb lower, the moment will increase giving you more and more backspin when you release the dice. Ideally, we want just enough spin to ward off the other rotational degrees of freedom. Too much backspin is bad because the dice will have to burn up all that spin energy before coming to rest. Any excess energy causes excess dice reaction and more volatility. If the *dice are coming out with too much backspin*, then chances are that your thumb is too low. Just raise the thumb slightly until the desired amount of spin is affected.

Another problem that you may encounter occurs when the *dice are not coming out together*. One die lags while the other leads; or, one die has a higher trajectory than the other, or a combination of both situations. In this event, you probably have more contact area on one die, which creates a greater release drag on that die. Try to determine which die is lagging and why. Go through the following checklist.

- First, check to make sure that your fingertips are parallel with the table surface. That is, if you were to draw an imaginary line across the tips of your fingers, they would be parallel with the bottom edge of the dice. Look back at Figure 7-2. You may have to rock your hand slightly to the left or right to affect this parallel line. If the right die is dragging, then rock your hand to the left and vice-versa. This will reduce drag on one side and increase it on the other.

- Check to make sure that your fingers are centered across the front, top edge of both dice. If two fingers are mostly on the left die, then do not be surprised if the right die comes out quicker. When you initially go to grip the dice, simply make sure that your fingers are reasonably well placed.

- Chances are that one of the first two suggestions will solve this problem but there is a remote possibility that your thumb needs to be better centered. If the thumb is too far over to one side, then that die will receive more *thrust force* causing it to come out earlier than the other die. Redistribute the thumb's contact area so that it is more centrally located. Shift the thumb over slightly from the *early* die to the *late* die.

Another situation that you might run into happens when the dice are coming out together with the same amount of spin; however, *they are spinning about different axes*. The dice are cocked, or angled to one side as they spin. Chances are that if you are doing everything else right then these axes will be parallel to each other but not to the table surface. This is more of a delivery problem than a grip problem but I will address it here.

- The first and most probable cause of this problem is using too much of a sidearm delivery. If your thumb or index finger is pointing up at the moment of release, then the dice are inclined to come out almost one on top of another. Depending upon the angle that your hand is at when releasing the dice, the dice will tend to come out parallel to your hand. Simply rotate your wrist so that your hand ends up flat (parallel to the tabletop) at the time of release. Usually in home practice, this problem does not surface but when you are at an actual craps table things may change. You find yourself leaning out over the middle of the layout, trying to shoot around the stickman and hit the flat part of the back wall. Especially if you are vertically challenged, you may be helping the dice out with a little bit of lateral motion. Remember to keep your hand flat at the release, even if it causes you to throw the dice a little off the perpendicular angle to the back wall.
- Another situation that may produce this problem occurs when one finger is much lower than the others are. This is especially true with the Two-Fingered Front grip. When initially gripping the dice, make sure that the fingertips are parallel to the table surface to rectify this problem.

As with any grip that you use, it is important that your fingertips are free from perspiration and oils. This could cause one die to stick momentarily, as the other is well on its way. The best way to prevent against this is to wash your hands with soap and water before playing. This will provide a clean, dry surface with which to grip the dice. It will also create a more consistent coefficient of friction on the finger surfaces. This will help the dice to exit the hand simultaneously and travel together. When the tables are busy and the dice have a lot of oil on them, I may try to wipe the worst sides inconspicuously on the table felt with short, quick strokes. The bosses may ask you not to do this if they spot you rubbing the felt. Another tactic is to spray a light coating of deodorant on the fingertips. This creates a constant coefficient of friction, even if the dice are heavily oiled. My personal favorites are Arid XX and Arm & Hammer, unscented.

I remember one occasion where Robin, Donnie, and I pulled up to the valet parking one Saturday night at the Main Street Station in downtown Vegas. As the car stopped, Donnie asked if we needed to "spray up." The trunk was popped and we all hopped out and headed for the luggage in the trunk. A can of Arid XX emerged and the three of us began to spray up, one after the other. The valet attendant stopped in his tracks as a white cloud wafted out of the trunk and around our bodies. "You take this one Charlie. I'm on break," he replied. The other attendant approached cautiously. "Don't worry, we always spray up before playing," Donnie informed the attendant as he handed him the keys. Somehow, this did little to comfort the poor fellow.

Other Dice Grips

Two-Fingered Front: The middle and ring fingers both oppose the thumb front-to-back, which is centered about both dice. The index and pinky fingers oppose each other laterally or side-to-side. Usually the person using this grip will bear down with his fingers all the way down to the table felt, totally enclosing the dice. The gripping force is minimal; however, this situation creates a great amount of release drag. Quite often, the shooter will compensate for this by snapping the wrist or arm harder than normal to get out of the dice. The dice may not come out together and will have excess spin or rotational energy to burn off. A variation of this grip would be to lift both the index and pinky fingers out and off the sides of the dice. The drag is then reduced, but the dice may splay out from the thumb. If your fingers are larger or thicker than average, this grip variation may work for you. I would recommend not bearing all the way down on the dice.

Figure 7-3
The Two-Fingered Front

One-Fingered Front: One finger, usually the middle finger, is centered in front and directly opposes the thumb that is placed on the back. This grip requires little clamping force and is easy to release out of. It may be a little tough to keep the dice from shifting, but overall it offers good control. Gently grab the dice one-third to one-half the way down and toss. If you get too much lateral rollout, consider another grip. One idea would be to grab the dice initially as shown, but then gently bring down the index and ring fingers on either side of the middle finger. This can actually be used as a prelude to mastering Sharpshooter's grip . . . the Three-Fingered Front. In fact, I use this technique to help students getting comfortable with the tougher-to-master Three-Fingered Front grip. You may find that this grip, on its own merit, works quite well. Some of my students who have physical limitations, such as arthritis, can easily and accurately throw with this grip.

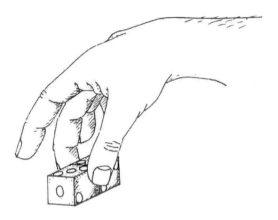

Figure 7-4
The One-Fingered Front

The Ice Tong: Another grip that can be used when the dice are side-by-side is the Ice Tong. The thumb is placed on the right side (right-handed) and one finger, the index, middle, or ring finger is placed on the opposing side, laterally. See Figure 7-5. No other fingers are used. Very little clamping force is needed and it is moderately easy to release the dice together. You may encounter the dice shifting relative to each other, because there is no fore/aft support. Uneven perspiration from the finger to the thumb will present different coefficients of friction on either side. This will also cause the dice to shift somewhat during the release. This grip is easy to master, but yields a moderate amount of control at best.

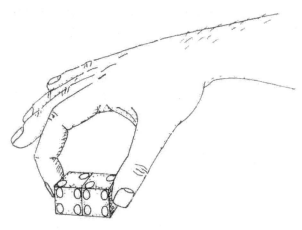

Figure 7-5
The Ice Tong

The Stacker: This is really not a grip, but a setting and delivery technique. You have probably seen this attempted countless times before. It involves stacking one die on top of the other. Most shooters who use this technique do not even understand the main concept behind its use. The idea here is to control, or freeze, the bottom die with the desired number set on top. If thrown just right, the dice land at the base of the back wall. The bottom die is boxed in at the bottom by the table bed. The back wall bumper stops its forward motion and the top die keeps it from bouncing upward. Nine out of ten shooters who pick up the dice and throw this way cannot even come close to freezing the bottom die. It is extremely tough to master. Here is how the advantage is supposed to be gained. Let's say that the point is 10. Our stacker will set a 5 or 6 on the top face of the bottom die. If he executes the throw just right and boxes in the die with the 5 or 6 still on top, he now has only one way to seven-out. At the same time, he has one way to throw a 10 and win. The odds of making the 10 versus sevening out are even, or one to one, while the payoff is two to one for any odds bet behind the Pass Line.

Now, to further take advantage of the situation, the shooter places the other high point numbers, 8 and 9 and let us say that he has double odds behind the Pass Line. (Incidentally, the strategy would be similar for a point of 8 or 9). If he can freeze one die with a 6 on top, then here is what will happen:

- The second die produces a 1 for a total of 7. The Pass Line 10 plus double odds and 8, 9 Place bets lose. There is one way to lose five units.
- The second die is a 2, making a total of 8. The 8 Place bet wins 7/6 of a unit.
- The second die is a 3, generating a total of 9. The 9 Place bet wins 7/5 of a unit.
- The second die is a 4, making the point of 10. Even money is made for the Pass Line bet and four units for the odds. Total net equals five units.
- The second die is a 5 or 6. A total of 11 or 12 has no effect on your wagers.

The 7, losing five units and the 10, winning five units, cancel each other out over the long haul. A total of 11 or 12 neither helps nor hurts things. The average net profit over a cycle of six throws is 7/6 + 7/5, or 2.567 units. The shooter who can expertly execute this grip and delivery will average over 2.5 units profit for every six controlled throws during the point cycle. This concept, of course, works in the same manner for a low point of 4, 5, or 6, only the bottom die is frozen with a 1 or 2 on top. In theory, this technique gives the shooter a huge 8.557 percent edge over the house after a point is established, but in practice, you might see one skilled thrower in a hundred who can perform this maneuver five percent of the time. If someone could figure out how to freeze one die on a certain face by using technique (not cheating) and bet accordingly, they would become wealthy in a short period.

In Conclusion

As with any grip that you endeavor to experiment with, you will want to make some general observations. These observations coupled with the outcome of the dice will clue you in on just how well your grip is working out. First, get comfortable with the grip. Throw the dice several times to see if it feels good. We are not worried about results here; you just want to determine if the grip is somewhat easy to employ for you. Second, if you feel that there is potential, then note the effects this grip may have on your delivery. Observe your arm and hand position after releasing the dice. Does your hand end up being parallel to the table surface after every throw? Is your middle finger pointing to the space just above the dies' initial landing spot? Are you able to duplicate the release and delivery each time with this grip? How are the dice reacting after they touch down? Are they popping in all directions? Or do they continue to roll end-over-end, kiss the back wall, and softly come to rest? You should have a feel for exactly where your thumb and fingers should be and what adjustments to make. Finally, what do the results look like? When trying out different grips, look for continuous improvement in your results.

I believe that the Three-Fingered Front is the best dice grip to employ with the One-Fingered Front running a close second. I would estimate that nine out of ten throwers can and should use this grip. It is the hardest to master (not including the stacker method), but provides the best control when gripping and releasing the dice. Well, now that the "grip" has been properly promoted to its own place of distinction as one of our primary mechanical elements and all is well in the land of dice control, you now have all the tools and techniques to develop your own controlled throw!

Part Three

Putting It All Together

Chapter 8

Developing a Powerful Practice Routine

Once you have found a delivery that you can duplicate from throw to throw with consistently good results, you should practice that delivery. I have half a craps table set up in my dining room where I practice about 45 minutes a day. You can liken it to playing just about any sport requiring a coordinated delivery. Much like the pro athlete who works on the delivery system for his particular sport, I practice my dice sets, my carefully balanced grip, and soft release. After I release the dice, they travel side-by-side and go through identical motions. They land together, hitting the table flat or on edge, still turning over together in a smaller parabolic trajectory, and possibly hitting the table a second time. They take what I call a "dead cat bounce" up just grazing the rubber pyramids slightly and coming down to rest. During the delivery, it looks as though only one die was thrown along the length of a mirror, and the second die is just its reflection. The key is to get both dice going through the same gyrations through space. You are developing control and using your muscle memory to breed greater consistency.

Creating a Physical Mock-Up

You will need an overall area that is about 3 by 10 feet for practicing. Build an appropriate practice rig and elevate it so that the bed is 28 inches off the floor. Plans for an elaborate practice box are included a little later. In a pinch, you can use one corrugated cardboard box lid for the bed, or landing area, and a second box lid for the back wall. This is a very quick and inexpensive way to get up and running. Pace off about eight feet from your back wall and situate a high-back, stationary chair (about 40 inches high) with the back towards you. Build up the seat area (phone book will do) so it is closer to 28 inches high and deposit the dice on top. If you like, you can wrap a swatch of felt around the book for a more realistic surface. Lean on the chair back with your non-throwing arm (like you would lean on the arm rail of a craps table) and reach over to set the dice that are resting on the seated area. You will grip and toss the cubes lightly onto the bed of your rig. If the practice box is to the right side of you, then you are practicing from the stick-left table position. Rotate the chair around and walk over to the backside. Now, the practice box should be to your left side. This will simulate the stick-right throwing position. You can easily move or reposition the chair to represent other throwing positions at the craps table if you desire.

Jack B. from Las Vegas, an early dice student of mine, suggested an idea for practicing on the road if you do not have a portable practice rig. Remove one of the drawers from your hotel dresser. Place it at the head of your bed, lengthwise, so the smaller side is up against the headboard. Make sure that the drawer sits level on the bed. Pull the covers flat and remove the pillows if need be. Grab a large terrycloth towel from the bathroom and line the bottom and back wall of the drawer with it. This will give surprisingly good bounce characteristics for your in-hotel practice session. Set your stationary desk chair up at the appropriate distance with a book on the seat. Lean on the chair back and reach over to set and grip the dice that are sitting on the book. Carefully toss the dice into the drawer and record your results. You now have a viable means for practicing on the road. Alternatively, you can build an elaborate practice box that works well at home and breaks down/sets up easily for travel practice.

If you wish to build a representative practice box that is portable, here is a plan that will help. I have to give credit to my friend, Gil Stead in New Jersey. He is a finish carpenter who designed and built dozens of these practice boxes for many of my students. If you are interested, he can build and ship one to you for about $200 US. You will have to call the phone number on the last page to check for exact prices and availability. If you are so inclined, you can build one for yourself. You will need a 4-by-4 foot sheet of high-grade 3/8-inch plywood. Using a circular saw with a fine to mid-cut blade, you will cut the sheet as shown below in Figure 8-1. Carefully sand and remove any burrs or splinters. If you like, stain the tapered sideboards, back wall, and edges of the plywood bed at this time. Purchase a thin, high-grade wool fabric that is about 3-by-3 feet in size. This should not be too thick, but like that used on a billiard table. Using a cheap paintbrush, lightly apply rubber cement to the front underside of your 30-by-30 inch table bed. You will anchor the wool fabric to the front underside and eventually fold it up and over the top surface of the bed. Apply a band of cement that is 3 to 4 inches wide and spans from right to left in what will be the front, underside of your box. Attach the wool fabric edge (also 3 to 4 inches) to the cemented underside. Pull the fabric across as you let it contact, then "iron" flat with your hand if necessary.

The fabric should have excess material on each side (about three inches) that you can trim later. Let the cement dry so the bonding takes affect. Use a light spray adhesive (not rubber cement) to coat the topside surface of the 30-by-30 inch plywood table bed. Now fold the fabric over to the top (with one edge securely bonded underneath). Gently pull taunt and let the wool contact the top bed area where the spray adhesive is applied. Iron out or reposition the fabric until no air gaps are present. Once positioned, fold the fabric back to expose the right and left edges of the plywood bedding. Apply a one-inch band of rubber cement on each side, from front to back on the plywood bed. Pull the wool carefully on both sides and let it contact the cement. You must make sure that the material is somewhat taut from side to side *and* front to back. Iron the wool down with a hardcover book or smooth block of wood and let dry. The wool fabric will now be attached to the plywood bed with rubber cement on the front underside and two thin bands up the right and left topside. The rest of the top surface will have the light adhesive to keep the fabric from shifting. Using heavy scissors or shears, carefully trim the excess fabric off the sides and down to the table bed edge. Now apply a three- to four-inch band on the back underside of the plywood bed (similar to what you did in front). You will fold the wool over to the underside around the back and attach it to the cement. Iron flat and let dry. Your wool fabric is now attached and trimmed to the plywood bed.

Next, you will need a minimum of seven aluminum hinges that are a half-inch wide (when folded over) by one-and-a-half inches long with two screw holes on each half. In addition, you will need 28 flat-head wood screws that fit the hinge hole diameters properly. Eighteen of these will fasten hinges through the thickness of the plywood and should be no more than 1/2-inch in length. Ten of your wood screws will fasten hinges into the ends of plywood sheets and should be 3/4 to one inch long. Before screwing in any of the hinges, you will measure out and drill pilot holes that are about half of the screw's diameter where needed. The tapered sides will stand up on edge and sit on top the right- and left-most edges of the plywood bed. This is directly on top of the fabric where you applied the one-inch band of rubber cement. Measure about three inches up along one side from the front corner, mark with a ballpoint pen and position the first folded hinge starting from the mark. The open side of the hinge should be flush with the table bed, side edge (the pinned side will be parallel to and 1/2- inch, off the side edge). Measure three inches back from the rear corner, mark and position the second hinge the same way. Drill four pilot holes that are aligned with the hinges and almost through the table bed thickness. Using four, 1/2-inch screws, fasten half of each hinge to the table bed.

Position a tapered sideboard so that it is flush with the front and back of the plywood table bed and sitting on top of the non-fastened hinge half. Fold the sideboard and hinge halves over so that the sideboard is lying flat on the table bed. Use the hinge holes as guides, drill four pilot holes that are about 3/4-inch deep, into the bottom edge of the tapered sideboard. Using the longer wood screws, fasten the second half of each hinge into the tapered side, bottom edge. The sideboard should lie flat on the table bed in its folded position. Now, swing the sideboard upward so that the outside surface is flush with the edge of the plywood bed. With some support from your hand, it should be able to stand straight up. Check Figure 8-1 to see the vertical and folded positions of the sideboards. You will fasten the other tapered sideboard in the same, but symmetric (or mirror image) manner. At this time you have used four hinges total, with eight 1/2-inch screws (into the table bed) and eight of the longer screws (into the bottom edge of the sideboard). Both sideboards will lie down against the plywood bed when stored and fold upward and outward for the assembled position. Remove the hinge pins from the three remaining hinges. You will need a screwdriver and hammer to pop them out. Buy three L-shaped pins that can be used to re-attach the hinge halves for assembly (removable hinge pins). Make sure that they fit snugly in place where the pins used to be.

Position the back wall piece vertically near the back edge of the top bed surface. It should span from the back of one tapered sideboard across to the back of the other and fit almost perfectly in between them (about 29 inches wide). Take two halves of one hinge and position it in back at the bottom, so one half will attach to the back edge of the ply-

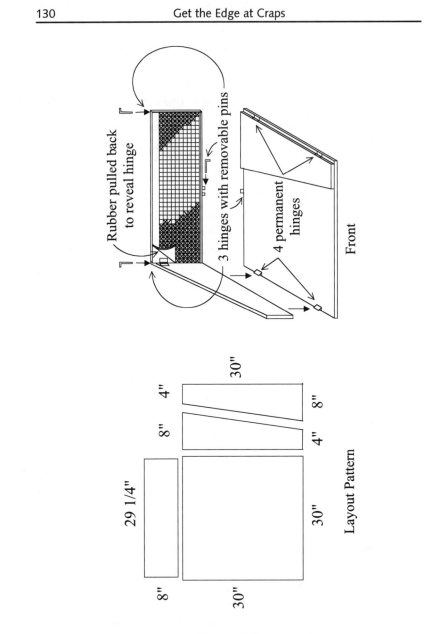

Figure 8-1
Portable Practice Box

wood bed (two longer screws) and the other mating half will attach to the back bottom of the back wall. Make sure they are centered from side to side. Drill two 3/4-inch pilot holes and screw in the back table bed hinge-half first. Position the mating hinge half and insert the removable pin to attach the two halves together. Reposition the back wall to the plywood bed and use the hinge holes as guides to drill two 1/2-inch pilot holes into the rear, bottom back wall. Screw in two 1/2-inch screws and the back wall is now attached at the bottom center. At the right, inside upper corner, where the back wall and sideboard meet, you will position two more hinge halves. Mark, drill, and fasten one half to the upper right back wall with two 1/2-inch screws. Remember that the back wall should fit nicely between the two sideboards so the hinge half should not hang out over the edge. The side where the hinge pin is inserted will be flush with the outboard edge of the back wall. Insert a removable pin to attach the mating hinge-half, position it up against the right sideboard, mark, drill, and fasten two 1/2-inch screws into the upper right sideboard to secure the second hinge half. Attach the remaining hinge halves to the left, inside upper corner, where the back wall and left sideboard meet, using the same technique.

Purchase a roll of the diamond crap table rubber that is eight inches high and at least 30 inches long. You can order these from most general gaming supply houses. The Gambler's General Store at 800 S. Main Street in Las Vegas sells a 4'-by-8" strip of the diamond pyramids for about $40. You can charge it over the phone and they will ship it to you. Their phone number, at the time of this writing, is 1-800-322-2447 and their Internet address is *www.ggss.com*. You can also order a 30-by-60 inch home-style craps layout for about $30, that you can spread over the top of your box bed when you practice. You can only fit about half of the layout on your box bed, so cut the layout in half, right up the middle of the proposition bets. Use the other half a year or two later after the first half gets a little worn. After you obtain your diamond pyramid sheet, cut it down to match your 29-inch wide back wall. Apply a strong rubber cement to the contact area of the plywood back wall and to the backside of the rubber diamond pyramidal sheet. The cement will set independently on both surfaces after a few minutes (very tacky to the touch). In any event, read the directions for application. The continuous rubber bumper should be positioned along the bottom of the back wall. The two-inch wide, flat surface should run across the top. Slowly attach the rubber to the plywood. Be very careful here because once they touch they are stuck! I first aligned and then attached the bottom edge of the rubber diamond sheet. Rolling a wooden dowel (positioned between both surfaces) slowly upward and away from the contact area, I gradually allowed the rubber to contact the plywood with no air gaps.

The flat portion of the rubber sheet will be glued over the top right and left hinge-halves that you mounted previously to the upper front surface of the plywood back wall. You may have to cut a small notch out of the flat rubber sheet, so the sideboard hinge-half will mate up with the back-wall hinge-half properly. Once the diamond pyramid sheet is fully attached, I would recommend placing weights on it and letting it set over night. After the back wall is complete, you are ready to assemble your practice rig. Fold the two tapered sides upward and outward to their proper positions. Move the back wall into place so that the three sets of hinge-halves now line up. Insert the three removable hinge pins and your box is set. Position your half home-style craps layout over the top of the permanently attached wool fabric and iron down with your hand. A Velcro effect will hold the two together for your practice session. This will simulate your average craps table bounce. Make sure that the end of the layout with the Pass Line betting area and Don't Come box is just up against and underneath the continuous rubber bumper of the back wall. If you have excess layout material on the right or left side, trim it, or simply fold the excess up along the inside, tapered sideboards. If you wish to practice for a hard table surface, do not use the half home-style layout. To break your rig down, simply pull out the three removable hinge pins and remove the back wall. Fold the sideboards down, lay the back wall on top and you are ready to store it. Congratulations, you now have a very representative practice setup to hone your skills on!

Creating Muscle Memory in Three Weeks

With the following process, you should be able to select, master, and effectively apply a new delivery technique in three weeks or less. The dice sets, the grip and throw will become second nature in relatively short order. Here is a week-to-week, systematic approach that you can execute:

Week 1—Decide upon and commit to a practice routine. Initially, this should be about 40 to 60 minutes a day with no interruptions or distractions. Whether an elaborate practice box or just two corrugated box lids, set up a representative practice mock-up. Select one or two table positions that you want to throw from and position your high-back chair accordingly. Try out the body stances and positions described in Chapter 6 and nail down the combination that feels right for your table position and anatomy. Do not record or worry about results at this time and do not concern yourself with setting the dice. Experiment with different delivery variations of the perfect pitch. Considerations should be given to comfort, control and consistency. Try out and settle upon a dice grip that allows you to keep the dice stable and is easy to get out of. Refer to Chapter 7 for gripping details. Use three pairs of dice with which to practice. This will allow you to throw one pair immediately after the other. You will "groove in" more quickly as you develop a feel and rhythm for your throw. Don't be afraid to experiment a little in the early days of your learning curve. Focus on your delivery technique. By the third or fourth day you should have a grip and delivery that feels comfortable. Practice your chosen technique for the remaining four or five practice sessions of your first week. Remember—you are developing your muscle memory!

Week 2—You will use the first day of the second week to practice setting the dice. Spend your first practice session just mixing up and resetting the Hard Ways Dice Set. You should get familiar with looking at and handling the dice. Your objective is to quickly formulate a setting plan each time and then implement it. Refer to Chapter 5 for a quick review. Practice setting first for accuracy and then for speed. By the end of this session, you should be able to create the Hard Ways Set in four seconds or less. This will be your set for all rolls except the come-out roll. After you feel comfortable with the Hard Way Set, you will incorporate it into your delivery routine. Practice the set, grip, and throw for four or five 45-minute sessions. Your objective is to smoothly incorporate setting the dice and maintaining consistency of your rhythm in the delivery. Again, do not record or worry about the dice outcomes at this time. Only concern yourself with setting and delivering the dice consistently to complete the development of your muscle memory. By now, the dice should be exiting your hand together, traveling and landing together. If you are having difficulty, review Chapters 6 and 7. At the end of your second week, you should be completing the Hard Ways Set in about two seconds with a smooth transition into a consistent grip and dice delivery.

Week 3—Once you have worked the Hard Way Set into your delivery routine, you will proceed to record your results. Spend your third week practicing for five 45-minute sessions. Now read and study the Practice Plan that follows. This will be your third week of solidifying your delivery as well as your regular method of practice from here on.

Establishing Your Practice Routine

Set up your practice rig and a high back chair about eight feet away from your back wall with the dice on the seat. With the high back directly in front of you, lean on it with your non-throwing arm like you would on the craps table rail and reach over with your throwing arm to set the dice that are situated in front. Carefully grip the dice and gently toss them onto your practice box. Record the results after your throw. You will fine-tune your delivery this way at home until you can demonstrate a lower frequency of 7s (or higher Sevens-to-Rolls Ratio) with the Hard Ways Set. Once you are proficient at avoiding the 7 during the point cycle, you can practice setting 7s for the come-out roll. Initially you will practice in private with no disturbances. Once you are comfortable with the delivery and recording the results, you will strive to create a realistic environment in which to practice. The first thing you will do is to generate some continuous noise. Turn on the radio or television to create background noise as you try to practice. One of my students actually entered a casino armed with a tape recorder and created a casino background noise tape, spanning several hours. When it's time to practice, he pops the tape in and goes into his routine. The next thing is to allow interruptions. Make yourself available to family members if they need to speak with you. This will cause you to stop in between tosses and interact with them. You are now simulating table talk and possible dialogue with the crew. See if you can re-establish your timing after a brief conversation.

Before any practice session, take about six to ten warm-up tosses. As the body begins to loosen up and the dice begin to feel right, you see a tighter formation of travel. You can start the actual practice session at this time. One method of practicing is to run virtual casino craps sessions. You will set aside an actual session buy in and make and press bets as you would at a live craps game. As you hit certain numbers and make your points, you will dispense payouts. You can practice various betting strategies as well as proper money management. It helps to have casino chips when practicing this way. I have several hundred casino chips that I purchased when the Regency Casino in Bell, California, closed its doors. These are actual clay chips with the correct weight and feel. I have many 50¢ values all the way up to the $500 denominations. You do not have to go to that extreme, but one rack (holding 100 clay or plastic chips) with three or four different colors (or denominations) will suffice. If you can, pick up 20 white singles, 40 red nickels, 30 green quarters, and 10 black hundreds. Also, a smaller, inexpensive on/off puck will come in handy to mark your point after the come-out. You can order these items from a gambling supply house. It is fun to start out with, say a $300 buy in, and try to run it up to $1500 in one of these virtual craps sessions.

The Sevens-to-Rolls Ratio

Before I talk about documenting your play, there are some concepts that need explaining. At this point, allow me to introduce a term that I call the *Sevens-to-Rolls Ratio*, or SRR for short. This is simply the average number of tosses it takes for one 7 to appear. The SRR provides a measurable means to track our success at altering the frequency of 7s as compared to random. If you believe that there is no way to influence the dice and it is purely a random game, then the Sevens-to-Rolls Ratio will always be 1 to 6. After all, there are six ways to throw a 7 out of 36 possible dice outcomes. For random shooters (I commonly refer to these guys as "chicken feeders"), a frequency histogram averaged over thousands of throws would converge to look like the numbers represented in Figure 8-2. This is the familiar distribution of outcomes that you see printed in every craps book. For every 36 tosses, on average six 7s would occur, five 6s or 8s, four 5s or 9s, etc. This is about as far as the mathematical experts of the game will take it. They have given absolutely no credence whatsoever to the laws that govern rigid body translation and rotation, conservation of energy, angles of incidence and reflectance, and so on.

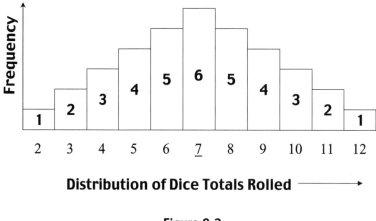

Distribution of Dice Totals Rolled ⟶

Figure 8-2
1:6 SRR Frequency Distribution
(Six 7s in 36 Trials)

Being able to set and deliver the dice at the craps table is analogous to a well-practiced croupier kicking the rotor up to some consistent speed and sniping out his own, heavily bet sector on the roulette wheel. If you are able to wager and then deal your own game, and know what you are doing, you can substantially swing the edge in your favor. As you become an accomplished dice shooter and you document your ratio of 7s against the number of total throws, you will see this number start to climb. I noticed this effect some six or seven years ago, so I began to track it. As I set and threw against the 7, I lowered my frequency of 7s, relative to random. This is important for extending your roll. Because there are two distinctly different directives in the game of craps, we need to distinguish between two different Sevens-to-Rolls Ratios. On the come-out roll, we set and shoot for the 7s. I refer to this as the *come-out SRR*. Hopefully, this SRR is less than 1:6, which means a higher frequency of 7s for the come-out will occur. During the point cycle, where we try to elude the sinister 7, we shoot for a *point cycle SRR* that is greater than 1:6, producing a lower 7s frequency. This second Sevens-to-Rolls Ratio is critical because it directly affects the life of the shooter's game. This is the chief SRR that I will be referring to herein, and may be as high as 1:8 for a well-practiced controlled thrower. Let's look at the frequency histogram for a shooter with an SRR of 1:7.

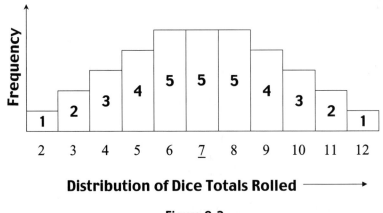

Distribution of Dice Totals Rolled ⟶

Figure 8-3
1:7 SRR Frequency Distribution
(Five 7s in 35 Trials)

For every 35 tosses, five 7s will occur for a ratio of 1:7. The remaining 30 throws have been normalized to pick up the slack. For example, if three 4s are random for 36 tosses, then 3 x (35/36) or 2.917 fours should occur on average for every 35 tosses. Because the frequency of 7s has been reduced through physical means, the remaining numbers will uniformly increase to fill in the void. The 4s frequency then increases from 2.917 to 3.000 for 35 throws. The other remaining numbers are weighted and calculated in a similar fashion. The 1:7 SRR model was chosen to illustrate this idea because it is realistic and works out nicely with whole integer values. Once you have determined your SRR, you can then calculate your mathematical edge, based on the type of bet and a modified frequency distribution of 7s. I have calculated the percent advantages for various craps wagers at different SRR skill levels in Chapter 15. Blackjack is a game of mathematics. As cards are removed from play without replacements, the composite of remaining cards will change. As a result, the mathematical edge will sway back and forth like a pendulum. When the pendulum is in the positive range for the player, he has the advantage and should bet accordingly.

Unlike blackjack, craps *is* a game with replacements. Just because a twelve is thrown on one toss, it doesn't mean it is removed for the next throw. In a game where two 3/4-inch cubes determine the outcome of that independent trial, you have to look at the rudimentary physics involved. Once you realize that this is a rigid body dynamics problem first, you realize that physical influence is the only way to beat this game consistently. As you develop dexterity at avoiding the 7, you can use statistics to confirm that the lower frequency of 7s is based on skill and not luck. Each toss of the dice is an independent, discrete binomial event. If the number of discrete trials is large enough and the probability of throwing a 7 is not too close to 0 or 1, then a *normal* continuous probability distribution can be used to closely approximate what will happen over a discrete sample space. At the center of this symmetric, normal or bell-shaped curve is the *mean*, or average number of occurrences of something we are interested in—like the frequency of 7s thrown as compared to random.

Statistical Confidence

Without getting too technical, just realize that the more you "deviate" from the mean of random 7s (measured in standard deviations), the better your validation that ability is responsible and not some statistical fluctuation. In addition, the larger the sample size of recorded throws to calculate the SRR, the higher confidence rating you will have. Table 8-4 below shows you how many recorded throws you will need to confirm a particular Sevens-to-Rolls Ratio at a 99.85 percent confidence level. This is based on using a continuous normal distribution of random 7s as compared against 7s recorded through controlled-throwing. Some of the calculations used to construct this table are included in Chapter 15. To gain 99.85 percent confidence in your skill, you must be three standard deviations lower than the average, or random, occurrence of 7s. Plus or minus three standard deviations from the mean covers 99.70 percent of the area under the bell-shaped curve. Half of the remaining 0.30 percent is an extraordinarily high number of 7s (mean, or average, plus three standard deviations) and the other half is an extraordinarily low number of 7s (mean minus three standard deviations). It is this second half, or lower frequency of 7s to rolls that we are interested in, when trying to avoid the seven-out.

Table 8-4
99.85% Confidence Levels for Different Sevens to Rolls Ratios

Skill Level	Rolls to Confirm	Average # of 7s	Max. # of 7s Allowed
SRR 1: 8	* 720 rolls	120	90
SRR 1: 7	2160 rolls	360	308
SRR 1: 6.75	3600 rolls	600	533
SRR 1: 6.5	7560 rolls	1260	1163
SRR 1: 6.35	14,760 rolls	2460	2324
SRR 1: 6.25	28,080 rolls	4680	4493
SRR 1: 6.20	43,200 rolls	7200	6968

* A probability of 1/6 is too close to 0 for only 720 rolls to confirm a 1:8 SRR. Record at least 3,600 rolls while attempting to avoid the 7 to be sure.

So, looking at the table, if you have 3,600 or more recorded throws and your SRR is 1 to 6.75 or higher, then there is a 99.85 percent chance that this SRR is due to skill and is not a statistical aberration. The average number of 7s expected from 3,600 rolls is 600, but because you have only thrown 533 or fewer 7s, your SRR has a very high confidence factor attached to it. If, however, your SRR is only 1 to 6.25, it will take 28,080 rolls to verify this SRR with a 99.85 percent confidence level. It is closer to random and will take a lot more rolls to be three standard deviations lower than the average occurrence of 7s. If you are willing to settle for two standard deviations (still not too shabby) at a confidence level of 97.73 percent, then you will need fewer rolls. (Plus or minus two standard deviations is 95.46 percent plus the high-end frequency of 2.27 equals 97.73 percent). To confirm an SRR of 1 to 6.5, you will only need 3,360 rolls. An SRR equal to 6.35 requires 6,600 rolls to verify and an SRR of 6.25 needs at least 12,480 rolls to validate your skill with 97.73 percent confidence. If you were to work with only minus one standard deviation from the mean, you would have an 84.13 percent factor of confidence (68.26 percent plus 15.87 percent), but I would advise against it.

Documenting Your Success

Another method of practicing is to set and throw against the 7 for the entire session. There is a practice form that follows with 120 spaces to record your results. See Figure 8-5. Fill out the date and dice set used at the top. Record the resulting dice pairs as they appear. For example, write 5-4 or 6-3 down, not just 9. In the leftmost column labeled, "ind" For result index. You will record a "P" for a primary hit, (i.e. 4-4 is a primary hit for the Hard Ways Set) or "S" for a secondary pitch or roll hit. "T" denotes thirds, or a number resulting from multi-axial movement and "*" is used to indicate a fatal 7 combination. Use the third column labeled, "remarks" to jot down any quick notes that are relevant to your throw at the time. Any observations or adjustments that you made would be perfect for this. I have included one of my actual practice sheets from a few years back to serve as an example. Refer to Figure 8-6. Your documented practice will act like a journal. You may see similar patterns or problems in future practice sessions and will now have a basis for making corrections. As your tendencies and idiosyncrasies become apparent to you, you will have a better idea what adjustments are needed. After you have thrown the dice 120 times, count up the number of asterisks you have recorded in the result index column. You can calculate your Sevens-to-Rolls Ratio (SRR) by dividing 120 results by the number of asterisks, or 7s thrown in that practice session.

If sixteen 7s were thrown, then 120 divided by 16 equals 7.50. Your SRR for that session is 1:7.5, or one 7 for every seven and a half throws. An SRR of 1:6 is random. When filling out a practice form, do not mix dice sets or objectives (come-out versus point cycle). You have my permission to copy the blank practice form found in Figure 8-5 in order to document your practice sessions. You are typically shooting to avoid the 7 for the whole practice sheet. Once you have mastered the mechanical elements of the controlled throw, your SRR should be higher than 1:6 when shooting against the 7. As you continue to practice, this ratio should steadily climb. I've heard students boast of having SRRs of 12 or even 15. While this may be possible over a short period of play, the edge held over the casino would be in the triple digits! For the past five years of documented play, my personal SRR is 1 to 7.53. If I only look at the past two years, it is a little higher— 1:7.81. This may not sound too impressive, but it is statistically significant because of the number of recorded throws. If you can achieve an SRR of 8 or higher over a population of 5,000 throws, write the publisher or contact me through the information found at the back of this book—I may have a place for you on my dice team.

Controlled Throw Practice Form

Date:_____   Dice Set:_____   7s to Rolls:_____   Initials:_____

Ind.	Pairs	Remarks	Ind.	Pairs	Remarks	Ind.	Pairs	Remarks	Ind.	Pairs	Remarks

Figure 8-5

Controlled Throw Practice Form

Date: __4-05-97__   Dice Set: __HardWays__   7s to Rolls: __1:8.0__   Initials: __S. S.__ .

Ind.	Pairs	Remarks	Ind.	Pairs	Remarks	Ind.	Pairs	Remarks	Ind.	Pairs	Remarks
S	4-1		P	4-4		S	4-5		S	2-3	
S	5-6		*	3-4	2x Pitch	*	4-3		S	6-2	
S	4-2		S	3-2		S	1-4		S	1-1	Roll, both dice
S	4-2		S	3-2		*	2-5	Sidearm?	S	5-6	
P	3-3		S	4-6		S	5-1		S	2-4	
S	5-1		P	2-2		S	4-1		*	3-4	
S	2-1		*	6-1		P	5-5		*	1-6	
S	4-5		S	1-5		P	3-3		S	3-5	
S	1-5		P	3-3		S	3-5		S	2-4	
*	3-4	2x Pitch	*	4-3		S	3-6		S	1-3	
P	3-3		*	1-6		P	2-2		P	4-4	
S	3-5		P	4-4		S	4-2		*	1-6	Opposing yaw
S	4-2		*	4-3		S	2-3		S	6-4	
P	4-4		S	5-3	Chgd. arc	S	1-2		S	5-6	
P	3-3		S	1-2		S	2-6		S	1-4	
P	4-4		S	1-3		P	3-3		S	1-5	
S	6-3		S	1-4		S	1-2		S	2-3	
P	4-4		S	5-4		S	6-2		S	5-6	
S	6-2		S	3-2		S	1-2		S	1-4	
S	6-2		P	4-4		S	4-6		*	5-2	2x Pitch
S	2-1		S	4-5		S	5-4		S	6-5	
S	6-6	Roll, both dice	S	4-5		P	2-2		*	2-5	2x Pitch
P	5-5		S	2-6		P	4-4		S	1-2	
S	6-2		P	2-2		S	2-3		S	6-6	Roll, both dice
S	6-4		S	3-2		S	1-1	Roll, both dice	S	6-3	
S	5-1		S	2-4		P	3-3		S	6-3	
P	2-2		S	4-6		*	3-4	Die off sideboard	S	4-1	
*	2-5	2x Pitch	S	3-2		S	4-1		S	5-4	
S	2-4		S	6-2		S	4-2		S	4-6	
S	5-1		P	3-3		S	3-5		S	1-4	

*120 rolls/fifteen total 7s thrown = 8.0 for a 1:8.0 Sevens-to-Rolls Ratio

Figure 8-6

The more minor come-out SRR, which is the least important of the two, occurs when you set 7s around as with the Come-Out Set and attempt to throw a 7. This might be useful on the come-out roll or if you are trying to seven-out. You are setting and attempting to throw a higher frequency of 7s than what is random. In this case, an SRR lower than 6 is desired. As mentioned earlier, this is not nearly as critical, unless you are shooting from the Don't side. If you are so inclined, you can track this ratio for trying to hit 7s, as well. For example, 120 tosses resulting in twenty-four 7s would yield an SRR of 1:5. If you are a Pass Line bettor and wish to track your *come-out SRR* as well as your *point cycle SRR*, then one practice sheet of come-out rolls for every four to five sheets of point cycle rolls would be about right. Just remember that avoiding the point cycle 7 is what lengthens our hand and increases our opportunity at the craps table. In the final chapter of this book, I have included some graphs and several calculations to show how your edge is affected when you elevate your point cycle SRR. As you influence the physical phenomena of the game, you are altering the frequency of occurrence for throwing a 7. This is measured by your SRR. Using your SRR, you can mathematically calculate your percent advantage over the house. If you plug a random SRR of 1:6 into the equations, you will come up with all the customary house edges reported in most craps books.

"Donnie B," King of Documentation

I received a letter a few years back from a new dice player residing in that fair country to the north of this Michigander. Donnie B. (a.k.a. 007) was quickly becoming an accomplished controlled thrower. Donnie was a proficient blackjack player, but for reasons that most of you can identify with, he wanted another weapon in his casino attack arsenal. Donnie tells in his letter how he attended the 1997 winter weekend clinic in Las Vegas.

> "After attending the clinic at which Sharpshooter spent so much time one-on-one with the students, I could really see and experience the rhythm roll. Most of all I learned how to fine-tune it. A picture is worth more than a thousand words!"

To his credit, he thoroughly read and studied the information and diligently practiced for a few months in a rig that he had specially set up. Donnie documented many of his practice sessions using the practice form in Figure 8-5. He calculated his Sevens-to-Rolls Ratio and analyzed trends with different grip or delivery adjustments. He also kept track of his primary and secondary number hit ratios, as well as his inside number hit ratio. His primary number hit ratio (hitting one of four combinations that are originally set on the dice) compared quite favorably to a random distribution. After all his study, practice, analysis and a clinic, here is how 007 progressed.

> "Starting February 16, up through March 24, 1998, here is how it went. The following (SRR) numbers represent one practice form equaling 120 rolls per page: 5.4, 6.3, 6.6, 7.1, and 8.5."

Notice the nice, steady improvement he experiences! He goes on to say:

> "On March 29, a monster roll ensued, 56 straight numbers with an SRR of 19.0! Then 6.6, 8.0, 8.0, 8.5, 8.0, 8.0, 6.6, 8.5, 10.9, 7.6 as of June 14 . . . The bottom line is 2,040 documented rolls and an overall Sevens-to-Rolls Ratio of 8.4."

Donnie's Story, Spring of 1998

Our good neighbor to the north now felt confident enough in his abilities to try them out in a real casino. In a subsequent correspondence, he writes:

> "Linda (wife) and I vacationed at Foxwoods in Connecticut a few weeks ago. She does not gamble but loves to watch, and enjoy the comps. We arrived Tuesday afternoon and in the evening went down to play. Betting a basic unit of $5 or $6 on the inside numbers, I felt a little apprehensive and nervous in very crowded conditions. I lost 18 units in 45 minutes due to poor playing conditions with overcrowded tables, so I called it a night. I went back down at 6 o'clock the next morning after 20 minutes of dresser drawer practice in my room and found an empty table. I placed a Pass Line bet, set 7s all around, and promptly threw five 7s and 11s in a row. I finally established a point number and proceeded to throw the dice for *one hour and 20 minutes* making pass after pass! Two of my passes took 20 to 30 rolls. I pressed my bets very slightly, until I had $64 across the board (up to two units). I went back to the room at 7:30 waking my wife with a fist full of hundreds. I had won $1,760 or (352) $5 units in one session! I only wish my units were higher, but I just wanted to protect the win."

Donnie managed to do a decent job of pounding the tables—even with his ultra-conservative betting progression. We have since put together a betting progression that makes more sense for his ability level. He then caps off his letter . . .

> "Over the next few days there was one more loss of 19 units and a few more smaller wins of 60 to

100 units . . ." (You call those *small* wins, Donnie?!) ". . . along with three ovations. What a great feeling! Thanks again, and see you in Vegas."

In June of 1998, I got a chance to shoot with Donnie at Bally's in Vegas. He averaged 13+ rolls per game for six hands (8.526 rolls per game is random). I made what Donnie would refer to as a "smaller win" of 65 units on his and my rolls collectively. A week after hooking up with 007 in Vegas, I got another update. After completing eleven more practice forms for 1,320 additional rolls, he has elevated his Sevens-to-Rolls Ratio to 8.53 for 3,360 total rolls! He is averaging one string of 19 rolls *or better* per practice form. In addition, he had recorded virtual casino wins of $1,065, $2,095, $3,488, and $1,433 with no losing sessions. This was after we worked on a betting strategy that made sense for ability level and delivery tendencies. Donnie B. went on to carry an SRR of just under 1:9 for the remainder of 1998. His level has dropped a little, but is still above 1:8 overall. He has since become a member of our professional dice team and more recently, one of my controlled throw instructors. You will read about another of 007's dinosaur rolls in Chapter 14.

Chapter 9
Betting Stratagems

Managing Your Money

Before we talk about specific betting tactics, I think a discussion on money management is warranted. You should have a separate, dedicated bankroll for your craps play. This makes documentation of your play more manageable and meaningful. You should keep some kind of accounting so you know how many units you won or lost on your hands and how you did on everyone else's rolls. I usually write down in a small notebook, the date, time, casino and which table I am playing on. Sometimes I will record, or have a partner record, the results of each roll for that session. I also jot down any ideas or items that stand out for that particular play. You can review your notes later to make some sense of it all. A general observation I have made from my notes is that I play better after lunch and even better yet in the evening hours. Unfortunately, these times tend to be the more crowded, but everything else being equal, I perform better in the evening. Another, more specific bit of information I have discovered, is that there are two particular tables at a local casino that I have *never* lost on. There may be various reasons why this is so and some of these I can even identify. Either way, these are the first two tables that I check on when I enter this casino. So, jot down a few pertinent notes as you play. There are things that you will recognize and then can capitalize on.

For your bankroll, I recommend that you have 200 units for a three- or four-day craps excursion. For a week or longer, make it 300 units. Divide your bankroll by the number of total gambling sessions that you will have for the trip. Each session is like a battle, and your goal is to win the war, one battle at a time. For example, if I plan to take a three-day trip with three sessions of play per day, I will partition off about 22 units per one- to two-hour playing session (200 units/9 sessions). Keep in mind that your allotted session stake must endure the whole session. If you run through most of your stake at the first table, then it will be a short session. I might play three tables during the course of one session, in one or two casinos. Once I complete a session (win, lose, or draw), I will not touch that session stake again for the remainder of the trip. By doing this, you are locking in session wins and minimizing session losses. This not only establishes proper discipline, but it attaches value to your session stake as well. You must have a decent enough overall bankroll to weather the trip. Yet, you must respect the individual session stake. If you blow through 22 units with total disregard during the course of one session, you might think, "No big deal, I've got another 180 units to play with." However, this is both wrong and reckless. You will find that *to consistently win the war, you must manage each battle.*

Another recommendation that I will extol is to set a *stop-loss* limit. Never leave more than half of your session stake at any one table, especially at the beginning of your controlled throwing career. If your buy in is 20 units, do not allow yourself to lose more than ten units at that table. I split my buy in into two equal amounts. One pile goes in the back, or *safe rack*, closer to me for safekeeping, and the active betting chips go in the front, or *active rack*. If my buy in is 20 units, then ten units is my table stop-loss and goes in the front rack for active wagering. The second ten units go in the safe rack. As you lose any units, they will come from the front, active rack. If the chips in the front rack disappear, then you have hit your stop-loss for that table. In extremely rare cases (like my last hand was great and I am the next shooter), I may extend my stay, but reaching a stop-loss is usually a sure sign to leave that table. You can try another table, but once the session stake is gone, you should conclude your session. If you do approach another table after hitting a stop-loss, you might consider re-splitting the remainder of your session stake into two equal piles again. Make the best call based on your circumstances at the time. By the way, you do not have to lose half of your buy in before you decide to leave a table. If the tables are too hard or too long or you observe something else that you don't like, then by all means, leave right away.

By the same token, if you are up a few units for that table, but the tide seems to be changing (i.e. the pit starts applying heat or you begin to feel tired), do not necessarily wait for the stop-loss to kick in. Preserve the small win and walk if you have just cause. Under any circumstances, do not lose more than the allocated session stake. You must live to fight other battles. Let's say that things go more favorably and you begin to win. Your stop-loss becomes a *trailing stop-loss* and your session stake will never be less than ten units off your peak. For example, your 20-unit buy in has grown to 27 units after the first shooter. Twenty-seven units is now your "high-water" mark. You will lock 17 units up in the back or safe rack and still have ten active operating units (the wagers out on the betting layout plus the chips in your front rack). The next shooter nets you four more units (ten active units and now 21 in the safe rack) so you are guaranteed, at least a one unit net win for this table. As you continue to win, you will maintain your ten-unit operating stake. The rest of the chips should be accruing in the safe rack, closest to you. You will not touch these safe chips so there is no excuse for not walking away from this table with a profit. As you lose a bet here or there but are predominantly winning, you can replenish your active betting stake so it remains at ten units. However, replenish it out of subsequent winnings and continue to place the excess winnings in the safe rack. Now, even if you start to lose, you can never be more than ten units off your highest balance.

Your first objective is to protect your table buy in. In this case, locking 20 units up in your safe rack. Your next goal is to start accumulating profits. As you continue to win, there is another point for your consideration. You should decide whether or not to tighten the trailing stop-loss parameter after you double your buy in. This is a personal decision that you should make before stepping into the casino to play. Some players get aggressive after they have more of the "house's money" to play with, but personally, I like going the other route. I figure that I have put in the effort and the money is now mine. If my 20-unit buy in turns into 40 units (especially from betting on other shooters), I will consider reducing my trailing stop-loss to seven or even five units. When you are throwing the dice and are in the middle of a long hand, use your discretion. If you are pounding numbers and continue to feel good about your form, then maintain your wagers (we'll talk about specific betting tactics and pressing your wins a little later). If, as mentioned before, the tide begins to change and you are throwing, there is no dishonor in reducing or calling off your non-contract bets. Either way, after having a long roll, I recommend ending the session to give yourself a breather. Enjoy the win, let your adrenaline stabilize, and allow your batteries to recharge.

Sharing Some Personal Experiences

Let me relay a quick example of what *not to do* as far as money management goes. I just played two sessions recently at a local casino. In the first session, I settled for a less than desirable table and shooting position. My first hand yielded a seven-unit win, but I knew I had been a little lucky. I was throwing the dice over a longer distance plus I was not yet warmed up. I did not possess the control necessary to create wins based on skill at that point. The dice traveled tightly together, but broke up too much after landing. I knew what was happening and figured it was time to walk—I almost did. Unfortunately, I decided to hang out until the dice came back to me. I began wagering on random throwers. The seven units of profit evaporated on the next two shooters; again, I thought about leaving. I blew another nine units (almost half my original session buy-in) waiting for the dice to finish coming around. Now the pressure had mounted and I felt the need to get back all the money on my next hand. I loaded up, established a point and promptly sevened out. I had blown seven units of profit *and* my entire session buy in of 20 units! I finally wised up and grabbed some dinner "on the house." It should not have gotten to this point. There were several warning signs, but I ignored them all, breaking at least three of my own rules in the process.

After dinner, I went back down for another play. The second session went much better, I'm happy to report. I found my favorite stick-left position open on a smaller table and the shooter was to my right. Just as I was buying in, the shooter sevened out and the dice came to me. A quarter on the Pass Line and two quick 7s were thrown for the come-out win. I established and made the 8 as my point three times with one point of 5 in the mix. I also pounded several inside numbers along the way. Eighteen minutes later, I sevened out. I was up 44 units for that roll so I quit and headed straight for the cashier's cage. Overall, I netted 24 units (44 minus the 20 I lost earlier) which is not so bad, you may think. However, It would have easily been a 44-unit win if I had been a little more patient and just waited for my favorite throwing position. I even had the opportunity to be up 51 units if I just laid off, after accurately assessing the situation. Then, after losing half of my session buy in, I had a third chance to leave with what would have been 35 units for the day, but chose to stay! I guess even veterans have discipline break downs from time to time. What I am stressing here is to respect every dollar in your bankroll, because a dollar saved is a dollar won. Now, let me illustrate what you should do in managing your bankroll.

A few years back, I flew out East to hook up with Long Arm and Eric N. for some dice play in Atlantic City. There were no classes or students, just three veteran rhythm rollers striking out to seek their fortune. The weekend went well. Usually, two of us kept the tables warm and every once in a while one of us would really heat things up. I felt confident enough in my form and ability to bet the standard $25 unit size that I like. As the weekend progressed, our profits steadily rose. There were no monster hands, just consistent money rolls. Three days later, as I was bidding adieu to my compadres, I was up (141) $25-units. The very next weekend I was in Vegas to teach and tape a class. There were a lot of preparations involved and I was focused on instructing. I could not get into the controlled throwing groove. There were just too many distractions to overcome. Recognizing this fact early on, I astutely reduced my playing time, minimized my exposure to random shooters and dramatically slashed my average unit size. I still managed to lose 125 units, but these were $7 units on average. I was not about to completely quit gambling (after all I was in Vegas), but realizing my dilemma, I made drastic adjustments. Even with a net gain of only 16 units for both weekends, I still emerged with over $2,600 of profit because of the adjustment to my unit size! It is very important to monitor yourself and the situation around you to effectively manage your money.

Once you become better at managing your money and have a good plan in place, you must have the *discipline* to stick with your plan. Last October, at a dice clinic I hosted in Vegas, Larry Edell came out as a special guest speaker with his wife Andrea. Larry and Andrea own and operate Leaf Press, a company that publishes gaming books. They also publish the longest running craps newsletter, "The Crapshooter." You can check out their online version at *www.crapshooter.com*. Larry is a fellow gaming author, and he and his wife are very disciplined players. For this particular trip, they were staying and playing at Caesar's Palace on the strip. Their plan was to win a realistic $300 per session. Their table buy in was $1,000, but most of this money was immediately locked up and never placed at risk. For reasons of earning casino comps, their buy in is usually much larger than what they intend to gamble with and they are disciplined enough not to touch their "show" money. They would bet $10 units sparingly on other shooters, and $30 units on their controlled rolls. By the time I caught up with them, Larry and Andrea had five consecutive winning sessions, hitting their ten-unit goal of at least $300 every time. They showed great discipline in sticking with their money management plans and were consistently hitting their win goals. As they were coloring up to head over to the cashier's cage, one of the dealers remarked, "Come back when you need another $300."

While we are talking about money management, it is very important to stick with the more intelligent wagers on the table. I am not going to review what we covered in Chapters 3 and 4, but I do want to stress the basic philosophy of putting your money where it will work the hardest for you. Let's assume that you have honed your throwing skill such that you can create a delta, or swing in the edge of five percent. This would be an expert-level shooter. If you make only Pass Line wagers with –1.414 percent, then your five percent skill will more than offset that with about 3.6 percent delta to spare. If you Place the 6 or 8 at –1.515 percent, you still are operating with a 3.5 percent positive edge over the house. Now, with that same skill level of five percent, you decide to put one unit on the Pass Line (–1.414 percent), one unit on the Any Craps (–11.111 percent), one unit on a "yo" (at –11.111 percent) and a fourth unit on Any Seven (–16.667 percent). At this point, your five percent swing is not even close to erasing the average ten-plus percent vigorish on all four units that you are giving the casino. The reason why I bring this up is that some students, who I know are skilled shooters, have bemoaned logging inconsistent winning patterns.

I decided to tag along and observe some of them in the casinos. Most of these students were serious, hard-working shooters. After seeing these guys in action, the problem became clear—25 to 50 percent of their wagers were made in the high-tax, center of the table area. Even if you possess a high aptitude for controlled throwing, you still must respect the mathematics. Why give yourself a mountain range to scale when you can just as easily choose a path with a slight hill, or mound to overcome. And if you are really stingy with your bets—just speed bumps. Many of these guys have been making these wagers for decades, and I guess old habits die hard. However, you must learn to divorce yourself from this style of wagering. Review Chapters 3 and 4 to get a good handle on which bets are overly dangerous to the bankroll. If you must, partition off five percent of your active buy in for making such bets, but no more. If your table buy in is $200, say twenty $10 units, then $100 will go in the front rack for active betting. Indulge yourself $5 of this stake for frivolous betting. Your hard fought-for skill can offset *some* of the casino's edge, but do not try to run through a brick wall unscathed or even at all. Before we jump into betting strategies, I have to address the classic Come betting versus Place betting debate.

Come Betting vs. Place Betting

I am often asked, after the point is established, what is the best way to bet on any additional numbers—to Come or Place? That is the question. This is an ongoing debate and there are arguments for both sides. Mathematically speaking, if the person holding the dice were throwing randomly, then the Come bet would have the smaller casino tax. This is true because that Come bet would have a huge edge over the

Don't Come, but *only on the next roll*. Just like the Pass Line bettor on his come-out roll, with eight ways to win versus four ways to lose, our Come bettor has a positive 33.333 percent edge. After the come-out roll, depending on which number you need to repeat, the edge takes a major turn for the worse. Unfortunately, you cannot remove the bet once a number is established (it is a contract bet), so you soften the blow by taking odds (more money at risk). And if the shooter does hit a 7 on your Come bet's come-out roll, then it would win, but all of your other bets would lose. Don't take it too hard though, you *did take full advantage* of that mathematical edge!

Because Come bets are made during the Pass Line bet's point cycle, they become "hedge" bets during their come-out roll. If you believe that it is impossible to influence the dice in any way, then you need not waste any more time. Bet the Pass Line with full odds, get a couple of Come bets working with odds and we'll still part friends. However, if you hate to hedge, or believe that it is possible for an accomplished controlled thrower to influence the outcome of the dice, then the answer becomes a little clearer. All of your wagers and efforts should be oriented toward avoiding the 7 during the point cycle. You are using your ability to avoid the 7 and extend the roll. This means that you are striving to wipe out any Come bet's come-out advantage. Why fight yourself? If you have developed the skill necessary to influence the cubes then "commonize" all your goals. Pick one objective and shoot for it. Aside from focusing on a single objective during the point cycle, there are other benefits to Place betting. Once the Come bet is established and goes to a number, it has a much higher house edge than the Place bet, unless you are prepared to take multiple odds. Look at the Table 9-1 on the following page.

Table 9-1
House Advantage After the Come Point is Established

Point No.	Come w/ 0 x odds	Come w/ 1 x odds	Come w/ 2 x odds	Come w/ 3 x odds	Come w/ 4 x odds	Come w/ 5 x odds	Place Bets
6 or 8	9.091%	4.545%	3.030%	2.273%	1.818%	*1.515%	1.515%
5 or 9	20.000%	10.000%	6.667%	5.000%	*4.000%	3.333%	4.000%
4 or 10	33.333%	16.667%	11.111%	8.333%	*6.667%	5.555%	6.667%

*The Come bet's house edge with multiple odds becomes equivalent to the Place bet's house edge.

These calculations are performed after the Come bet is established and do not take the come-out roll into account. If the Come bet with no odds goes to the 6 or 8, then you are paid even money, say 5 to 5, instead of 6 to 5. The amount you are shorted times the probability, 5/11, of making the point is the house advantage once your Come bet is established as a 6 or 8.

(5/5 – 6/5) x 5/11 x 100% = –9.091 percent

If a $5 Come bet is established on a 4 or 10, for example, and you take three times odds, the edge can be determined for the remainder of the contract bet. Your Come bet of $5 will win even money, but the $15 in odds will win $30 at a correct payoff of 2 to 1. So, $20 returns $35. $40 would be a fair payoff for a $20 bet at this juncture. The probability of repeating the 4 or 10 before a seven-out is 1/3. The calculation follows:

(35/20 – 40/20) x 1/3 x 100% = –8.333 percent

The Come bettor needs to take higher odds to soften the blow. Often placing five or six times more money at risk. And when the odds amount is high enough to cause an equivalent advantage to that of the Place bet, the Place bettor can simply Buy the 4, 5, 9, or 10 and create an even lower house edge with the same funds. (Revisit Graphs 4-3 and 4-4 in Chapter 4). Remember that the Place bet can be reduced, moved to another number, turned off and even removed if the thrower experiences heat from the pit or starts to lose his influence on the dice. The Come bets are frozen until a decision is rendered. In general, always Place the 6 or 8. For unit sizes of $25 or more, try to Buy the 5 or 9 for $1 each. For unit sizes over $15 or more, you will Buy the 4 or 10 for a buck each. If the shooter is throwing randomly, then Come bet along with your Pass Line wager or consider taking a hike.

Betting Stratagems

We are all humans and, as gamblers, we crave the action to a point. So the trick is to create enough action to satisfy our desire, but minimize the tax we pay and give ourselves a chance to profit. There are two main questions that you must ask yourself in order to form your betting strategies:

- What is my current skill level, or SRR when throwing against the 7?
- What is my temperament for risk taking?

I will give you four sensible betting styles that can be tied in with your Sevens-to-Rolls Ratio. You can adjust the style depending upon whether you are more conservative or more aggressive. Then, I will outline two related methods for pressing your wagers such that you maximize your wagers; yet retain most of your winnings. You will learn in this section that Come bets should be used in the early part of your career as a controlled thrower or on random rollers. They deliver some insurance against an early seven-out. You are not risking all your Place bets at once and a quick seven-out will win even money for your Come bet. As you develop your skill with the dice or bet on others who have honed their ability to do so, you will divert from Come betting in favor of conservative Place betting or buying the number if appropriate.

Ultra-Conservative: Pass Line with Come Bet

Step 1—This wagering system is for novice throwers or random rollers. Wager one unit on the Pass Line. If a 7 or 11 is thrown for a natural win, place the winnings in the rack and maintain one unit on the Pass Line. If craps is thrown, try one more unit on the Pass Line for this shooter. If a second craps is thrown, wait for the shooter to make his point or seven-out (next come-out roll) before betting again. After the point is established, take single odds and make no more bets until a decision is rendered. In this first phase, you will have no more than two units at risk simultaneously.

Step 2—If the point is made, bet one unit again on the Pass Line. Since most casinos allow you to take up to twice your Pass Line bet as an odds bet, you will take double odds after the point is established for a total of three units at risk. Some casinos may allow up to five or ten times odds. In this case, limit yourself to double odds.

Step 3—If the previous Pass Line bet is won with double odds, you will add in one Come bet. Place one unit on the Pass Line, establish a point and take single odds. Now, bet one unit on the Come and take single odds. From here, you will maintain four units on the betting layout. If the Come bet hits, then put another unit up in the Come box. After the point is established, take single odds. Continue in this manner, until the roll has concluded.

You will never be more than four units off your peak with this highly conservative method. The worst case would be a seven-out with Pass Line and Come bet established, both with single odds. If you seven-out with a unit in the Come box (that is waiting to go to the next number), then you will only lose one unit off your high-water mark for that roll. Your Pass Line wager with single odds will lose (minus two units), but the Come bet will win even money (plus one unit). With this method, you will keep the lid on your losses while gaining valuable live-table experience, practicing your controlled throw. An early 7 won't hurt you too much because you are not up on that many numbers—one, maybe two. A 7 on the Come bet's come-out roll pays even money. Remember to pick it up!

Conservative: The Super Sniper

This tactic involves making a Pass Line wager and placing the 6, 8. You are "sniping" at the 6 and 8. These numbers have the highest frequency of occurrence with the lowest house edge. This strategy is ideal for a skilled shooter with a Sevens-to-Rolls Ratio in the 6.5 to 7.0 range. In Chapter 15, I demonstrate mathematically, how an SRR of 6.143 is high enough to erase the 1.515 percent house edge on the 6, 8 Place bets. This is the break-even SRR for placing the 6 or 8. Starting with four units, you will bet the Pass Line for one unit and take single odds once a point is established. Next, Place the 6, 8 for one unit each. If the 6 or 8 becomes your point, you will pull down (or do not bet on) that particular number. In this event, double up on the odds bet. You will have a Pass Line and double odds on the point and one unit on the other number as a Place bet. For any given cycle, there are ten to 15 ways working for you versus six ways to seven-out. Because the Pass Line wager yields an even smaller house edge then the 6, 8 Place bets, a shooter with an SRR of about 6.2 or higher is playing with a bona fide edge over the casino.

Moderate: The Place Bet Pyramid

This is actually the betting tactic that I have settled upon using. It is a hybrid of the Sniper and Sharpshooter. You will have five units at risk with the pyramid. This tactic gets its name from the fact that you will have one full unit placed on the 6 and 8 each. You will have a half unit on the 5 and 9 each. There will be nothing on the 4 and 10, so you can see how the pyramid is formed. Assuming double odds are allowed, bet one unit on the Pass Line and take odds as follows:

- If a point of 4 or 10 is established, then take single odds.
- If 5 or 9 becomes the point, pull down the appropriate Place bet and take 1.5 times odds.
- If the 6 or 8 is the point, pull down its Place bet to finance double odds.

If you are playing at a casino that allows higher odds, you can reduce the Pass Line bet to a half unit and transfer it to the odds. For example, if you were playing on the Vegas strip and they offered 3-4-5 odds, then you would wager a *half unit* on the Pass Line. Your total risk is still five units. Take odds as follows for a half unit Pass Line wager:

- If 4 or 10 is the point, take 1.5 units in odds (this would actually be 3 x odds)
- If 5 or 9 is the point, take 2 units worth of odds (this would actually be 4 x odds)
- If 6 or 8 is the point, take 2.5 units in odds (this would actually be 5 x odds)

Because you are taking higher odds, this second situation is more ideal. Your Sevens-to-Rolls Ratio should be in the 6.5 to 7.5 range and you should be fully warmed up. If you are forced into playing with larger unit sizes because of a high-limit table, then stake one unit on the Pass Line and Place one unit on the 6 and 8 if they are not the point. Instead of placing the 5 *and* the 9 for a half unit each, you will select either the 5 *or* the 9 and Place it for one full unit. If the 5, 6, 8, or 9 becomes the point, then take double odds. You will have three inside numbers covered. If 4 or 10 is the point, take single odds and Place either the 5 or 9 with the 6 and 8. In this higher limit scenario, I usually Place the number next to the point. For example, if the 4 or the 6 becomes the point, I will Place the 5 over the 9. Again, you are risking five total units. Remember that if you are at a higher limit table, you can always fall back to the more conservative Sniper tactic.

Aggressive: The Sharpshooter Tactic

With the Sharpshooter tactic, you are taking a little broader aim. Your total risk is six units. You are placing the inside numbers, or the 5, 6, 8, and 9 for one unit each. First, bet one unit on the Pass Line. If an inside number becomes your point, then do not Place it. Take double odds instead. You will Place the other three numbers for a unit each. If the 4 or 10 becomes your point, take single odds and Place the four inside numbers for a unit each. The assumption is that you are grooved in for that roll and your Sevens-to-Rolls Ratio is in excess of 7.0. The break-even SRR for placing the 5 and 9 is 1 to 6.357 as shown in Chapter 15.

Too Aggressive: The Shotgun Tactic

The Shotgun tactic is very aggressive. You are aiming at everything all at once, or as the veteran players call it, "across the board." You will have action on the 4, 5, 6, 8, 9, and 10. This places seven or eight units at risk (depending on whether you take single or double odds). You would Place the inside numbers for a unit each and buy the 4, 10. To even consider such a strategy, the shooter should be carrying an SRR of 8.0 or higher over the past 3,600 throws. His unit size should be high enough to be able to buy the 4 and 10. This tactic is not recommended.

Pressing Your Winnings

My general rule for pressing is simple. Press every third hit that you make. You will keep 2/3 of your winnings this way, locking up almost 70 percent in the safe rack. Plus, you are pressing aggressively enough to take advantage of a moderate to hot roll, should one ensue. Another, slightly more aggressive variation would be to take 1/3 of your winnings on each hit and press with that. You are still using 1/3 of your winnings, but you are pressing a little earlier. By pressing earlier, but in smaller amounts, you may lose a little more money up front. However, the compounding effect of pressing a little after each win is powerful. In addition to deciding how much, or how often you will press, you must decide which bets to press. For example, you can press the "hot number" alone or possibly with its mate, (i.e. the 6 with the 8 or the 5 with the 9, etc.). If you use the exact same dice set each time with a consistent delivery, then an interesting thing may happen. You will see the same results start to repeat. We refer to this as a *signature*. If this is the case when you are throwing, then by all means, exploit this phenomenon. Press the hot number. If your results vary somewhat, or you are not using the exact same dice set each time, then press from the inside out. Start with the 6, 8 and work outward from there to the 5, 9 and eventually the 4, 10 (when you are able to buy them for $15 or $20). With this second strategy, focus on pressing the point numbers with the highest frequency of occurrence and the lowest house edge first.

Summing It Up

Go back and review this section, keeping the following questions in mind:

- What is my tolerance to risk? Am I conservative, moderate or aggressive?
- What are my gambling objectives for playing craps? Are they recreational, consistent income or professional?

- What will be my unit size and dedicated starting bankroll for craps?
- What playing styles and betting tactics will I use? For example, warm up with the Super Sniper and go on to Place bet pyramid. Play with a partner and document each other's rolls.
- What will be my overall money management strategy? What will be my stop loss, stop win, trailing stop loss? How will I press my winnings?
- When will I play and what will be the length of my typical playing session?

Even though accomplished controlled throwers possess an edge over the casino, it is important for you to understand that they will not win every time. If your documented Sevens-to-Rolls Ratio is 1:7.0 or higher, which is a reasonable goal, you should win three out of four sessions. At 1 to 7.81, I am winning seven out of eight casino sessions. If you lose three sessions in a row, then something may be wrong. Take a step back and re-evaluate your situation. Are you betting too much on the other shooters? Re-assess your SRR. Check your delivery. Are you warmed up and grooved in? If necessary, look back at Chapters 5 through 8 and review each aspect of your throw until you find the problem. Remember to stay focused on your *muscle memory*, and not the betting. If your betting strategy (left brain activity) is getting in the way of focusing on your delivery, or rhythm roll (right brain intensive), then become a super sniper and simplify!

Chapter 10
Playing Variations

When you play in the casino, you will encounter two basic situations: The opportunity to bet on skilled throwers and the chance to wager on random rollers. In this chapter, we will look to maximize our opportunities by wagering on ourselves and other controlled throwers. At the same time we will bet very conservatively, or not at all on random "chicken feeders." Unfortunately, the later circumstance is the one that we find ourselves in most times. As a controlled thrower, you will gravitate towards playing at empty tables. This will maximize your exposure to shooting the dice. The first suggestion is to plan your playing sessions around non-crowded times. A Friday or Saturday evening session would be the worst time to play, unless your *only* concern is the camaraderie. However, if your aim is to maximize your time shooting the dice and hopefully your profits, then you will be better served by playing at 6 o'clock on a Tuesday morning, for example. Even though fewer tables are opened, the early morning to lunchtime weekday sessions will give you more exposure with the dice. Another idea is to look for places to play off the beaten path. Try to avoid the mainstream casinos if you must play in the evening hours. The idea is to open up empty tables and play. Groove in with minimal units and get the dice right back and go. After two or three games you should feel comfortable without having to outlay too much. When the table fills up—walk over to the next table and start again.

The casinos may figure out what you are up to, but most won't care. You are acting as a *shill* to attract other players and fill the table. After you leave, many of these players will stay, believing that they have found a hot table. Most of these guys will give it all back, plus. Of course, your first consideration should always be to play casinos with playable tables. If you have no control over the cubes at a particular casino or table, then there is no sense in playing there no matter how often you can shoot. Assuming that you have found some casinos that have shorter tables with good bounce characteristics, and that the pit does not give you too much heat for setting the dice, you will still need some tactics for handling the conditions or play variations you will encounter. In fact, displaying the discipline necessary to deal with all of these issues is probably the toughest part of being a profitable controlled shooter, not the skill factor. Once you have developed the skill, you will always take it with you. Imagine yourself as the perfect card counter playing blackjack where the dealer gets one hand and the players get and bet on the second. All of the players, each with varying skill levels, take turns playing out the one player's hand. If you wish to remain at the table, you are required to bet at least the table minimum when the other, less skilled players, decide how to play the hand. You find yourself winning larger sized units when you play out the hand, but dribbling most of it back (even with smaller wagers) on the other less skilled players. This is nearly the scenario we face at the craps table. I will address specific techniques for dealing with these situations.

My first choice is to open new tables and employ the *Hit and Run Strategy,* discussed a little earlier, but this is not always practical. Let's assume that you are at a very playable craps table and you have just had a hot roll. The other tables are full and chances are, so are the other casinos. You are not ready to end the session, so what do you do? The quick answer is, you keep your spot at that table and try to wait out the dice for your next roll. There are a few things that you can do while you are waiting. You can abstain from betting (or maybe throw just a buck out on a hard way number for you or the crew), play with your chips or act like you see something that you don't like and are waiting for some kind of a signal to wager (craps players are a superstitious bunch). The casino may recognize what you are doing. You might get away with this *stalling ploy* a little here and there. At the very least, you should bet something on the shooter just before you. Many times if I am too blatant about not betting on the other shooters, the boxman might instruct the stickman to pass me by when it is my turn to shoot. Sometimes, when I first approach a table, I may not walk right up and buy in. I might stand back a few feet from a vacant position that I wish to occupy and watch until the dice get closer. If the dice are one or two shooters away, or someone else looks like they may take the spot, then I will jump into my position and take my time buying in and organizing my chips.

6, 8 Regression/Progression

This is a conservative strategy that you can run on random shooters. With this method, you will *not* play the Pass Line. Place the 6 and 8 for 1-1/2 to 2 units each initially. For example, at a $5 table, you would Place each number for $12. At a $10 table, you can Place the 6 and 8 for $18 each. Give the shooter five tries to hit a 6 or 8, otherwise turn the bets "off" for the remainder of this shooter's point cycle. Wait until after the next come-out roll to turn them back on. If this shooter sevens-out, you will bet after the next thrower establishes a point. If the present shooter makes his point, you will wait until after his next point is established to Place the 6 and 8. Once a 6 or 8 has been hit with your Place bets up, take the winnings and regress both Place bets down to one basic betting unit. At the $10 table, for example, your $18 Place bet of 6 or 8 will win $21. Regress both bets down to $12 each and you now only have $3 at risk ($24 in bets minus the $21 win). Collect on the next two hits and press your winnings on every third hit from here out. The first press (fourth hit) will raise your Place bets back up to the initial betting level that you were at, before you regressed. Use most or all of every third hit to press both numbers as this shooter continues to throw.

If, at any time, the shooter stops throwing 6s or 8s for five consecutive throws, turn your bets off until after the next come-out cycle. Make sure that the *dealer* hears you and places an *Off* lamer on top of your bets, but do not speak too loudly. The supervisor in the pit may also hear your request and mark it against your comp rating. If you are not too concerned about comps or you don't care if the pit personal notices that you are not betting all the time, you can completely take the bets down if you like. After the next come-out cycle, start the progression all over again. I cannot tell you how many times I pressed up to $48 or $78 each for the 6 and 8, only to have the shooter hit a dry spell and then seven-out after five misses. With ten ways out of 36 possibilities being a 6 or 8, five consecutive throws is enough opportunity to hit one of them. If you are waiting at the table with a friend or partner, you can each Place one number and agree to split all profits and losses. After the first hit, you will split the winnings. Both of you will then regress your adopted number down to one betting unit and put the proceeds in your racks. Press the 6 and 8 uniformly on every third hit and collect in between. Any "odd" dollars can be put into a pool or separate pile and split later. Typically, I will use the final odd chip (if one exists) to tip the waitress who brings us both a soda or coffee.

The Don't Come Hedge

Another system for betting on other rollers that risks less money, but also wins less, is one I call the "D.C. Hedge." I will usually employ this hedge-type strategy on random throwers, while I am waiting for the dice. After the shooter comes out and establishes a point, let him throw three or four more times and bet one unit on Don't Come. This is similar to betting the Don't Pass, but it is less conspicuous. Make sure that the dealer places your wager in the Don't Come box. If a 7 or 11 is thrown you will immediately lose. A 2 or 3 is a winner. Chances are that your D.C. Bet will go against a point number. At that time, Place the same number for one unit so you cannot lose. You will have one unit against the number and approximately one unit placed for the number to repeat. For example, you put $10 on D.C. and a 5 is thrown. Your $10 goes in the back portion of the 5, point box. You immediately slide another $10 towards the dealer and ask him to Place the 5 for $10. If a seven-out occurs, your D.C. Bet wins even money and your Place bet on 5 loses—a break-even scenario. If the 5 is repeated before a 7, then the D.C. bet loses and the Place bet wins 7 to 5. You will either break even or net 2/5, (40 percent) of a unit in this case.

If the Don't Come point becomes a 4 or 10, you will either break even or net 4/5, or 80 percent of a unit. A 6 or 8 will either lose 1/5 of a unit (seven-out) or win 2/5 of a unit if the number is repeated. The thing that I like about this system is that you are rooting *for* the shooter along the way, even though you are betting the Don't. Consider the fact that when your bet is in the Don't Come box, you are rooting against the 7 like everyone else at the table. A 2 or 3 wins for you but probably does not hurt the other players (unless they have just made a Come bet). And, after placing the D.C. number, you are actually hoping for the shooter to continue throwing and repeat this number. That way you will make, say 2/5 of a unit in profit if the point is a 5 or 9. If the shooter does seven-out, you are not hurt. The only risk is a quick 7 or 11 on the next roll after you make the Don't Come bet. Your maximum risk on this point cycle is one unit and that only occurs on the first roll. The crew seems to figure out what I am doing after a short while. They make a comment or two, but I have never gotten any heat or ridicule. If you are feeling pessimistic for a particular shooter, you can leave the Don't Come bet naked, with no Place bet. After all, you will have six ways to win and fewer ways to lose at this juncture.

The final method I might try using to stall a little on a random roller is the *ultra-conservative* method I described in the previous chapter. Bet one unit on the Pass Line and take single odds, for a total of two units at risk. If the point is successfully repeated (now up two units plus), bet one unit on the Pass Line with double odds. If the shooter sevens-out at this time, you will lose less than one unit. After the second point is made, you will be up around six units. Bet one unit on the Pass Line with single odds and make one Come bet with single odds. Bet another unit in the Come box if your Come bet is made. Take single odds after the Come point is established. You will remain at this four unit betting level for the duration of this shooter's roll. Each time a Pass Line or Come point is repeated, you will gain 2.2 to 3.0 units in profit. If you stick with these guidelines, you can never be more than four units off your peak and may even catch a hot roller. At the end of Chapter 12, I will share another, more set intensive strategy that creates more options for playing in crowded conditions.

The High Roller Hedge

This tactic is for wagering on high limit tables, but it can be used for wagering on random rollers throwing at lower limit tables under crowded conditions. I call this one the High Roller Hedge. Ordinarily I do not advocate using a hedge-type system unless betting on random rollers. After all, we as controlled throwers are single minded in our craps play objective. We bet on certain numbers, and we focus on hitting these particular numbers. A hedge is a situation where you have placed two or more bets that actually oppose each other. Each bet has a negative expectation or a negative edge. As you know, if you sum up a group of negative numbers, you only get a much larger negative number. There is no way to arrange bets with negative expectations to create a positive expectation. Now after all that harping against a hedge, here is one hedge system that I have had good success with. Let me explain. While it is true that some places give me heat when I play, others are neutral, just carefully watching me, still others are trying to gain my loyalty. Several of the casinos in this latter category have decent craps tables for serious play. Some of these places are comping my room, food and beverage. I am frequently offered show tickets, and some have paid for my flights. I wanted to enhance my complimentary rating situation and try to get *everything* covered.

To get the full treatment, you have to be willing to lose at least $10,000 at that casino for that trip, or at least give the *appearance* of someone who is willing to lose close to that. There are plenty of books written on this subject so I'll spare you all the little "cute" ideas like giving your host a fruit basket, or buying your favorite pit boss a splashy, colorful tie. The bottom line is what is your average bet, and how much table time do you put in? They will also look at the type of bets that you make and how much money you have won or lost. All of these items can somewhat be controlled except for the third, the type of bets that you make. We will never make *stupid* bets with any serious amount of money to gain comps! That leaves average bet size, table time, and session win/loss. After pondering the comp situation, I have come up with what I believe to be the best hedge method for appearing to be a high roller in the game of craps. The idea behind this hedge method is to remain close to even (0 to +2 unit range), while giving the illusion of being a high roller. But first, here are some points of interest:

- This system works ideally with two or three players, building up all of their comp levels.
- Two or three partners can play this strategy with smaller units, at crowded, low-limit tables, to wait out the dice.
- This system reduces your exposure to the lowest possible point while giving the maximum protection.
- This system helps to build confidence for the shooter while betting at higher unit levels with minimum risk.
- Yes, you can use your controlled shooting knowledge and skills to gain a positive edge when you are holding the dice.

First, you will form a team of two or three people that you are staying with at some casino destination. It helps if at least one of you is a practiced, controlled shooter. You will pool to a bankroll that will later be split. If your team consists of two people, then each puts up equal amounts to a *common* bankroll. If there are three teammates, for example, then each can contribute $300 for a total bankroll of $900. At the end of the session, all stakes will be recombined and divided by the number of players involved. The shooter will make a $100 Pass Line wager, while his confederate(s) make opposing Don't Pass wagers equal to the $100. For example, if just one other partner is involved, then he would make a $100 Don't Pass bet, (great for a $100 minimum table). If two other partners are involved, then they would each make $50 Don't Pass bets totaling $100. They can stand together at the other end of the table and lightly banter the shooter between shots (like buddies might) with comments such as, "If you shoot like you did earlier, I should make all my money back on the Don't" or something similar. Otherwise, the Don't players can keep quiet and act like they do not know the shooter. In crowded conditions where you are just waiting out the dice, so that you or your partners can throw, you can bet much smaller, offsetting amounts.

The *only* outcome that will hurt you is a 12 on the come-out roll. If you are shooting the dice, you should actually try to pass successfully; whether it is a natural 7 or 11 on the come-out or by making the point. The shooter should use the 5-2, 3-4 Come-Out Set for the come-out roll to avoid the 12. This practice will give the shooter confidence at making the point while betting with larger units and he just might begin to heat it up. There are five different scenarios you will be faced with, as illustrated below with a $100 unit size, as you shoot for each decision.

- Shooter throws a 7 or 11 on the come-out roll, eight ways out of 36. The Pass Line bet wins $100 and the Don't Pass loses $100 for a net gain/loss of zero dollars.
- Shooter throws a 2 or 3 on the come-out roll, three ways out of 36. The Pass Line bet loses $100, but the Don't Pass wins $100—again a wash.
- Shooter establishes a number in one of 24 ways and makes his point. The Pass Line wins $100 and the Don't Pass loses $100 for $0 gained or lost.
- Shooter establishes a number (one of 24 ways) but sevens-out. The Don't Pass wager(s) win $100 and the Pass Line loses $100.
- Based on random, one time out of 36, the shooter will throw a 12 on the come-out roll. The Don't Pass players will push (if it were a fair game they would win) and the Pass Line bettor loses $100. This is the only negative situation possible.

The idea here is to have the controlled shooter avoid the 12 on the come-out roll. Everything else is a push. The shooter who directly establishes a point number and then takes his time to reach a decision will get the most mileage out of this system. This is true because it is only during the come-out roll that the $100 Pass Line bet is at risk.

Some Additional Points

The prime objective is to play even with the house, but if after making two or three passes with *black* on the line, and confidence is high, then take single odds. The house has zero percent edge on this bet, so even at random, you will break even over the long run. However, if you have warmed up and can exhibit some level of skill, you may bag a few of the larger units by winning your odds wager. If the shooter gets "hot" and has made two odds bet wins, then the team might consider one of the following strategies:

- You can Place the 6, 8 for $60 to $120 each. If, after three rolls, the shooter has not hit a 6 or 8, then pull them both down. As soon as one 6 or 8 is hit, regress both bets to $60 on the 6, 8 if possible, otherwise pull down the one that didn't hit. Placing the 6, 8 is a bold move aimed at trying to make some larger units, so allow yourself only three rolls to produce, better minimizing your risk and exposure.

- The second strategy involves the shooter making one $100 Come bet (two total numbers working) or two $50 Come bets (three total numbers working) while his confederates make the opposing Don't Come wagers. Again, with the exception of a 12 appearing on the very next roll, these bets are a complete wash. The shooter will take double odds on each $50 Come bet or double odds on the $100 Come bet. These odds bets have no house edge and hopefully the shooter is heating up at this juncture. The house edge may be nil at this point, but it sure looks like a lot of heavy action is being thrown around.

When the shooter does seven-out, the Don't players will pass the dice back (not wanting to shoot the dice themselves) and the shooter may or may not continue at his discretion or if an agreed upon time limit or win/loss point has been reached. Another variation would have the next shooter, a former Don't player, switching to the Pass Line and electing to shoot. The other partner(s) then would wager the offsetting amount on the Don't. This methodology requires two or three players with good team chemistry. If you are being comped at a casino for three days say, play this system on one shift the first day for an hour to try it out. The next day you can play for one to two hours, but on a different shift. The third day, you might go back to the first shift or play the third remaining shift. If you are playing with larger unit sizes and lose two units at any time, halt play and take a break. If you are playing to boost your comp rating, then playing this system for a total of four hours for the trip at the $100 unit level should raise your average bet substantially. If you are typically a $5 or $10 bettor, then you can use this method with $30, $40, or $50 on the Pass Line. If you are a *green* bettor, then go with the *black* action as described.

As a team looking to play with more aggressive-sized units and a shared bankroll, you should establish parameters ahead of time. For instance, you should set an approximate session time but let the shooter have the final say based upon how he feels while shooting. The team should agree, if and when the shooter is allowed to take odds (i.e., shooter makes two points and feels confident). The team must carefully consider if and when the 6 and 8 should ever be placed or if the Come/Don't Come strategy should be used. But don't get too carried away. Remember that the main idea is to avoid the come-out 12 and break even over an hour or two of time. The shooter should buy in with half of the session stake. If the bankroll is $900 for three players, the shooter should buy in with $400. Each Don't player will buy in for $250. If only two players exist, each can buy in for half. The shooter will regulate the speed of the game so it does not move too fast (we are limiting exposure here). The attitude that you will portray here is "this is a nice friendly relaxed high rollers game."

The "Tax" to Play

What is the cost to play this system? Well, that can depend on several different parameters including your Sevens-to-Rolls Ratio. But, if we assume that no skill is involved (like when the shooter is throwing randomly), there are only two questions that need to be answered to determine this:

1. What is the average number of throws needed to reach a decision (average length of a game)?
2. What percentage of this game, or one complete cycle, does the come-out roll consist of?

Starting with the first question, let's define what is meant by a decision. A decision means that a determination has come about as to whether the bet has won or lost. So, for example, a 7 on the come-out roll is a win and that decision only took one roll. As a matter of fact, twelve out of 36 or 1/3 of the come-out rolls result in a one-roll decision. Twenty-four out of 36 come-out rolls will establish a point. Let's look at the average number of rolls to a decision for each of the point pairs:

Table 10-1
Number of Rolls to a Decision

Point Established	6 or 8	5 or 9	4 or 10
Ways to Win:	5	4	3
Ways to Lose (seven-out):	6	6	6
Ways to Win or Lose:	11	10	9
Dice Possibilities:	36	36	36
Number of Rolls to Establish:	1	1	1
Avg. Rolls to a Decision:	$36/11 = 3.273$	$36/10 = 3.600$	$36/9 = 4.000$
Total # of Rolls:	**1+ 3.273 = 4.273**	**1+ 3.600 = 4.600**	**1+ 4.00 = 5.000**

- We already demonstrated that 12/36 or 1/3 of the cycles would last exactly one roll (2, 3, 7, 11, or 12 on the come-out).
- We now know that (5/36 + 5/36) or 5/18 of the cycles will last 4.273 rolls on average (point of 6 or 8).
- We also know that (4/36 + 4/36) or 2/9 of the cycles will average 4.600 rolls (5 or 9 point).
- And finally, (3/36 + 3/36) or 1/6 of the shooter's cycles will last 5.000 rolls (point of 4 or 10).

The average length of a Pass Line decision cycle can thus be calculated:

$$(1/3 \times 1 \text{ roll}) + (5/18 \times 4.273) + (2/9 \times 4.6 \text{ rolls}) + (1/6 \times 5 \text{ rolls}) =$$
$$3.376 \text{ rolls}$$

The percentage of rolls spent during the come-out portion of the decision cycle is simply one come-out roll divided by 3.376 cycle rolls or about 29.62 percent of the rolls. This equates almost exactly to eight rolls in 27. The average Pass Line game lasts about 3.376 throws before a decision is reached (the first of which is the come-out roll). Based on random, the shooter's Pass Line wager will have a 2.78 percent chance (one in 36) of being lost, but only on the first roll of 3.376 rolls. So, at a relaxed pace of about 40 throws per hour, one 12 should appear on the come-out roll once in about 122 throws. At a faster clip of 60 rolls per hour, one 12 will appear, on average, once every two hours.

This means that controlled throwing skills not withstanding, you would on average be able to play for two to three hours and only lose one unit. Please note, though, that the exposure to the 12 on the come-out roll increases if you employ the Come/Don't Come strategy. Based on a random 40 throws per hour, you will average minus one unit per three hours of play while employing the basic hedge strategy, even if you take odds. A $100 unit divided by 122 rolls (about 82¢) and then again divided by three players equates to a cost of about 27.5¢ per player, per roll. Even if odds are taken, this cost will not increase over the long haul because the odds bet has no house edge. So, for a little more than a quarter a throw, three players can get comped like high rollers and maybe even scalp off a few black units on the odds bet. At the same time, three players "waiting out the dice," at the $10 Pass Line unit level will pay a little less than 3¢ per roll, to each keep their position at the table.

Looking for Veteran Rollers

If you are playing in crowded conditions, take the time to size up each shooter. There are other veteran throwers out there who can influence the cubes. Some of these grizzled players have picked up the major components of the controlled throw through trial and error. Through the school of hard knocks, they have discovered that certain dice sets, along with a consistent delivery and an air of confidence can tip the scales in their favor somewhat. They may not understand the physical phenomena behind what they are doing, only that they can garner a slight edge by playing this way. When the casinos are busy, you should be on watch for these players. These rare breeds are tough to find, but they are out there. Here's what you should be looking for when evaluating unknown shooters who may be controlled throwers:

- Are they setting the dice? This is important. Look at the dice set they are using when shooting to avoid the 7. It should be a variation of the Hard Ways, 3-V, 2-V, 6-T, or Parallel 6 Dice Sets (more on these other dice sets in Chapter 12). At least make sure that the shooter is removing 7s from the top and front before he throws.
- The first thing you will probably notice is a smooth and consistent delivery. Are they tossing the dice in the same manner and landing them in the same target area

each time? They should be using a light and carefully balanced grip. The dice should be traveling together and undergoing similar motions. How well are the dice maintaining the initial set relationship after they touch down?

- Watch for their focus and confidence level. High confidence is usually a sign of past success (unless the shooter has been drinking heavily). Observe to see if they are easily distracted and whether or not this affects their delivery. At the time that they throw the dice, they should be focusing exclusively on their form.

If a shooter exhibits all three characteristics, then consider betting a few units. Use the Pass Line with Come bet tactic or the Super Sniper Strategy discussed in Chapter 9. I have picked up some nice wins over the years betting on other veteran rollers.

Playing with a Partner

Once a month, before I got caught up in writing and instructing on dice control, I would fly out to Atlantic City and hook up with Eric N. and Long Arm for some serious dice play. Sometimes we did fantastic and other times we did okay. Overall, I averaged slightly more than 80 units of profit for two or three days of play. I looked back and thought about our success and came up with several reasons why we did so well; reasons why I performed better when shooting with one or two partners than when I went solo. One thing I noticed is that while one guy throws, the other observes and documents the results. By recording your hand, you will have valuable feedback for that session and that particular table. Keep a small notebook handy and document each other's rolls. A second benefit is that your partner may notice something wrong with your form and can critique you on the fly. You can then take the necessary corrective actions and extend the life of the roll. In addition to all this, a partner can nurture your roll and feed you positive reinforcement for your confidence. He can talk you through a roll when you think you are struggling.

At one such instance, I was throwing at the A.C. Hilton one Saturday morning. After five minutes into the roll, I remarked, "Eric, I don't think this hand will last too long. Watch your betting. " Eric answered back, "Relax, every roll looks a little better. You're just getting warmed up. " As it turned out, I was able to relax and added another 25 minutes on the back end of that particular roll. After I got comfortable, we were both able to milk an additional 20+ units off the table.

A fourth possible benefit to partner play is not having to worry about making or manipulating bets. You can instruct your partner to place your bets for you as you focus exclusively on throwing the dice. You can, in turn, return the favor when he shoots the dice. Discuss all the betting details before you approach the tables. Things like what size units, which bets, and how to press come to mind. The simpler your betting tactics are, the better. And if both of you can adopt the same wagering pattern, then better yet. Making wagers is an analytical process, utilizing your brain's left hemisphere. By having your partner place the bets while you throw, you are able to operate in the right hemisphere where things like coordination, feeling, balance, and timing all dominate. Switching back and forth between the left and right hemispheres is difficult and exhaustive. You want to be in your "right mind" when exercising your muscle memory to deliver the dice!

Part Four

Going for the Gold

Chapter 11

Organizing a Professional Play Team

Imagine heading off to the casino knowing that you will have an excellent shot at bringing home some serious dinero! You know that you will be working with a crackerjack team of crapshooters, capable of shooting out the lights. Chances are that at least one or two of you will be on fire . . . and if more of you can heat up, look out! What I'm talking about here is working with a pro-play team. Although we are like pro athletes in the way we practice and consistently execute in our "sport," we probably don't rely on the game as our primary means of income. Yet, we still may play for serious money on a part-time basis. Whether controlled shooting becomes a vocation of sorts or just a hobby that pays nicely, you may want to network with other interested players to build up a team. Team play is serious business. There are certain considerations and guidelines that should be established when constructing such a team. The guidelines I will discuss are parameters that my team has elected to use. They are for general reference and you can modify or borrow any ideas that you like.

Building a Team

Putting together a dice control team is not a trivial task. Careful thought must be put into team management, style of play, geography of play, skill level of its members, unit size, betting strategies, etc. We did not even mention team chemistry, which is a big consideration. When selecting candidates for the team, you do not want to broadcast all over town what you are doing. Yet, you want to attract the right kind of players. The best way to recruit members is probably to go to the casinos where you plan to play and watch for skilled shooters. We discussed how to look for other veteran rollers a little earlier in the book. I have found that the younger, more technical types are open to this sort of venture. Talk quietly and discretely off in the corner somewhere, and set up a formal meeting away from the casino. I have been spoiled with regard to recruiting. Having personally trained over 600 (and counting) controlled throwers to date, I am able to choose the cream of the crop for assembling pro-play teams. As a result, *all* of my teams were successful, with only one losing weekend experienced over the past three years. My typical team consisted of four or five members, but anywhere from three to six may work out. Two or three members might be considered partner play, while six or more might be too much to manage. Let's start off with a description of the team members and their responsibilities.

Team Captain—Each pro-play team will have one member who is designated as a team manager or captain. The team captain may be the member who initially organizes the team or he may be chosen by his teammates in some mutually agreed upon process. In the beginning, the team captain should be a strong veteran player, dedicated to building up the skills of the other members. After a while, the responsibility can be rotated, for each team trip. The captain must be able to organize all the details and effectively communicate them to the other teammates. The team captain may have many responsibilities. He will probably decide which players shall be accepted for team play. The captain will develop a training plan and work with team players to develop their skills to the optimum. He may coordinate home practice sessions and review practice records and documented play of team members to determine their strengths and weaknesses. The captain will decide on which team play strategy to use. He will decide on whether a pooled bankroll is feasible for the team and whether it will be with equal contributions or by selling shares. He will discuss with the members and decide on which betting strategies to use for any given team play session. The captain may terminate the session at his discretion, or if a table departure criterion is met, by coloring up or using the code word *color*. He will assign session shooters for the next play and may decide on a designated shooter if one player is especially hot.

As you can see, the team captain has many responsibilities and his *management style* will determine how he makes decisions. If he is a strong veteran player who is responsible for developing the team, he may wish to operate as a dictator in the beginning, making decisions with little or no input from the team members. The captain will set up the sessions, determine the betting style and instill team discipline. He will coordinate a loose session schedule with the team members, after he learns which casinos they prefer to shoot at. Each teammate will submit their top five casinos in order of preference. The captain is responsible for keeping the team on track. He collects team notes and statistical data from the session recorder and looks for any pertinent trends. For example, Player B cannot handle any heat from the pit when he shoots. Player C needs to work on his betting execution, while Player E is taking too much time to set the dice. The captain will prescribe individual work plans to eliminate weaknesses. He will work closely with the team accountant to reconcile the bankroll balance after each session. After the team is up and running with multiple senior members, many of the decisions can be made with team consensus. Each team member should understand the management style of the team manager before agreeing to participate in the team.

Team Accountant—Operates during the course of the entire weekend or excursion as the money manager for the team. He will sell "shares" and collect contributions for the team bankroll. The accountant rations out session stakes before each session and makes a notation in his book. Each shooter/bettor (usually three at a table) will receive five units with which to operate. At the conclusion of each playing session, the accountant will collect all of the session money from the shooters and the notes from the session recorder. The accountant will record the individual amounts returned by each bettor/shooter and initial the notation. Using the session records of each roll and knowing the betting sequence used by the team, the accountant can reconstruct exactly where the resultant bankroll should be. He will compare this to the actual count and check for discrepancies. After he has reconciled the bankroll to the satisfaction of the team captain, the captain can then set the next team session. The team accountant will perform his function during the course of the entire excursion. At times he will double as a session shooter, bettor, or recorder, but he is always looking after the team's money. The team accountant manages and is responsible for the team bankroll.

Session Shooters/Bettors—We will rotate, or have three designated shooters per session, usually with each making two attempts. However, if something is "wrong" at that table, a second attempt may not be tried. The three shooters will usually try to take the stick-right, stick-left, and x-left table positions. The shooters/bettors will alternate shooting and betting duties during the session. A fourth team member will position himself at one of the table's ends and record each roll for that session. For the first shooting cycle, or wave, each shooter will make one attempt at sustaining a roll. While the first shooter has the dice and bets the Pass Line, the next shooter acts as a Come bettor. He will wait for the Pass Line point to be established and then places a Come bet with odds.

After the Come point is established, the second shooter out will place another Come bet and take odds so that three different numbers are working. As the Pass Line or Come bet points are made, the bettor responsible will put the bets back up to be re-established. After the first shooter sevens-out, the second shooter has the dice and will place the Pass Line wager. The third shooter will now make the first Come bet and the previous shooter will then operate the second Come bet. The shooting and betting duties continue to rotate in this manner during the course of the session.

The shooter will bet the Pass Line and take double odds (or more). That is it. The Shooter will then focus exclusively on grooving in and maximizing a long hand. Typically, the shooter should select and stay with one primary dice set (i.e. the Hard Ways with, maybe 3-3 on top and 2-2 on front) to take advantage of any developing signature trend and the Come betting strategy that we use. However, those shooters experienced in "set transposition" (described in the next chapter) may, after careful consideration and close observation, elect to transpose the dice set if a latent signature appears, causing the Pass Line and Come bets to become marooned. The session bettors will run the Come bets and may offer coaching or moral support to the shooter if it helps. Because the team has Come bets working on the next Pass Line come-out roll (contract bets), the shooter will *set against the 7 on subsequent come-out rolls*. The session bettors will tell the dealer that their odds bets are always working on the come-out roll. With Come betting, the shooter must always try to avoid the 7. It then pays to minimize the amount bet on the Pass Line or Come and maximize the odds bet.

If nobody is able to generate even a small profit, the captain may call the session after the first wave, or shooting cycle. He will color in to signal that the session is over. If, however, one or more shooters does okay on the first attempt and feels confident, then a second round is tried. The shooter(s) who feels "all thumbs," will pass the dice ahead to the others. Sometimes the captain will give input on who shoots, overriding everyone else. If the captain waves his hand flat and side-to-side over his chip rack (same hand motion as standing on a Blackjack hand), that shooter will pass the dice. If the captain nods his head or scratches with his fingers front-to-back on the armrest (like a Blackjack player signaling for a hit), then the indication is to shoot. After the second round of shooters attempt a roll, the table session is usually over. However, keep an eye on the captain. If he does not color in, this will indicate that a third wave of shooting is warranted. At this point, one shooter has probably gotten hot and the team should try to capitalize on him further. During the entire table session, the shooter makes a Pass Line bet with odds, while the other potential shooters make their respective Come bets. Another variation is to forego the second Come bet and run an aggressive 6, 8 Place bet progression–regression strategy instead.

Session Recorder—Designated for that session, he will record the casino, date, time, and shooters' names. In addition, the unit size and odds amount should be documented. It is important to correctly track the team's play. For this reason, the session recorder will usually not bet and will never shoot the dice. He will position himself at one end of the table and document the play. He may help to ensure that a clear path is maintained on the Pass Line, near his end, so the shooter can land the dice without hitting chips and stay on their axis of rotation. The recorder will note the shooter and write down each number pair thrown in order. After a Pass Line or Come bet point is made, he will circle the number after recording it. A seven-out is signified with a star next to it. Records are turned over to the team accountant after each session to help reconcile the bankroll. The responsibility of the session recorder is rotated from session to session.

Establishing the Bankroll and Betting Tactics

The easiest way to establish the team bankroll is by having all members contribute equally to a common bankroll. Everyone will then have an equal stake. Another approach is to offer *shares* for sale. Team members can purchase from two to four shares in the team bankroll. Each share might cost $500. If, for example, three members each buy four shares at $2,000 and two members purchase three shares at $1,500 each, then the resultant bankroll will be $9,000. The team accountant will initial and issue a slip of *stock*, reflecting the bankroll contribution. The team's session buy in should be about 15 percent of the team total bankroll. This is aggressive enough to pull down respectable profits, yet conservative enough to permit at least eight to ten team session attempts (at the worst). A one percent unit size works well with this arrangement. For the above bankroll amount, a unit size of approximately one percent would dictate a $90 betting unit. Our team has elected to use larger-sized units with a very conservative betting strategy—one Pass Line wager with one or two Come bets in play.

The shooter will place a Pass Line wager and take double odds. From there he will focus on extending the roll. The next shooter will place a Come bet after the Pass Line point is established and take double odds. The third shooter will place a second Come bet with double odds, once the first Come bet has been established. This will put a total of nine units in play. The idea is to get three different numbers in play with all three session-shooters involved. This way each potential shooter will share in the betting responsibility and have action attributed to him. The shooter will risk three total units on the Pass Line and the Come bettors will risk three units for each Come bet. If the casino allows higher than double odds, then fractional units can be used on the Pass Line and the higher odds amount then taken. For example, if the betting unit were $90 (one percent of the total bankroll), then based on the odds allowed, any Pass Line or Come bets would be made as follows:

- Double odds allowed = $90 Pass Line or Come bet + $180 odds = 3 units total
- Triple odds allowed = $70 Pass Line or Come bet + $200 odds = 3 units total
- Five times odds taken = $45 Pass Line or Come bet + $225 odds = 3 units total

Know the odds amount allowed at your casino and plan ahead. If the Pass Line and Come bets are executed properly, there will be three different numbers (more diversity) out on the layout most of the time. We are not risking all our money in the very beginning. Instead, we are gradually introducing it to the layout. The second Come bet gives us a little more insurance further into the roll. It also gives the shooter a little more time to establish a signature delivery. Sometimes, the team will opt to run one Pass Line, one Come bet and a 6, 8 Place bet progression with one unit total. This particular 6, 8 Progression–Regression is more aggressive than the one we outlined for random shooters. Place the 6 and 8 for a half unit each. You will press on the first and third hits, then regress on the fifth, back to the original wager amount. Using the $90 or $100 unit size, as an example, the 6, 8 Progression/ Regression would work as follows:

Start: Take $100 and Place the 6, 8 for $48 each. You now have $96 at risk.

Hit 1: Take the $56 win plus $4 in change and press both bets up to $78 each.

Hit 2: You will lock in the win of $91. Your total risk at this point is only $9.

Hit 3: Take $84 from your $91 win and press both Place bets up to $120 each.

Hit 4: Collect the $140 win and lock it up. You are now guaranteed $138 profit.

Hit 5: Collect another $140 and regress both bets back down to $48 each. Put the extra $144 in the rack along with the $140 win.

After the fifth hit, you will regress both Place bets down to $48 each and begin the cycle again. You will be $138 ahead from Hit 4, plus another $140 from Hit 5. You will also have $144 from regressing both bets down ($120 – $48 = $72 x both bets). This gives you a total of $422 locked up in winnings plus the $48, 6 and 8 Place bets are now fully funded for the next cycle ($518 ahead). The third shooter will run this bet instead of a second Come bet. When the second shooter takes the dice, he will make a Pass Line bet with odds, the third shooter will now run the Come bet with odds and the first shooter will then run the 6, 8 Progression, maintaining the betting rotation. Recently, I conducted a dice control clinic in Las Vegas. This progression was attempted and made by several of my students. One noteworthy student, Scott W., a stockbroker from Wichita Kansas, hit twenty 6s and 8s in one hand! Some of these were come-out rolls, but the progression was made three successive times in one roll. This occurred at a recent clinic weekend, immediately after attending our dealer school practice session on Sunday afternoon.

Guidelines for Team Play

The team members have to be able to trust each other to make this work. Certain guidelines or rules are established so everyone knows how to conduct himself. If a team rule is broken, then the team must meet and decide what action, if any, is to be initiated. Depending on the offense, and the history of infractions, a team member may be suspended or even voted off the team. Sometimes the team may be dissolved for that trip at the team captain's discretion. Because we are playing with each other's money, trust and mutual respect is of the utmost importance. Any breakdown in team discipline creates unnecessary risks for the other teammate's bankroll. One of our rules was, absolutely no *free styling* in between sessions. Free styling is when one player sneaks off on his own to put on an unscheduled play. We had one instance in Atlantic City where one of the teammates played early in the morning. His motive was to tune up his throw so he could perform better when he threw for the team. As luck would have it, he held the dice for 45 minutes and another team member spotted him at the table. Needless to say, the other team members were very upset that we didn't have team money riding on the roll, and a team meeting was called.

As a result, the captain elected to dissolve the team for that trip and everyone then played individually. It's too bad, because we always profit more as an organized unit, than as a collection of renegades. As you can see, the team is regimented and plays very disciplined. The rules and strategies are discussed and agreed upon in advance, so no one member should change things that were preset by the collective group. Our team has very strict guidelines. For example, no unscheduled play is permitted (as already discussed) and no betting is allowed on random shooters. The team will look for and play at empty tables to help ensure against it. The team will usually play at higher limit tables that have few or no other players. The session bettors will wager in exactly the agreed upon manner. They must play close attention so that mistakes are not made when wagering. The session shooter will select and stick with exactly one dice set for avoiding the 7 (i.e. the Hard Ways Set with 4s on top and 5s on the front). By staying with one exact dice set and consistently throwing the dice the same way, a signature develops and numbers are repeated more frequently.

Another rule that we have adopted states that every player must warm up for 20 to 30 rolls before playing on the tables. The team will assemble in one of the members' hotel rooms, to practice in the portable practice box. The practice box described in Chapter 8 fills the bill nicely. Another guideline we have established is the table departure criteria. Instead of a certain stop-win or stop-loss unit size, we play in waves. As long as things are going well, we will continue to play. There will be two or three designated shooters for a particular session. In the first wave, all designated shooters will take one shot. If nobody can get anything going (all lose money), then the team will depart. If one or more shooters are able to scratch out some profit and build confidence, then those particular shooters will attempt another hand (second wave). The others will pass the dice around. Hopefully one member will really heat up and the overall session will be profitable. It may be possible to cycle through a third time if one or more of the shooters are still performing well, but after three waves, a break is warranted. A chance to unwind and let the adrenaline flow is advised. The captain will signal table departure by coloring in or saying the code word *color*. The team will color up, hit the cashier's cage and reconvene at a nearby restaurant or lounge (no drinking is another rule).

The money and records for the session are turned over to the team accountant. He will then reconcile the bankroll along with the captain. The team captain can set up the next play session. The next casino is selected and two or three session shooters and their table positions are set. Session members will rotate betting responsibilities as different members shoot the dice. No team member who is feeling ill, hungry, or tired will be permitted to roll the bones. This strategy is ideal for multi-casino locations like Las Vegas, where teams can leave one casino if it becomes too crowded and drive a short distance to the next one. Also, in Atlantic City, where higher limit tables abound, the team can usually procure their own table. Other casinos are within a short walking distance along the boardwalk. If casinos are few, and the tables are crowded, then the teammates must be patient and insert themselves in the best table positions. These will probably be stick-left, stick-right, and x-left or x-right. When the other rollers are throwing, the shooters will refrain from wagering or possibly employ the High Roller Hedge Strategy, using offsetting table minimum bets to secure their table positions. The team captain will decide if conditions do not warrant a play and may terminate the session.

Breaking the Bank

The bank is usually split and redistributed if one of three things happens: First, the team loses 50 percent of the bankroll (this has never happened). Second, the weekend is over and time is up. Third, the bankroll has doubled in size. If this latter event happens early in the weekend, then the original bank is redistributed to the members and a second phase of team play takes place with the profits; again, the goal being to double the bank. Early on in the team's history, I recommend that you simply divide the bankroll based on contribution percentage and not performance. Give the team a chance to develop. Team members should become skilled at throwing and flawless in their betting execution. Once the team has evolved into a professional playing machine, then the team may elect to reward the stronger shooters. Keep in mind that for this to work out, very detailed records must be kept. The following example is an actual payout scenario, used on a recent pro-play weekend. The percentages used below can be changed to reflect a more conservative split (i.e. 25 percent bonus versus 75 percent equity).

A 40 percent performance bonus is added to reward top shooters. After play concludes, the bankroll will be broken down and redistributed. If a break even or net loss occurs, then the remaining bankroll will be divided by the number of shares outstanding and allocated according to straight percentage contribution. If a net win results, the *original* bankroll is returned according to contribution percentage. The first 60 percent of net profit is also distributed according to percentage contribution or number of shares purchased. The remaining 40 percent profit will be allocated using the following criteria:

- The amount of profit generated by each player will be calculated from the detailed records.
- Any shooter with an overall losing record is eliminated from the 40 percent bonus round.
- The percentage of profit generated by each team member is calculated relative to the other team members. Each eligible teammate is awarded that percentage of the 40 percent profit.

Here is an illustrative example:

Five team members each contribute $1,500 for a total $7,500 bankroll. At the end of the weekend, the bankroll has grown to $11,500. Members 1 through 5 receive their original $1,500 back, leaving $4,000 in profit. They also receive 60 percent of $4000 times their share percentage (in this case $2,400 divided by five or $480 each). But, team member 1 is "minus" for the weekend. He will have to be content with getting $1,980 back. Members 2 and 3 have each generated 20 percent of the net profit. They will each receive $320, or 20 percent of $1,600 plus $1,980, for a total of $2,300. Team member 4 accounts for 10 percent of the profit, receiving $1,500 + $480 + $160 = $2,140. Teammate 5 has a two-hour roll and produces 50 percent of the profit! He would be awarded $1,500 + $480 + $800 = $2,780.

Teammate # 1	$1,980 (Tin Man)
Teammate # 2	$2,300 (Silver Arm)
Teammate # 3	$2,300 (Silver Arm)
Teammate # 4	$2,140 (Bronze Arm)
Teammate # 5	$2,780 (Golden Arm)
Total:	**$11,500**

Without penalizing the poor performers too much, we are adding a nice incentive to those that more than pull their weight. Again, this is for an experienced team of veterans, who have ten or twelve successful pro-play weekends under their belts and keep very detailed books. For our team of senior players, the "Golden Arm" shooter earns the honor and responsibility of team captain for the next pro-play weekend.

Playing in the Casino for a Living

I have been asked many times, "What does it take to draw a living off the tables?" and I am not necessarily talking just about dice here. First, I know many knowledgeable players who have tried to make a living by gambling. I can count on one hand the number of players that were able to successfully do this for longer than twelve months. I am not talking about professional team play here. I have trained and helped dozens of successful pro-play teams across North America. They meet up once a month or so for some serious play, but they have other sources of income as well. I'm talking about individuals who wish to do nothing other than professional gambling for a livelihood. I can tell you that it is not the glamorous life of a celebrity or superstar. Your abilities will not be appreciated by the casinos. In fact you will be a thorn in their sides. Now that I've set the stage, here are some tips and ideas of what you will have to contend with:

   1) You must have *extensive knowledge* of your game of choice. That means becoming a top expert on that game and all its variations. You should know all its rules and protocol. You should understand all the mathematics and physics involved that affect how a result comes about. You will need the ability to make real-time adjustments on the fly.
   2) A *viable methodology* for legitimately beating this game is very important. Do not overlook this point. For every viable approach, I could show you 9,999 nonviable approaches that are being peddled about. If you find a system that seems too good to be true, chances are great that it is just that.

Mathematical betting schemes alone will never make you a living, but a mathematically-based system, such as card counting for Blackjack, is a viable approach. Any skill worthwhile will take a concerted effort to master.

3) *Test-drive* your methodology for an extended period with minimal pressure. Document and successfully play this system for at least 100 casino sessions before you quit your daytime job. You should then have adequate data to plan and project your income. Prove to yourself that: A) It is indeed a viable system and B) That you can execute the system properly under pressure and make money with it.

4) You must have *adequate bankroll* to weather any storms. A 1,000-unit bankroll is an absolute minimum. A 2,000-unit bankroll is better. If you wager with $10 units, you will need $10,000 to $20,000. If condition #2 above is not met or you have not properly test driven your approach, then you will quickly burn through your gambling stake.

5) You should keep six months worth of *living expenses* saved up and put somewhere safe. This money is separate and aside from your dedicated bankroll.

6) *Being single* helps because you will not get away with playing in the same area all the time (assuming you are skillful enough to win consistently). Unless your significant other is a motivated and skilled player, he or she may not be happy with such a lifestyle. Having children further complicates things as you might imagine.

7) You may become *nomadic*, hopping around from one venue to the next. As you wear out your welcome, you will spend more time living out of cheap motels and eating fast food (the casinos will stop comping you after a while). One exception might be buying a house or condo and operating out of the Las Vegas area. I do know a few successful players whose children have grown and they are supplementing their retirement off the casino tables. If this sounds like something you might enjoy, then this could be for you.

8) Being *thick-skinned* and able to work under pressure is necessary to your survival. You must be able to handle any heat that the casino personnel will throw your way and the experience to know when to leave a situation altogether. Even if you can perform flawlessly under controlled conditions but struggle in the heat of the real battle, you may not be cut out for this lifestyle.

9) Being *very disciplined* and well organized in your approach and play is critical. Document everything so you can learn from your experiences and are not reinventing the wheel. Once you have a well-developed plan for money management, stick with it.

10) Eventually, you will want to learn *multiple games.* For example, *Get the Edge at Roulette,* by Christopher Pawlicki, is an excellent book for advantage roulette play. Either way, you should develop the ability to play more than one game proficiently. It provides better cover and opens up more options. Put in the same amount of effort and attention to details that you put forth in learning your initial casino game.

A final word about playing for a living; be careful. I do not know how experienced a player you might be, but please realize that it is not the glamorous life that you may be envisioning. The casinos do not like advantage or professional players. As one boss pointed out to me, "My side of the table is business. Your side is recreation." These guys will look at you like you are snatching breadcrumbs from the mouths of their families. It is also important that you become an expert-level player. Read everything you can find and invest the necessary time to learn the right approach. This process is what actually drove me to uncover and develop the techniques you are reading about in this book. Once you have the correct method, then practice. Play your approach part-time for six to twelve months and prove its success. Save up at least 1,000 units plus six months worth of living expenses. Do not test how deep the lake is by plunging in headfirst!

Chapter 12

Specialized Sets and Dynamic Dimensions

Grab a pair of dice and follow along. I want to share some powerful new dice sets and techniques with you. Over the last several years, I have enjoyed an increasing number of peak experiences at the dice tables. During these experiences, I have been able to predict the exact dice results before I picked up the dice and threw them. What a feeling! Imagine throwing down a $25 chip and announcing, "Sixty-three on the hop," and then proceeding to throw it and getting paid 15 to 1. That's right, this Sharpshooter (the same Sharpshooter who shuns high-edge proposition bets) has been known to make a calculated hop bet or two (just ask Robin or Donnie), but only if I am highly consistent. I can make certain delivery and set adjustments that will take better advantage of my controlled throw. Early in the book, you read about one experience I had at Bally's in Vegas. As I called the second hop bet, one stickman off-handedly remarked, "You must have ESPN," but after accurately calling four hop bets, I had the whole pit intently watching me. The table was dumping and the patrons were lapping it up. After calling another hard 8 and making my point, they closed down the table!

On another excursion while playing in the A. C. Hilton, I was shooting from stick-left, while Eric N. watched from stick-right. I held the dice for over 45 minutes on this particular roll. At one point in my roll, I began to pound the top primary set combination, setting something I refer to as the 3-V formation on top and throwing hard 6s. The dice were flowing effortlessly from my hand in a nice, fluid motion. Although I did not advertise the hard 6 as my intended target, people began to load up on it after I hit two hard 6s back-to-back. In the next eight attempts of throwing the hard 6, I nailed five 3-3s! The chances of shooting a hard 6 on the very next throw are one in 36, but the chances of throwing five of them in eight tries is astronomical. At one instance when I missed the 3-3, I shot a 3-5 instead, making my point of 8. The table (good-naturedly) booed me for missing the 3-3. "Now I've seen just about everything!" intoned the bewildered boxwoman. One gentleman, standing at the far end where the dice were landing, ran a progression on the hard 6 from $5 all the way up to the table maximum of $500. On the next throw, I nailed the hard 6 for the fifth time. He and his wife squealed with delight. After the dealer pushed $4,500 worth of chips his way, he tossed me $150. At the end of my roll, I received a standing ovation (what other kind is there at the craps table?) that seemed to last several minutes.

I have had many other such experiences. It's wonderful to say the least. You feel like you are a "folk hero" or something. How do I do it? In the next few pages, I will describe the techniques I have developed and employ at the tables for peak performance. These are advanced methodologies that you should not attempt unless you are very experienced with controlled throwing and can demonstrate a highly consistent delivery. This stuff is bleeding edge technology straight from the Sharpshooter. The first section of this chapter introduces some expert-level dice sets that will take further advantage of your well-developed controlled throw. Next I will share three advanced techniques that can be employed for even greater dice control. I call these the "Dynamic Dimensions." The first two techniques can be attempted after mastering the controlled throwing skills needed to produce a very high level of consistency. The first method uses grip/delivery adjustments to minimize "pitching" revolutions on the dice, or what I call *reducing the revs*. You will then pinpoint a particular pair of faces (one-quarter revolution out of the full revolution) and tune the revolutions in order to hit these faces, referred to as *tuning the revs*. Once you are able to control the revolutions on the dice, you can employ the third technique. This one has you comparing the original dice set to the final result, making the appropriate set adjustment and sniping out your desired number. I call this approach, *transposing the sets*. These techniques are quite effective when used individually, but really dynamite when used in tandem. Then we will wrap it up with a set intensive strategy for playing the Don't.

Degrees of Freedom

The physical approach that we use to influence the dice is based upon the laws of "rigid body dynamics." You do not need to know all the laws or equations of motion involved, but some basic understanding of how objects move through space is warranted. If you have not read the introduction to this book, which is really an introduction to controlled throwing, or need a quick review, please read it now. As you recall, there are three ways to move or translate through space. You can shift front-to-back, side-to-side, and up and down to describe these three different axes. You can translate in a skew or off-axis direction by combining motions of two or three of these axes. As the dice travel through space, they can also spin, or rotate about any of these three axes, individually or in combination. That gives us six total degrees of freedom (components of motion), and countless possible combinations of the six in which the dice may move. The more degrees of freedom that you can eliminate in getting the dice from point A to B, the more control you will have.

Unfortunately, the dice have to be thrown and must land on the bed of the craps table. All or even most of the die's energy is not absorbed on the first impact. Because the table is nearly rigid itself, it exerts an equal but opposite reaction force back onto the dice. That means that the dice have to burn off the excess energy through multiple reactions with the table. Friction, gravity, air resistance and other obstacles will cause the dice to come to rest eventually, but the trick is to get the dice to stop in a synchronized fashion. Using the perfect pitch delivery, we will eliminate side-to-side translation, and roll and yaw rotations. We will control the remaining forward and vertical translations, as well as the pitch rotation. Once the dice touch down, they should continue to bounce in controlled, but successively smaller parabolic trajectories. In this way, the dice remain in their 2-D plane with slight end-over-end rotation. The other degrees of freedom do not come into play and the dice subside in a controlled and predictable fashion. We are working with the forces of nature, not against them. This is a bit of a review, but important for setting up the optimal dice reactions needed to qualify as an expert-level throw.

Optimal Dice Reactions

Before we even get started with this section, you need to exhibit near perfect delivery mechanics. Observe the dice motions and reactions after you release them:

- Is your technique flawless during that session? Are you perfectly pitching the dice? They should be traveling and landing together. Be honest with yourself.
- Is the table bounce allowing the end-over-end pitching motion to sustain itself? The parabolic trajectory should be maintained after striking the table.

● Is the back wall having only a minimal effect on the pitching motion? The dice should lightly strike the wall and repel back, staying on axis as they come to rest.

Only if the answer to all three of the above is yes, will you benefit from using the dice sets and techniques we will discuss in this chapter. When taking *all* six degrees of freedom into account (and any of their possible combinations), the Hard Way Set is the safest to use, but when the perfect pitch delivery is executed correctly, the "V" family of dice sets work best. The "V" that we speak of is created when we imagine a line connecting the spots on both dice faces. The first of these sets is the 3-V Set. The hard 6 is set and the 3s are arranged to form the "V" pattern. The 3-V Set is used for sniping out the inside numbers, 6 and 8. The next two sets I will discuss, are variations of the 2-V Set, which places the hard 4 in a "V" formation. I have discovered that the 2-V Sets are most effective for targeting the extreme outside numbers, 4 and 10.

The 3-V Dice Set

At this point, the delivery mechanics are ingrained in your routine. You will have been practicing on a regular basis for several months with the Hard Ways Set. Hopefully, over the last 3,600 or so documented rolls, you will be sporting a SRR of 6.5 or higher. The dice are reacting as described above, meeting the optimal conditions. You are now ready to attempt using the more advanced "V" sets. If you can keep the dice rotating end-over-end, or pitching, in a two-dimensional plane as they travel, then the "V" family of dice sets will actually give you better protection against the dreaded 7. You must be able to limit the DOFs down to the three ranges of motion just described, in order to shoot effectively against the 7.

3-V Set with   3-V Set with
5-1 on Front   6-2 on Top

Figure 12-1
Two Examples of the "6-8" 3-V Set

Figure 12-1 above depicts two examples of the 3-V Dice Set. The 3-V pattern can be on top, front, back, or bottom. All told, there are 32 variations of the 3-V Set, but 16 of these are much more powerful. You should use the variations that result in 6s and 8s set all around. That way any primary hit will be a 6 or 8. Some of the secondary hits will also produce a 6 or an 8. The left picture above shows the 6 on top in a V formation, with a 5-1 on front. That would indicate that the hard 8 is on the bottom and a 2-6 combination is on the back— all totaling 6 or 8. The right graphic shows a 6-2 on top with the 3-V formation on the front. It follows that the 1-5 is at the bottom, and the hard 8 is in back. These are two examples of the more effective 3-V Sets. If you set a hard 6 or 8 on top, just remember to set 5-1 or 6-2 on front. Figure 12-2 below, portrays the results if both dice pitch together, creating a primary hit from the "all 6-8" 3-V Set.

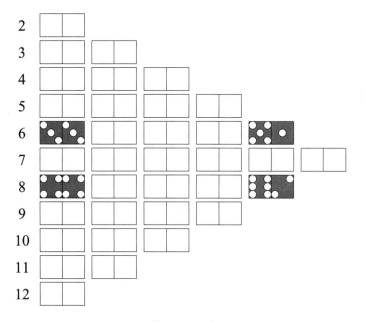

Figure 12-2
3-V Set, Primary Pitch Combinations

You will have four possibilities, all being 6s and 8s. I love to use this set when my point is a 6 or 8, I'm running a Place bet progression on the 6, 8, or I'm using the Super Sniper betting tactic. If I happen to pitch one die an extra face forward or backward, relative to the other, then the possible results are represented in Figure 12-3 on the following page. You will notice that another 6 and 8 are possible, but you will pick up two 5s, two 9s and an easy 4 and 10 to round things out. You are still pounding out point numbers.

Space will not permit me to include all of the secondary and third hit combinations like I did for the Hard Way Set in Chapter 5. Pick up a pair of matching dice and check them out for yourself. Certain secondary roll and yaw combinations will introduce some 7s as possible outcomes, so be careful to remove all elements of roll and yaw from your dice delivery! If you can keep the dice on their lateral axis, then there are only two 7s that can appear when you *double pitch*

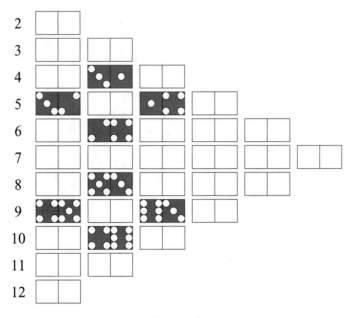

Figure 12-3
3-V Set, Secondary Pitch Combinations

one die (two faces) relative to the other. If you observe the dice pitching end-over-end with the 3-V Set and you are getting 4-3 combinations, or 3s and 11s, then realize that you are probably double pitching the dice (more on how to attack double pitching a little later). However, if you are sevening out with the 5-2 and 6-1 combinations off the 3-V Set, then a secondary roll or yaw is occurring. Revert back to the Hard Way Set for maximum protection against these ranges of rotation.

The 2-V Dice Set

This set is created when the 2s of the hard 4 form a "V" pattern. The 2-V Set is also an expert-level dice set that requires the dice to maintain their pitching axis of rotation. As with the

3-V Set, your Sevens-to-Rolls Ratio should be 6.5 or higher with the Hard Way Set. There are 32 total variations of the 2-V Set. Sixteen of these have all 4s and 10s set around. Figure 12-4 below depicts two examples of this set. On the left graphic, the 2-V, or hard 4 is on top, so the hard 10 is at the bottom. The 3-1 on front will dictate that a 4-6 is paired up on back. For the right hand picture, the 6-4 on top means that a 1-3 combination is at the bottom. Whether the 2-V is on front or top, etc. or the V is pointing up or down will not matter. As long as you have 4s and 10s all around, you have one of the 16 "all 4-10" 2-V Sets. Your primary hit combinations (not shown) are 2-2, 3-1, 5-5, and 6-4. As you might probably imagine, I will use this set if my point is a 4 or 10. Taking a pair of dice, you can check out all the secondary pitch, roll, and yaw combinations that can occur. As with the 3-V Set, some secondary roll and yaw pairings will result in 7s. The dice must maintain their pitching axis of rotation.

2-V Set with   2-V Set with
3-1 on Front   6-4 on Top

Figure 12-4
Two Examples of the "4-10" 2-V Set

There are 16 additional variations of the 2-V Set that contain the hard 4 and hard 10, but in conjunction with a 4-1 and 6-3. You are including a 5 and 9 with the hard 4 and hard 10. If you wish to create this dice set, place the 2-V formation on top. Check to make sure that a 1-4, 4-1, 6-3, or 3-6 is paired up on the front. If an easy 4 or 10 is on front, then simply spin one die around two faces like a top (this is a yaw rotation). The 2-V pattern is recreated and a 5 or 9 is now on front. Your primary set and hit combinations are 2-2, 5-5, 4-1, and 6-3. This is a good set variation if you would rather have a 5 and 9 included as a primary hit. Figure 12-5 below depicts two examples of the "5-9" 2-V Set.

2-V Set with   2-V Set with
4-1 on Front   6-3 on Top

Figure 12-5
Two Examples of the "5-9" 2-V Set

Whether with 5s and 9s or all 4s and 10s set around, all 32 variations of the 2-V Set will produce one of the secondary pitch combinations shown below in Figure 12-6. Think about it. A certain "4-10" 2-V Set with the right die pitching back one face will equate to a certain "5-9" 2-V Set with the right die pitching forward one face.

There are some other specialized dice sets that are worth mentioning. The 6-T Set occurs when you pair up two 6s, with the pips, or spots, oriented in perpendicular directions. There will be times when you are using the 3-V or 2-V Sets and are struggling a bit. You are throwing well enough to avoid the 7, but not good enough to hit meaningful point numbers. You are pounding nothing but Horn numbers in the process and just cannot make that necessary final adjustment needed to hit your Place or Come bets. You can use the 6-T Dice Set to "force" the inside numbers to appear. Because you set the 3-V and are consistently hitting Horn numbers, you will now set the 6-T and hit inside numbers with the same relative dice movements. This is a simplified version of "Set Transposition," which we will get into a little later in this chapter. Realize though, that you might be on borrowed time

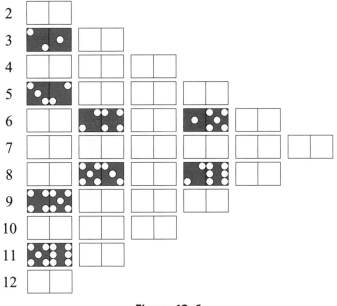

Figure 12-6
2-V Set with Secondary Pitch

and should find and make the correct adjustment to your grip or delivery. The 6-T Set will help you hit a few more inside numbers under these circumstances. If you make the proper adjustments and are now throwing Horn numbers with the 6-T Set, then revert back to the 3-V dice set to hit inside numbers again. Figure 12-7 below shows two examples of the 6-T Set.

6-T on Top with
a 3-2 Front

6-T Front with a
5-3 on Top

Figure 12-7
Two Examples of the 6-T Set

You can couple the 6-T formation with a 5, 9 or 6, 8. The primary hit pairs (which are the combinations that you originally set on the dice) are 6-6, 1-1, 3-2, and 4-5 for the "5, 9" 6-T variation and 6-6, 1-1, 3-5, and 4-2 for the "6, 8" 6-T variation. Depending on which 6-T set you use and how the dice pitch, the secondary pitch outcomes include the following: 6-2, 1-5, 3-6, 1-4, 3-1, 4-6, 1-2, and 6-5. This covers everything from 3 up to 11 while avoiding any 7s. Another noteworthy dice set is the horizontal, or *Inline 6 Dice Set*. This set is great for sniping out the horn and outside number combinations. If you enjoy playing the Field (2, 3, 4, 9, 10, 11, and 12), then this is the set for you. Look for a craps table that pays triple on the 12 or 2 Field roll and your mathematical edge is only –2.778 percent. Use this dice set along with your controlled throw to tip the edge in your favor. Figure 12-8 depicts two examples of this particular dice set.

Inline 6 with a   Snake Eyes with a
Hard 10 Front   Hard 4 Front

Figure 12-8
Two Examples of the Inline 6 Set

With the Inline 6 Set, there are four primary Field hits of 6-6, 1-1, 5-5, and 2-2. A secondary pitch produces two ways each to create a 3, 11, 6, and 8, or four ways out of eight to throw a Field number. A secondary roll produces seven Field numbers out of eight outcomes. A secondary yaw creates the same seven Field numbers in eight possibilities. (By the way, the eighth number in both cases is a no Field 5). If you can keep the dice perfectly aligned, or just one relative face away (in any direction), then you will have 22 Field possibilities out of 28 total results. That is almost 79 percent Field numbers with no 7s to be seen!

Dynamic Dimensions of Controlled Throwing

These next three techniques are very powerful. They will allow you to maximize your ability to control the cubes. The first technique, *reducing the revs*, will almost immediately improve your control. To better understand and see the effects of these techniques, you must select a specific dice set to use. Sticking with one particular set permutation will make it possible to track your progress. One example, if you are using the 3-V Set, might be a 3-3 on top with 1-5 on front (left to right). Make sure the dice are reacting in unison after you throw them. Once you have the dice reacting consistently and you are employing a specific dice set, you will be ready to try out these new techniques.

Reducing the Revs

It is highly unlikely that we will get from point A to B without some reaction after touch-down. Hence, there are two things that we must do:

- *Reduce* the amount of dice reaction after they touch down. That is why I always say to use as least amount of force as possible to get the dice from A to B. The less excess energy to burn off, the fewer reactions and less volatile the dice will be.
- *Control* what reactions still remain as best as possible. This is why we must introduce a third DOF, the end-over-end *pitch* rotation that we speak of. Imparting a backspin on the dice eliminates the other rotational

DOFs. A body in motion will retain that particular motion, unless acted upon by some external force. In addition, there is a secondary "braking" benefit that occurs when the dice touch down. The backspin helps to neutralize the forward momentum.

When the dice touch down, we want *minimal* energy left to burn and we want that energy to subside in a *controlled* fashion. Some backspin or pitching is preferred to control the reaction, but too much spin is as bad as no spin at all. The more backspin used, the more spin energy that has to be burned off after touch-down (conservation of momentum). So, minimize both the locomotive force transporting the dice from A to B and the rotational force (backspin) they experience while in flight. Practicing from stick left, I have been able to cut my revolutions from roughly six revs to about one or two and still avoid the other rotational DOFs, roll and yaw. The dice land and react with minimal surplus energy and, as a result, will stay better aligned to each other. Remember that too much backspin will transform into bounce energy, lateral rollout, and other undesirable gyrations. If you are using a grip where the dice are side by side and the fingers oppose the thumb, front-to-back, then this should be easy to accomplish. Examples of these grips would be the One-, Two-, and Three-Fingered Front grips. With the fingers positioned high in front and the thumb slid down in back, a lot of backspin is created. By raising your thumb relative to the lateral axis of rotation (that passes through both die's center of gravity), you can reduce the rotational moment of inertia. This results in less backspin on the dice. As you raise your thumb higher, the moment is reduced. The trick is to create just enough backspin to keep the dice pitching, while warding off the other two rotational degrees of freedom, roll and yaw.

Tuning the Revs

After you are able to successfully minimize the number of revolutions that the dice undergo in flight but still retain the end-over-end motion, you are ready for the next step. You will now attempt to make those fewer number of revs consistent for that session. Through very slight front-to-back grip adjustments you should be able to augment or reduce the amount of spin that the dice experience more precisely. For example, with the Three-Fingered Front grip, I can control the amount of spin imparted on the dice by merely lowering the fingers on the front or raising the thumb on the back. If you need to, review Chapter 7, where extensive details concerning grip adjustments are covered. You will need to use the exact same dice set (top and front combinations) each time during the point cycle, in order to monitor your progress. If you can throw two revolutions consistently on an eight-foot table, for example, and the dice turn over two more times after touchdown, then you will start to see more consistent outcomes. Say that you set 4-4 on top with 6-2 on front (a variation of the 3-V Set). You know that for your throw, the dice will travel two complete revolutions in the air and two revs after landing; then you would be four total rotations from where you started, putting you right back with the 4-4 on top. In this example, the person who can hit what was set on the top would be referred to as a *full-roller*.

You might successfully reduce your revs down to three, with two and a half more after landing. This would result in five and a half total revolutions. We would refer to you as a *half-roller*. If you frequently hit the back face, set combination, that would indicate a *quarter-roller*, and the front faces would constitute a *three-quarter-roller* tendency. Just a quick note—if you consider the back faces to be the ones that face the boxman and you are throwing with a backspin, then those faces will immediately appear on top, as the top faces now show on the front. Hence, the back faces have rolled one-quarter spin. Personally, I found that I am primarily a full-roller with a secondary tendency to three-quarter rolling. Remember that we are looking for a consistent number of revolutions, from dice set to outcome. Each time you walk up to a different table and re-establish the mechanics of your delivery, you will probably need to retune the revolutions. Different sized tables with different bounce characteristics will need to be re-gauged. With practice, you will become adept at *tuning the revs* in two or three throws. *Reducing the revs*, however, is a learned skill that you will carry with you from table to table without having to readjust. If you can reduce the number of revs down to two, then you are sniping one-quarter rotation (one pair of faces) out of eight when attempting to maintain consistency. This isn't too terribly tough for a skilled shooter, but when you are throwing with eight revolutions, for example, and you are trying to pinpoint one set of faces out of 32, this is much more difficult to do. This fact presents another good argument for minimizing the number of dice revolutions.

Eliminating Double Pitch

The dreaded double pitch will be your biggest problem to deal with once you are able to consistently reduce both dies' degrees of freedom to the horizontal and vertical motions and pitching rotation. Assuming you are somewhat warmed up, you will use your come-out roll to gauge how the dice are reacting for you at that particular table during that session. It is free practice (no seven-out) and you will use subsequent come-out rolls to experiment with other adjustments if needed. If, for example, you had set the 3-4 on top and you threw a hard 6 or hard 8 to establish the point, and the dice maintained the pitching motion, then you are double pitching the dice. If you had set the hard 6 during the point cycle and delivered the dice the same way, you would have sevened-out. Double pitching occurs when one die rotates two quarter-spins relative to the other. When perfectly pitching, the double pitch is the only way to affect the fatal 7. Another thing to keep in mind is that one die is a *full-roller* and the other is a *half-roller* based on what you had originally set on top. Armed with this information, we would use the 3-V Set (with a primary 6 and 8, and secondary 5 and 9) or the 2-V set (primary 4 and 10, with a secondary 5 and 9) if we weren't using them already. Next, we would pre-pitch both dice one-quarter rotation forward or backward. The main idea here is to rotate the hard 6 or 8 from the top to the front or back when you set the dice. Now if you double pitch with a full and half revolution, you will have an outcome of 3 or 11 (for the 3-V Set). This will tell you, without sevening out, that you are still double pitching. You have given yourself an added layer of protection, albeit a thin one. You still need to *eliminate the double pitching* itself, but now have some room to operate.

If, on that same come-out roll with the 3-4 set on top (and the 5-2 on front or back), you now rolled a hard 10 or hard 4, then you are double pitching one die with a one-quarter rev and the other with a three-quarter revolution. You would then use the 3-V Set during the point cycle, but with the hard 6 or hard 8 *on top*. That way if you occasionally double pitch as you make grip adjustments, you will see the telltale 3 or 11 result—a nonfatal outcome. You now have some latitude to try adjusting, but you are still on borrowed time. Observe the release and travel of the dice to assess the problem. Try to pinpoint the cause, then make the adjustment to eliminate the problem. The problem will be with the grip 95+ percent of the time. For example, if one die is coming out of my hand a little lower or later than the other, I might rock my hand slightly to the left or to the right. Watch the dice motions and check the results. If the problem disappears, then great. But be watchful; it may return again later. If you cannot shake the problem with a minor adjustment, then you have bigger problems and should not be attempting Rev Tuning or Set Transpositions at this time. In any event, review Chapter 7 on the grip, and perhaps 6 (delivery) as well, if you are having difficulty keeping the dice together.

Here are some emergency measures that you may want to try just to sustain your roll in a live craps game. If you have money committed on the craps table and just cannot shake the double pitch (one in four times or greater), then as a final measure, go to the 2-V Set exclusively. Do this even if your point is 6 or 8. Let me explain what this does for you under these circumstances. The 2-V Set, when exposed to double pitching (and with the right revs set), will still yield point numbers. The 2-V with a 4-1 or 6-3 will double pitch to reveal a 3-1 or 6-4. If a single pitch occurs, then totals of 6 and 8 primarily and 5 and 9 secondarily will appear. Conversely, the 2-V Set with a 3-1 or 6-4 will double pitch to yield a 4-1 and 6-3 combination, or a 5 and 9 respectively. If a single pitch occurs, then again 6 and 8 will predominate followed by 5 and 9. At this point, you are not able to correct the root cause of the problem, only trying to add a few extra throws to the overall life of the roll. You should consider turning your non-contract bets off until you are able to make the proper adjustments.

Some Quick Examples

Problem 1: You are double pitching one die at full revs and the other at half revs.

Solution 1: Try the 3-V Set with the hard 6 or hard 8 on the front of the set. Adjust the grip or delivery as necessary. If the problem remains, then go to the 2-V Set with the hard 4 or 10 on the front.

Problem 2: You are double pitching one die at one-quarter revs and the other at three-quarters revs.

Solution 2: Use the 3-V Set with hard 6 or hard 8 on top. Try adjusting the grip or delivery. If the problem persists, then go to the 2-V Set with the hard 4 or hard 10 on top.

At this point you would not proceed to the remaining advantage measures until the problem with your grip and double pitching is eliminated! However, the fact that you are able to recognize that one die is full-rolling and the other is half-rolling, for example, will better help you understand the next section.

Transposing the Sets

If things are going smoothly and your results are showing consistency, then you are probably ready for the next step. If you are setting 7s on the come-out roll (no Come bets working), then pick a specific set and stick with it during the point cycle part of the game. Because I tend to be a *full-roller*, I want a 5 spot face on the top left coupled with a 2, top right. If I indeed throw a full-roll, then I will hit 5-2 for a come-out winning natural. If the 2 rolls off, then I still have a chance to catch the 6 for a winning 5-6 combination. On my last casino trip, just before writing these words, I threw four 11s in a row on one of my come-out rolls at the Motor City Casino in Detroit, using this technique. Assuming that the 5 face stays on top, I will have two chances in six of winning on the come-out roll. If I were setting 5-2 on top, but for some reason I was consistently throwing numbers with a 4 or a 3 spot face as part of the combination, then I would rotate my 5-2 set from the top to the front or back. Hopefully, I will start to see a 5 or 2 spot face show up consistently on one die. If it is the 2, then I would simply exchange the left die with the right die when I set them next. Now I should have 5s appearing and, as I said earlier, I will have two chances in six (a 5-2 and 5-6) to throw a winning natural as compared to two chances in nine (or eight ways in 36) for a random thrower.

I typically throw both dice in full-roller fashion, but sometimes the right die will consistently undergo a three-quarter roll, revealing what was initially set on the front. Let's say that my dice are reacting this way and my point is 9.

Having units also placed on the 6 and 8, I would then use one of the two following variations of the 3-V Set:

Initial Set with
3-V on Top

Quarter Pitch
Resulting in 3-6

Figure 12-9
Variation # 1

Initial Set with
Hard 8 on Top

Quarter Pitch
Resulting in 4-5

Figure 12-10
Variation # 2

For the first variation, the hard 6 would be my full-roll hit. If the right die quarter pitched forward (same as three-quarter pitch backward), then I'll gladly take a 3-6, making my point of 9. Likewise, with the second variation, hard 8 is my full-roll target, but I will not be too disappointed if the front face continues to pitch at three-quarters instead, revealing a 4-5. In the beginning of this chapter, I spoke of making five hard 6s in eight attempts, one session, at the A.C. Hilton. On one of the unsuccessful hard 6 attempts, I instead made the point of 8 with a 3-5 combination. For the most part I was full rolling. I was setting 3-3 on top and nailing the hard 6. Knowing my secondary tendency, I set 1-5 on the front. The right die turned over one less face while coming to rest and the 5-3 appeared for the point.

Two Quick Sample Problems

Problem 1: You are primarily a half roller, but a secondary tendency causing the right die to rotate an extra face (three-quarter-roller) appears. The point is 10, but you also have a Come bet situated on the 5. What should you do?

   Solution 1: Sometimes, as with the first example, there may be more than one acceptable answer, depending upon which number you wish to make first or which multiple tendency is stronger. Because you are a half-roller, whatever is set on the bottom should appear on top for the outcome. There are several different answers, most of which involve the 2-V Set. You will hope that both dice either half-roll or three-quarter-roll together.

   A) Set 5-5 on bottom with 4-1 or 1-4 on the front, giving you a crack at both the 10 and the 5.
   B) Set 4-1 or 1-4 on bottom with 5-5 on the front, ditto A above.
   C) Set 5-5 on the bottom with 4-6 or 6-4 on the front, giving you two cracks at the 10.
   D) Set 4-6 or 6-4 on the bottom with 5-5 on the front, giving you two chances for the 10.

   If the quarter pitch tendency is stronger, then use one of the two Hard Way Sets as follows:

   E) Set 3-3 on the bottom with 2-2 on the front, with a chance of throwing a 3-2 or 2-3 combo.
   F) Set 2-2 on the bottom with 3-3 on the front, ditto E above.

   Problem 2: You are a full roller with a minor tendency for either the right or left die to three-quarter roll. What is the optimal set to use if your point is 6?

   Solution 2: The best set to employ would be the Hard Way Set with one of two permutations:

A) Setting 3-3 on top with 5-5 on the front will give you one full-roll hit of 3-3 and two quarter-pitch rolls of 3-5 or 5-3. Use this combination if the full-roll tendency is more promising.

B) Setting 4-4 on top with 2-2 on the front will give you a full-roll result of 4-4 and two quarter-pitch possibilities of 4-2 or 2-4. Use this set if the quarter-pitch bias is stronger.

Not everyone will exhibit the same pitching characteristics in their throw. However, once you are consistent enough to establish a pattern, and observant enough to see what that pattern is, you can similarly transpose the sets for any point or number that you wish to throw. Essentially, you will see the result, remember what your starting set was and piece together in your mind what relative dice movements occurred to get that result. You will then substitute your desired result in place of the actual one and transpose the relative movements back to get an optimal starting dice set. There will be several starting dice sets that can work. When shooting to avoid the 7, you will choose a dice set that is a variation of the Hard Way, 3-V, or 2-V Dice Sets. It sounds a little tougher than it actually is, but as you gain experience through practice and observation, this process will become second nature. It's exciting to be able to throw a little money out for a hop bet and then punch it out on the next toss of the dice. I consider the concepts in this chapter to be expert level, used only by those dedicated veterans who have solidly mastered the basics and weathered a few seasons. If you are having any problems maintaining consistency, go back and hammer on the basics. Remember that the root cause is probably in the grip or delivery. Modifying the set alone can buy you a little extra time, but you will need to fix whatever is wrong. Work to produce a high enough level of consistency to see patterns starting to emerge, then Sharpshooter's Dynamic Dimensions can elevate your game to the next level!

Sharpshooting from the Don't

Here is an expert strategy that I almost inserted in Chapter 9 or 10, but because it is so dice-set intensive, I have included it here. There will be times when you feel like you are on the brink of grooving in and then an unexpected 7 takes the dice away. Or, conditions are so crowded that even if you could get your favorite throwing position and the dice before your session stake runs out, you will create an inordinate amount of pressure on yourself to immediately perform. Otherwise, you will likely not see the cubes for another 40 or 50 minutes. Maybe you live near a one-casino town and there just aren't that many options. These circumstances can make it difficult to shoot and hence, profit from your skilled throws. For those of us who would like a little more opportunity at shooting the dice, necessity has become the mother of invention! My Sharpshooter Don't Strategy solves these problems. It gives you increased exposure to the dice without killing your bankroll, even in crowded conditions. Sharpshooting from the Don't takes advantage of our perfect pitch delivery through use of carefully devised dice sets. Unlike the right-way shooter, our objective is to set against the point and seven-out. But wait, you say, when the shooter sevens out, doesn't he or she give up the dice? Yes, this is true, but here's the trick—you play at higher limit tables with fewer or no other people. You will get the dice back much quicker and will only risk *one larger unit* on the Don't Pass while you shoot.

Many times on a Saturday or some other busy night, the $5 and $10 tables are jammed. I have been able to stroll right up to a $100, or even $25 minimum table, pick up the dice and shoot with nobody else at the table. As soon as I seven-out, the dice come right back and I quickly tune my delivery and develop my rhythm. "But I can't afford to bet black, or even green" you say. Nonsense. The average $5 Pass Line bettor has $5 on the line, $10 to $20 in odds, at least $6 on the 6 and 8 each, $5 on the 5 and 9, pushing close to $50, and that goes double for the $10 bettor. Remember that you will only risk *one* green (or black) unit initially and you will *never lay the odds*. Once you are grooved in, you can continue to flat bet, play a positive progression, or even switch to the right side and play the Super Sniper Tactic if you are up six or eight units. I had one session a couple of summers back at the Luxor one busy night, where I was pounding the Don'ts with this system. At one point, I hit a personal best of eleven Don'ts in a row! People from the casino were crowding around to see what all the excitement was. Eventually the table filled up with Don't bettors, who were rooting against the point and passing the dice back to me. One of the players at the table nicknamed me "Dr. Freeze," because I had made the table so cold. Every time I sevened-out, the table went wild. The boxman remarked to one of the dealers, "In all of my twenty-two years in this business, I've never seen anything like this!"

Okay, let's get to it. Because this Don't method is set intensive, you will need to know and practice with four specialized dice sets. Once you have mastered these sets, the rest is a breeze.

- The Don't Come-out Set(s): shooting against the 7, or for instant craps
- The Don't 6, 8 Set: shooting to seven-out against the point of 6 or 8
- The Don't 5, 9 Set: shooting to seven-out against the point of 5 or 9
- The Don't 4, 10 Set: shooting to seven-out against the point of 4 or 10

Rolling on the Come-out

On the come-out roll, your safest bet is to use a set I call the 2-V formation. We discussed this set earlier in the chapter. The hard 4 is arranged such that connecting the dots of the 2 faces, form a V. Look at the examples below in Figure 12-11 and recognize how this set appears. You will use the 2-V on the come-out to avoid the 7 or 11 and, hopefully make the 4 or 10 your point to shoot against. Even if the 5 or 9 become your point, you will command a large advantage. The 2-V formation can be found on the top, front, bottom, or back. It doesn't matter what other combinations of faces are on the other three sides, unless you are using set transpositions. They will automatically be either 3-1 with a 6-4, or 4-1 with a 6-3, and of course the 5-5 or hard 10 will be opposite the 2-V (hard 4). Once the 7 or 11 is avoided on the come-out roll, the Don't player has a *huge* edge! All you need to remember on the come-out roll, for now, is to set the 2-V.

2-V Set   2-V Set
on Top   on Front

Figure 12-11

There is a more expert level set that I hesitate to share with you. I know some of you will become accomplished shooters and may wish to try this out. You can try using the *Inline 6 Set* on the come-out if your skill is highly developed. One pair of faces will have horizontally orientated 6s and another will have the hard 10 set. Opposing these faces will be "snake eyes" and the hard 4, respectively. If you are comfortably grooved in and have successfully "tuned" the revolutions on your dice, then you can shoot for hitting craps right out of the gate. The advantage is that you don't relinquish the dice when throwing a craps on the come-out, yet you have a winning decision. In addition, you can win at a more rapid pace. The face combinations you will need to remember are 1-1 with 2-2. On the opposite sides will appear "box-cars" and the hard 10, respectively. I tend to throw full revolutions, with a secondary tendency towards the front face combination. What this means is that most of the time one or both dice will end up with the number on top that I originally had set on top, or a full revolution. Typically, if a top-set face does not appear, then a front-set face probably will. Because of this fact, I will set snake-eyes on top, with the hard 4 on front. This way I have all three craps possibilities covered. If the top comes in, I hit *double aces*, or snake-eyes. If the right front pitches upward, I hit *ace-deuce*. An extra pitch of the left front yields *deuce-ace*.

This set neatly avoids the 7; however, you must be on the lookout for the 11. If you are getting inconsistent revs on the dice, then you may be more prone to hitting 12 (no problem), or 11 (big problem), which is found on the opposite side of the ace-deuce or deuce-ace combination. If I hit an 11 on the come-out, I will turn the initial set over and try again, shooting for the 3. If I hit an 11 a second time on any come-out roll, I will then abandon the craps set in lieu of the 2-V Set. Following are some examples of the craps, or Inline 6 Set that we covered in the last section when we spoke about setting for the Field bet.

Full-Revs
Craps Set

Half-Revs
Craps Set

Figure 12-12

The simplest and most conservative approach is just to use the 2-V set on the come-out. Now that we have covered the Don't Come-Out Set, we will move on to the seven-out sets.

Shooting Against the Point

Unlike the right bettor who cheers for the point to come and has to take odds to soothe the sting of the house edge, the Don't bettor is now in the catbird's seat. At this point in the game's cycle, he has a 9.09 percent edge over the 6 or 8, an even 20 percent over the 5 or 9, and a whopping 33.33 percent edge over the 4 or 10. Moreover, these figures are based on a random game! They do not take our shooter's skill into account. Of course, the Don't bettor has a large disadvantage on the come-out roll. That is why avoidance of the 7 or 11 on the come-out roll is paramount. Assume that we've survived the critical come-out and established a point of 6 or 8. This is a tough point to beat, but you have a solid advantage over the house. Letting your perfect pitch delivery system go to work for you, you will simply set 7s all around. The only thing you must remember is: Do not use the 5-2, seven combination in the mix. The reason we must avoid the 5-2 or 2-5 combination is that if one die quarter pitches relative to the other die, the likelihood of hitting a 6 or 8 is greatly increased. Any permutation of 6-1 with 3-4 set on any of the four possible face pairings is correct. Here is a little memory device that I use in the heat of battle to remember the correct 7s set: "Don't 6, 8 means 6, half of 8." The full translation is, you don't want a 6 or 8 repeated, so set the 7s such that a 6 (with a 1) is one pairing, and half of 8, or 4 (with a 3) is the second pairing. This will help ensure that a 5-2 combination is not used. Figure 12-13 depicts two examples of the Don't 6, 8 Set.

Figure 12-13
The Don't 6 or 8, Seven-out Set

What if you have a point of 5 or 9? With the added controlled throw edge, you should be in the 25+ percent range! With the Don't 5, 9 Set that I have developed, it may be even higher. As long as you keep the dice rotating about the lateral axis (perfect pitch), there is no possibility of any pitching combination that will yield an outcome of 5 or 9. They are removed from the four face pairs that rotate about the lateral axis. All you need to do is set 7s all around, avoiding the 3-4 or 4-3, seven combination. The pneumatic device here is, "Don't 5, 9 means 5, upside down 9." In Figure 12-14 below, a 5 coupled with a 2, or an upside 9 (or 6) paired up with a 1 is found on the top or front face pairings.

Figure 12-14
The Don't 5 or 9, Seven-out Set

If the 4 or 10 is your point, you will set 7s all around, steering clear of the 6-1 or 1-6 combination. The 6 coupled with the 4 (or 4-6) gives us two ways to make the 10 out of three possibilities. Likewise, the 1 with the 3 (or 3-1) gives us two of three ways to make the 4. If we keep the dice pitching like cartwheels, we only have one chance in 16 of popping the 4 or 10, (both hardways). Your edge in this situation should be in the 35 to 40 percent range, winning close to 70 percent of the time! For this set remember, "Don't 4, 10 means 4, half of 10." Use the 4-3 and 5-2 combination. Study the following sets in Figure 12-15.

Figure 12-15
The Don't 4 or 10, Seven-Out Set

If you can shoot with an SRR of 1:7 on the come-out while trying to avoid the 7; and an SRR of 1:5 while trying to avoid the point and seven-out, then your overall edge for this system will be +7.43 percent. The calculations supporting this figure are included in Chapter 15.

Now I will summarize the critical components for the Sharpshooter Don't Strategy:

- Use the 2-V set (or possibly the Inline 6 Set) for come-out rolls.
- Against the point of 6 or 8, use "6, half of 8," or (6-1) with (4-3).
- Against the point of 5 or 9, use "5, upside down 9," or (5-2) and (6-1).
- Against the point of 4 or 10, use "4, half of 10," or (4-3) with (5-2).

Once you have learned the sets, decide what unit size and which alternate betting strategy you may employ and that's it!

Chapter 13

Regaining the Psychological Edge

The casinos have spent tens of millions of dollars to study how they can efficiently and expediently part the patrons from their bankrolls. They use all kinds of psychological tricks that get us to let down our guards and play recklessly. They euphemistically refer to it as "gaming" or "entertainment," but never gambling. You must walk through the entire casino to get to your room, the restaurant, the pool, or whatever. When you first walk through the casino, you are bombarded with sensory overload. The carpeting is overly busy and too colorful. If you stare long enough, you will get a headache. The casino ceilings are plain and boring. Your attention is directed from waist high to eye-level where all the action is. Then there are the harsh noises that can put you over the edge—the incessant clanging of coins or tokens, the bells, and the little audio snippets you hear repeatedly from those theme-type slot machines. Even the payout of a minor jackpot is enough to drive you to the asylum and back. And if you are driven to drink instead, the beautiful cocktail waitresses are scantily clad and the alcohol is freely flowing. There are no clocks and there are no windows. There is no clue as to what is happening in the "real world." Time seems to be standing still but, in fact, that is merely the impression that the casinos want to create.

In casinos, people are driven to behave strangely, and do things they ordinarily would not do. I know guys who will drive across town to save 5¢ a gallon on their gas fill up, yet will drop $500 at the gaming tables with little or no thought behind what they are doing. Other patrons may be minding their money, but not their manners. People one stride ahead of you will stop suddenly in their tracks to scope out a Blackjack game, not realizing (or caring) that you are now scrambling to maintain your balance and keep from piling into them at the same time. Then there are those that experience the "casino stare." Their jaw drops and their heads pivot in all directions as they maintain a painful, one-and-a-half mile per hour pace. You can try cutting through the maze of narrow-aisled slot machines, but there will more than likely be obstructions that will further slow you down. Those painfully slow folks will still end up five or six people ahead of you in the buffet line. In the casinos, the players do not bet with real money, they stake with colorful clay chips. The idea being, if you wager with and see a Benjamin go by the wayside you might be a little alarmed. However, in this place where time stands still, you think, "just another black chip, I have a few more." So the casino has got you brainwashed into thinking it's okay to lose your money and sense of time. People are rude, you are constantly being bumped into and wafts of cigar smoke blow your way! With all these disruptions, how can a thinking man operate? Nevertheless, it gets even more interesting if you are attempting to play with an advantage.

Experiencing Heat at the Tables

When you do buy in and attempt to use a controlled throw, you may face additional obstacles. Many of you know what I mean when I talk about the casinos applying heat to a good roll. For the others, I'm not talking about warming up your buns at the dinner buffet. Anything that the casino injects to disrupt a good hand at the craps table is what I am referring to here. Sometimes the bosses might be sweating the game if the house is dumping on a good roll. You will see them hovering over the table, criticizing dealers, telling the shooter to hit the back wall on every throw and with both dice. They may slow down the pace by examining the dice, rechecking every payout, and sometimes ordering an unnecessary chip refill. Other times the heat will be subtle, like the time the boxman at the Taj Mahal (knowing I was a big Red Wings hockey fan) engaged me in conversation about their run to the Stanley Cup. "Your boys look poised to take the cup," he said, just as I was leaning over to pick up the dice. Of course, I put the dice back down and looked up to talk with him. As I finally picked the dice up to throw, I was not focusing on my grip or my delivery. I was still finishing up with my commentary as I let the dice go. The dice came out of my hand horribly. The rotations were badly off and after touching down, they separated and hit the back wall about 18 inches apart! I don't need to tell you what the result was. This treatment was more diplomatic, and I give the boxman credit for being tactful about how he handled it.

I have had some rather unpleasant experiences at eight or ten Vegas casinos and a downtown club (where I thought they were gonna rough me up in the back room). I have been back to most of these establishments and have gotten better treatment, with the exception of the Monte Carlo and the Horseshoe Club. Another interesting experience happened at the Las Vegas MGM. I noticed that the back area where the high rollers tend to play craps was empty, so I walked over. They had green and black action tables open. I found a nice quarter table and bought in for $500. I placed $25 on the Don't and set for craps, hitting an ace-deuce on the come out. "Let it ride," I said as I already had my craps dice set positioned. This time, I established and was shooting against the point of

9. I was setting 7s all around and throwing. Two throws later—seven-out. "Press it up to $100," I instructed. Then the throw . . . "Snake Eyes," the call from the stick. "Take it up to $200," I said with a ring of confidence in my voice. Now the pit boss was hovering over the table. I kept getting the dice right back because no one else was at the table. The point was 4 this time. I had six ways to seven-out (and win) versus three ways to make the point (a 2-to-1 proposition for an even-money payoff). I decided not to be as meticulous with my grip and throw since I was in the driver's seat, mathematically, and I now had several "suits" watching me.

I still set 7s around, but my throw was a little looser than the previous tosses. The dice were in synch and came to rest. "Seven-out, pay the Don'ts," was the call. Before I could utter a word, the pit boss spoke in a businesslike tone, "Sir, you're done." To which I began to reply, "What do you mean, I still . . ." He cut me off, "I've seen enough sir. You're simply done." As I picked up all my chips, I half-inquired, "See you in a couple of days?" After a brief pause, "That will be fine sir," was his response. Some of my students have had similar experiences. Most times, I believe that the particular shift that I played on was not doing well. Maybe the bosses were reamed out at the last meeting with the shift manager or V. P. of Operations and were not in the best of spirits. Then some upstart dice control artist comes in to rub salt in the wound! You can see where they might be a little peeved at times. The casinos are business centers. They are corporations with stockholders to answer to. First, do not take any of this in a personal way. These guys are trying to protect their turf. Second, be polite and businesslike yourself. You may want to come back and play there later. I have read Blackjack books where the author bragged about how many casinos he had been barred from, but I contend that the real trick is to play without getting permanently uninvited. This is not always possible, but being respectful of the personnel will extend your playing longevity. Realize that it becomes a game within a game that we sometimes have to play.

There are a few things that you can do to mitigate the situation. Your attitude towards the casino personnel can dictate how you, in turn, are treated. If you come in acting like a tough guy or bragging about how you bagged the last casino for a few grand, then do not expect them to roll out the red carpet. If you are friendly and personable, it will make it that much tougher for the boss to come down on you. One veteran player I know, who uses the casino handle "Heavy," has a way with people and a way with words. With his southern drawl, he affectionately calls the bosses, "pit critters" and presents them with professional looking, laminated cards that say things like, "Bearer is entitled to one free seven-out. Present this card to the Floor Supervisor on duty." The cards have graphics on them and look official. Many times, the boss first presented with this card will have to look twice before busting out laughing. The card then is circulated around the table for the dealers to look at. This helps to set up a fun, friendly environment in which to play. You do not necessarily have to go to this extent to break the ice, but being friendly and polite goes a long way. A more unimaginative, but fully effective way to warm up the crew, is to use judicious tipping.

Tipping the dealers may result in less heat, especially from the stickman who controls the pace of the game. Many dealers depend on tokes to supplement their income. Their hourly rate is low and they will appreciate your gesture. The dealers are quick to learn your betting patterns. They will help you to keep your betting consistent and insure that your payoffs are accurate. Instead of barking something like, "Shooter, stop fixing the dice," the stickman may even preset the cubes for you with your combination on top. If your point is a 6, for example, then place the crew on the hard 6 for a buck. The stickman may set 3-3 on top for you with his stick and even encourage you to roll it. Place a buck out for the crew on either the Pass Line or hard ways and let them ride along with you. Usually this conduct will buy you some loyalty, but if their attitude does not change for the better, then save your money. Moreover, if things get worse, (casino personnel are getting short and may even start to ridicule you) consider leaving this table or even the casino altogether. There is no sense in trying to perform under such stressful conditions. How you are able to handle the casino environment is important and if you cannot handle a particular situation, then leave. Like the professional athlete, you need to retain the mental edge once you have found it . . . and maintaining a keen focus when you are shooting. Do not allow anything to faze you.

A third thing that will help you to control heat is to know what you are doing. Know ahead of time which bets you will be making and how you will press those wagers. Develop a routine for placing and pressing bets, as well as setting and throwing the dice. With any dice set you are using, you must learn to execute this set in two seconds or less. Otherwise, you will bring undue attention and anxiety to yourself as you prepare to throw. Once tension and anxiety sets in, your game will lose its consistency. Idio-motor responses (small involuntary twitches or muscle contractions) will cause your muscles to react differently from throw to throw. In addition, your breathing will be adversely affected, throwing off your posture. Your delivery will not be nearly as consistent as it should be. This is generally true of anything that causes you to feel tense or anxious, but this particular aspect is one we can control. Thoroughly practice your dice sets along with your throw. Why give the pit a needless excuse to break your rhythm and put the pressure on? Also, know what your own betting patterns are. Each time you stop and struggle with how to wager or press, you are taking yourself right out of the game. You will compromise your focus on the delivery. By developing a smooth routine for setting and throwing, along with a system of making wagers and raising them, you can focus on the finer aspects of your throw and keep the game moving along. By keeping the game more efficient (without rushing), you can keep the heat from the bosses down to a minimum.

Other Performance Inhibitors

Stress and anxiety cause us to tighten up, reducing the effectiveness of our throw. Physical exercise and relaxation techniques can allow us to play more calmly and improve our consistency. Certain breathing exercises will relax the body and reduce nervous energy. Here is an exercise I learned from Eric N. When you have a few moments to yourself, close your eyes and try this technique. Get comfortable and breathe in slowly for four full seconds. As you breathe in, visualize pure, white energy entering your body. Hold the air for another count of four seconds and see this white cloud permeate throughout your body. Now exhale slowly for four seconds. See a dark gray cloud exit through your mouth as you blow. With your eyes still closed, take in another dose of pure, white energy for four seconds. Hold this and allow it to travel throughout your body. Now exhaling slowly, see the gray cloud leaving your body, only this time it is not so dark gray. Repeat in this manner eight to ten times. At the end of this exercise, the cloud leaving your body when you exhale should be pure and white like the air you are breathing in. How do you feel? Hopefully you are calm and relaxed. I use this technique to help fall asleep after a hectic day. You can further enhance your ability to relax by listening to Baroque-type classical music, or some other appropriate music, as you do the breathing exercises.

Inactivity in our daily lives may dampen our prospects for profits. Physical exercises such as briskly walking, swimming, and light aerobics can set the stage for good cardiovascular and respiratory health. You will breathe easily, think more clearly, and have more stamina as well. Other exercises like bike riding, inline skating, or jumping rope will improve your sense of balance and timing. This will aid in your execution of the dice delivery. Aside from the physical health and performance benefits you will realize, you will find your mental endurance vastly improved. Another benefit of physical activity is better flexibility. Some stretching exercises that are great for the legs and back are toe touches. You can do windmills for the arms and shoulders. I usually loosen up at the table with a few neck rolls. Do a few in the clockwise direction, then follow it up with a few counter-clockwise rolls. Hand stretches are always good. Bring the fingertips of your hands together and press slowly until both hands entirely contact each other. Now rotate your fingers toward your chest (thumbs down) and hold. Now rotate outward until your thumbs point up. These are all good stretching techniques. Sometimes to help warm up, I will tuck my throwing hand up to my collar bone and unwrap it slowly outward. This helps me to relax, stretch out my throwing arm, help my muscle memory kick in and burn extra adrenaline. Inflexibility, injury, arthritis, and even tension can limit your range of motion. Exercise and relaxation techniques can eliminate some of these problems, but therapy may be needed for more serious ailments.

For some of us, the size of our bets will adversely affect our ability to focus. Even if we can fully afford to wager with the buy in we have designated and have sound money management practices, we still may become uncomfortable or even afraid to wager with larger units at times. Fear makes us overly cautious and hesitant in our actions, resulting in an unnatural, forced delivery. Our consistency will disappear. One of my students raises an interesting point on exceeding his comfort level of wagering when shooting with the dice. This student presses his bets more aggressively, raising on every other hit. He discovered that when the bets get above his comfort level, he loses his focus, and often sevens-out, leaving too much of his profit on the table. His solution was to assess his discomfort level and upon reaching it, cut all his bets in half. This is working well for him and eventually, with more experience, he will be able to raise that top bet and increase his comfort level. I have played craps with purple units in action on my roll. I am not afraid to wager at this level, but I do feel more comfortable capping my bets off at the $100 or $120 level. Once I press my bets up to black sized units, I often stop pressing and retain all the winnings from then on. This sets a pressing goal for me to reach and takes the pressure off at the same time. I feel comfortable, yet I am playing aggressively enough to capture a nice win. You may want to consider a maximum betting plateau and what that amount should be. Anything that makes you squeamish is suspect.

Keying in Your Throw

How long does it take to key in your throw? The answer may be a little different from person to person. Depending on things like table experience, coordination, skill, and timing, different shooters will take varying amounts of time to warm up. Whenever possible, I warm up with my practice box before driving off for the local casinos. Even with this warm-up (I don't hit the tables until maybe an hour later), I find that it may take me eight to ten rolls to get in the groove. To key it in as quickly as possible, I play the hit-and-run style whenever I can, not waiting for the dice to come back around. If you are able, try playing during the week in the early morning hours. Look for empty, low-limit games to get back-to-back chances to throw. Right after I miss-out, I am looking for the next table where I can get another quick shooting opportunity. I might stay at this table if there are just one or two other shooters and the other tables appear to be full. The ideal scenario is several open tables with me hopping from one to the other. As I open them up and get my throwing arm warm, I am acting as the house shill, attracting other players. How many rolls will it take you to warm up? That depends on you. Nevertheless, remember that it is important to get grooved in. Even though you have the edge, you will have to "key in" your muscle memory for that situation. Every one of us will tune in a little differently and keying in your muscle memory is critical. Each casino is different and even in the same casino; every table (although similar in design) may play a little differently.

Maintaining Peak Performance

Peak performing takes place when you have developed the muscle memory necessary to execute the throw and can concentrate fully on doing it correctly. Muscle memory is the programmed motions that your body goes through to accomplish a repeatable task. When you go to dial a familiar phone number, for example, your fingers are able to dance nimbly across the keypad. The same is true with any well-rehearsed physical motion. Once you are producing your best physical performance, you want to maintain this level by placing yourself in a certain state of mind. This can be done by using a form of *experiential visualization*. That is, you create a vision where you are experiencing the event in the first person frame of mind. You will visualize continued performance perfection in your throw. You are directing your attention to the proper objective that you have in mind and are letting the rest flow. You will project confidence and execute with authority. You may even find yourself in a trance-like state, where all the outside distractions seem to melt away. You react automatically and consistently, with no conscious effort. A rhythm or cadence to your throw develops and your delivery flows naturally, without being forced. You begin to visualize a precision shot each time, so you simply pick up the dice and execute it as imagined.

Let's assume that you are a very seasoned controlled thrower. You have developed your throw to the point where you can walk up to a table, make a few quick adjustments and adapt to your playing conditions. The mechanics of your throw are second nature and your muscle memory is well ingrained. At this point, the game becomes 90 percent psychological. The first objective is to keep a positive, healthy frame of mind. Relax and have fun. Enjoy what you are doing. The second goal is to play with confidence and stay focused on the task at hand. Some people even enter a self-induced hypnotic state. Professional athletes often speak of being "in the zone." You will use mental imagery to create this state of mind. I want you to try this experiment, right now. Visualize yourself at the table, shooting the dice. You calmly assess the conditions, make the appropriate wagers and select the dice set you will use. As the stickman slides the cubes over, you already know what hand motions you will use to create your set. Now, you go into your pre-shot routine, quickly and accurately executing your set and grip on the dice. Your sense of feel is piqued and you sense that the dice are perfectly balanced in your hand. As you lift your arm to deliver the dice, you already know where and how they will land. The dice float off your fingertips and are perfectly synchronized—gently arcing and rotating together. The dice land and slowly bounce up to kiss the back wall, then gently come down to rest on the desired result. Sound far-fetched? Not really.

You are using mental imaging to elevate your game. Through experiential visualization, you are seeing success in your mind's eye. You merely step into the stance and execute the shot, allowing your muscle memory to replay all the little details, like proper grip, delivery motion, timing, and focus. Through this mental imagery, you are using all of your senses to create a realistic experience in the mind. As you get proficient at doing this, the same brain activity will take place as if you were really executing the delivery. You may even experience increased adrenaline and heart rate. Reread the paragraph above adding in even finer and more vivid details. For example, actually *feel* the dice as you pick them up in your mind's eye and grip them. *See* the dice coming off your hand perfectly and landing. *Hear* the other players get excited as you make your point. Use all your senses to add in as many fine details as you can. When you do this correctly, your brain will not be able to decipher between the visualized experience and an actual one. As you gain experience shooting in actual crap games, you will have several great rolls that will make you feel proud; rolls that made yourself and the other players a lot of money. Select one of your most impressive games and actually visualize yourself re-living that game. Using your internal memory, you can recall one of your own peak performances. Transport yourself back to that experience as you actually throw at a real live craps game. This form of experiential visualization is called *power imagery*. It can keep you calm and build high confidence for your present roll.

When you vividly imagine a highly successful roll, or re-live one of your great games, you should feel strong and in control. We want to recapture that *calm sense of purpose* and be able to conjure it up when we are shooting the dice at a later game. As you practice your power visualization in private, circle the index finger and thumb together from your non-throwing hand. Say something to yourself like, "I feel GR-E-E-A-A-T!" or "I am POWERFUL!" Do this while you are still visualizing your peak performance. This little action on your part helps to *anchor* that feeling of calm confidence to the power phrase and finger circling action you just did. Psychologists call this a "post-hypnotic queue." When you are at the dice table feeling tense and overly nervous, just circle your thumb and finger together and say your phrase quietly. Your brain has now been programmed to make you calm and confident when you use this queue. This is very important. If you are feeling calm and confident, then there is no room to feel tense and afraid. Practice seeing your power image ten minutes a day for about a week. Remember to include your anchor phrase and action. Later, when you are shooting in the casino, you can easily conjure up this experience, and the confidence it brings, by simply circling the thumb and finger and silently repeating your key phrase. You can also use experiential visualization to mentally practice your shooting routine. If you are sick or unable to get to an actual table to practice, you can imagine yourself shooting the dice in your mind. Visualize a series of throws, or even an extended game without being at a real table.

Walking It Through

When I first approach a craps table to shoot, I immediately size the table up. How hard is the table bed? I will rap with my knuckles to check. How long is the table and where should I be landing my dice? How do I expect them to react when they touch down? My first few throws are used to better gauge the table. I will key my throw in for this particular table. I make any corrections and finer adjustments to my grip and delivery. Hopefully this can be done while I am still coming out (and cannot lose the dice). When I start to feel keyed in for this table, I circle my thumb and finger together, saying, "I am powerful," or some other appropriate phrase. As the dice are being slid over to me, I decide which set to use and how to quickly create it. The dice set is executed and I now close my eyes to focus on the feel, for the proper grip. I glance at my target area at the other end of the table and look for a runway or clear path, about 4" or 5" between bets, that I can use as a landing strip. I imagine a cereal bowl sitting where my target circle is and I try to float the dice carefully into the bowl so they will stay in it. This approach will help you to develop the target accuracy and soft touch to better control the dice.

As I am releasing the dice, I am thinking of an exact combination I want to see as the result. Never say to yourself, "I hope it's not a 7" or "Whatever you do, don't throw a 7." These are actually negative suggestions that play on your fear. Instead, say something positive that includes the combination you set on top, for example. If you set the hard 8, say to yourself "Give me a forty-four." As we continue to avoid the seven-out, we are happy, but if we hit our 4-4, or other designated pairing, this becomes a bonus and a big confidence booster. The dice are released and I imagine a positive outcome. As the table fills up with players, things such as buy ins, placing wagers, and making payoffs take longer. Your rhythm and focus may begin to deteriorate. You can maintain your focus by reducing outside distractions between shots. Direct your eyes upward, maybe 20 or 30 feet in front of you or off to the side and look at the plain ceiling. Allow your mind to go blank and just hear your cadence or favorite song for throwing the dice. Do not think about anything else. When it looks like the stickman is ready to start things up again, circle your thumb and finger and silently say your power phrase. Go into your pre-shot routine and repeat the whole procedure.

Some Final Words

Now you will get the lecture about not being reckless with your bankroll. Do not play when you are feeling tired or in the wrong frame of mind. Realize that chasing your losses will usually result in greater losses. The following are six important rules for all controlled-throw dice players:

1. As my scoutmaster used to say, "Be prepared." That means knowing your dice sets and betting patterns so you can keep the game running efficiently. This will reduce heat from the pit personnel. That also means being physically well rested, practiced and mentally ready to dedicate yourself to focusing on your goals. You should have a craps bankroll and a solid money management plan established. Plan as much of your playing sessions as practical and eliminate unwanted surprises.

2. Play when *you* want to play, when you are at your personal best. Do not let anyone else dictate the terms of

your play, unless you have discussed these terms in detail and fully agree to them. You should do this long before you enter the casino to play. Try not to gamble on the last leg of a journey.

3. Never play with "scared money." Realize that you could lose. If you are winning and pressing your wagers, find your betting unit comfort level. When you are losing, reduce your bets. When you are winning, that is the time to press the situation. Develop the habit of quitting when you are ahead. Never go chasing a falling piano!

4. Keep a positive frame of mind. Never play when depressed, tired, sick, or under the influence of alcohol. For the majority of players, alcohol has no part in a successful session. Being calm and confident when you shoot is ideal, but being loose or too relaxed will kill your consistency. You may even adopt a false sense of confidence.

5. Do not let dealers or other players annoy you or distract you. If this is not possible, simply leave the table at the earliest time suitable. Being courteous and making dollar bets for the dealers may nullify any heat from the stick. Do not get caught up in the excitement of the game as the other players urge you on to make your point. Maintain focus until after your roll concludes. Clear your mind between shots.

6. Finally, do not let your guard down. Remain cool and calculated. Set your goals and stay focused on the mechanics of reaching them. Think about what you might do with the money you win. Develop tunnel vision at the tables. Some players go into a trance-like state when focusing and achieve a higher state of awareness when handling the dice. You will practice bringing up your power image and blocking out distractions.

Try to develop a sense of mental toughness. Play the table—nothing else matters. It's just you, the dice and the task to be completed. Focus on your form and show no emotion until after your roll concludes. Then take a break and let the adrenaline flow. Accept the accolades and high-fives from the other players, color up and walk away. After the session is over, review the good things that you did and write them down. Also, write down the things that you might have done differently. Target areas that need more work and formulate a plan. If you have a long layoff, be careful when you tiptoe back in. Certain aspects of your muscle memory may lapse. Immediately check the fundamentals. Review the basics and play with a partner who is familiar with your form and knows the game. Ask him or her to comment on your throws. If there is a problem, review your records or practice journals to see if you had a similar problem before and what you did to correct it. Once you get the mechanics back on line, work on re-establishing the mental edge.

Part Five

Wrapping It All Up

Chapter 14
Tales from Two Cities

With apologies to Charles Dickens, this chapter is not about London and Paris, and actually, it is two unrelated tales of dice play. The first one is based out east, in Atlantic City and the other, in that western oasis known as Las Vegas. We will relive the experiences of Donnie B. in A.C. during the monster roll he sported. Then we will move on to the trials of Sharpshooter as he works his way up and down the south Strip.

Donnie Does A.C.—Spring 2001

Donnie writes . . .

> On Saturday night, I enjoyed a great dinner with Long Arm, Robin F., and Bob C. and his lovely wife at the Oaks Restaurant. Our friends went back to their rooms for the evening, while Robin and I went back to Resorts to put in a few hours play before retiring. We did a casino sweep for a playable blackjack game, but the tables were

badly overcrowded. We then scouted roulette to
no avail. Robin suggested that the high roller pit
may be better, and worth a look. The minimum
was $200 and, there were quite a few empty
seats, with only one or two players at most of
the tables. There was one table that caught our
eye with a Japanese player sitting at first base
and three large stacks of black chips. We
observed about five hands and decided to buy
in for two units, ($400) and give it a shot. We
played for about a half hour, winning five units
(a cool $1,000 win). Little did we know that this
was just the beginning of a terrific casino session.

We walked back into the busy main floor only to
be jostled around by the crowd. Very frustrated,
we spotted a lone craps table along one wall that
was in a room by itself, with about six people
playing. We went to have a look, figuring that it
must be a high roller pit. It turned out to be a $10
minimum and we each bought in for $200. The
dice slowly moved around to stick left where we
were standing and I was the first to shoot. The
table was older, but nice and short, with manageable bounce. A few more people joined the
table as I began, and it quickly filled up. I set for
7s on the come-out and had an immediate hit.
The next roll produced a 6 as the point. I usually favor the 2-V Set, rather than going for the
point with the 3-V. I decided to stay with the 2-
V Set. I Placed the rest of the inside numbers and
for the first 20 minutes, I could not hit the
damned 6. All I could hit was the rest of the
inside numbers with lots of pressing going on.

Finally, the 6 came and I was rewarded with a round of applause. For the next 30 minutes, I was on a mission. I continued making point after point and the other players were ecstatic about the chips that were building up in their racks. Two girls, who were playing at the end of the table, were debating whether or not to catch their bus that was soon departing. They decided to make alternate travel arrangements. At one instance, after the completion of another successful point, a gentleman in the corner threw out a $25 chip to the dealer and said, "Bet for the shooter on Any Seven." Thanking him, I said I would give it a shot. He answered back, "It's your tip if you can do it." Setting 7s around for the next come-out, I arced the dice through the air, landing them for an 11. Yes a come-out win, but not the one he had hoped for. "Here's another quarter for you. I know you can do it," he replied. The dice arced once more, and bam, the 7 appeared! That gave me a $125 tip for which I thanked the gentleman, very much.

Robin was there all the time, encouraging me to stay focused by reminding me, as I picked up the dice, "fingers all the way down, deep breath, and focus." At this point, the crowd and the dealers (for whom we were making and winning bets) had gotten used to the idea, that in order for me to be totally focused, they would keep silent until after the throw. The stick man to my right even started to say to me, "fingers all the way down, deep breath, focus." At the one-hour mark, I had an audience of five bosses observing my rhythm roll. One of them started talking to me (I don't believe to distract me), but to compliment my controlled throw. Being careful not to lose my attention, I cut the conversation short and went back to work. In the three years that I have been playing craps, it is the first time that a craps table *had* to bring in chip refills. Most of the $5, $25, and $100 chips were now in the racks in front of the players. Finally, after an hour and 25 minutes, the inevitable happened. The 7 reared its ugly head. A great cheer and applause broke out and everyone was thanking me, and giving the thumbs up.

I looked at them, and feeling like a real hero, I said, "You know it doesn't have to end." A look of confusion came over their faces. "If everyone passes the dice," I explained, "I would give it one more try." They all eagerly agreed. As skill would have it, the second roll lasted another half hour—two rolls, for two hours! At one point, Robin started with a dollar on each of the hard ways and was able to press them up to $100 each. This time when the seven-out came, Robin and I colored up and left to get some sleep. We have no idea of the total amount taken from the table, but Robin and I had close to $7,000 in our pockets, starting off with very conservative betting units. One outstanding point I should mention is that with practice, the muscle memory for controlled throwing is just like riding a bike. Once you learn it, you never forget. I had played craps four times in the past four months and only slight adjustments were needed to zone in on my throw.

The best of luck to all my friends, and the new students in the program,

Donnie B. (a.k.a. 007)

Over the last four years, Don has enjoyed several dozen rolls in excess of 30 minutes, but as I take this tale to print, he did it again! Our friend has turned in another hour plus hand. This one, in the winter of 2002, at the Casino-rama, in Orillia, Ontario, lasted 70 minutes.

Diary of a Sharpshooter

I kept a detailed journal on a recent trip to Vegas, as I usually do. This particular trip was nothing special. It was far from being my best outing nor was it one of my worst. I thought this would be a realistic experience to share with the reader. I made some mistakes and I made some nice recoveries. I also kept a detailed log of Sharpshooter insights. The team wasn't with me on this one, so I had three full days to frolic on the Strip's south side as I saw fit.

November 25th

7:00 A.M. (EST)—I awoke to the alarm. Happy Thanksgiving! After a shower, shave, etc. I headed off to pick up my brother, Rich. We arrived at the International terminal at about 9:00 A.M. Check in went smoothly and so did the 3-1/2 hour flight. We arrived in Vegas at 1:30 P.M., uh, make that 10:30 A.M. Pacific Standard Time. The bags were forwarded over to Bally's, where we were staying. I spotted a driver holding a sign with my last name on it as we walked down "rental car row" in the main terminal. "We get a limo? . . . Cool!" my brother responded. "Stick with me, kid, and you'll do alright," I replied. A black limousine whisked us off to the hotel; so far, so good. My brother and I got to the VIP line for what was supposed to be a quick check in. I don't know what the delay was about, but finally, after close to an hour, one of our junket hosts flagged us aside and had us taken care of.

2:00 P.M. (PST)—We relaxed at the Sidewalk Café. I had matzo ball soup and a Rueben sandwich. My brother had a turkey club with a salad. After our satisfying dinner/lunch, we headed up to check out our room. "Where are we at?" Rich inquired as we approached the elevators. "Room 2222," I answered. "Think you can remember that one?" He just gave me a look. Up in the room, our bags were already waiting for us. He took the bed near the TV and I got the one by the bathroom. We unpacked and unwound for a half-hour. I set up my practice rig and began throwing the dice. Thirty tosses and only three 7s; I felt good. But then the dice starting popping on me a little and I threw three more 7s in the next six throws! After analyzing the situation, I came to the conclusion that for some reason my revolutions on the dice had shifted slightly. Instead of landing flat, the dice were more on edge and were a little too lively. I brought my thumb up a little higher on the grip to kill some of the backspin. That did the trick and I threw twelve more times with only one 7. I felt ready to take on the tables.

4:30 P.M.—We bellied up to a table. I had the dice and my favorite table position . . . stick left. I bought in for $300 and began betting $25 units, but after five attempts with the dice, I was almost even (maybe one or two units down). These tables were a little softer than my practice box and I hadn't quite turned the corner yet. Rich grew impatient and went off to the blackjack pit. I changed tables and got my position and the dice again. This time things looked better. I held the cubes for over 20 minutes. My $300 turned into $700! I had made four point passes and hit several inside numbers along the way. I liked the way the dice were reacting at that table. I decided to stay, hoping to get the dice back at some later time, with minimal damage to my bankroll. I Placed the 6 and 8 for $30 each. My plan was to take one hit for $35 and regress down to $18 each. At that point I would only have $1 at risk, but a quick seven-out took my 60 bucks. I tried again on the next shooter. Three throws later . . . you guessed it— "Seven-out, line away," the stick called out. All right, let's try the Don't side, but a quick 7 on the come-out claimed my quarter. Two hundred dollars later, I concluded I would leave the table with *some* profit. I walked around the pit, but all of the stick left positions were taken.

6:00 P.M.—I found my brother at a quarter blackjack table. It was a hand-held double-deck game. He seemed to be holding his own. I asked him, "How are the cards treating you?" which, translated means, "What's the count?" "Decent," he answered, meaning slightly positive. I put four green chips aside and sat down. "We're meeting a friend at 7:30," Rich said. "She's picking us up at the set of doors across from the Sports Book," he added. "Anyone I know?" I asked. "No, she's a boss at New York, New York," he answered. "A table boss?!" I inquired, sounding more interested. "Don't get any ideas. She's got the day off and doesn't want to talk shop, I'm sure," he affirmed. "Alright, what's on the agenda?" I asked. "Well, there's some performer at the Rio in the lounge," he said. "She says he puts on a hell-of-a show. We won't be disappointed."

7:25 P.M.—"Hey, we got to go!" Rich exclaimed, looking down at his watch. "Are you sure? I've got these guys right where I want them!" I replied with a grin. The dealer shook her head (I was up a whopping $25). We hit the cashier's cage and made a break for the Sports Book. After we hooked up with our friend, we headed west on Flamingo Road. It was a beautiful, clear night. I could see all the lights down the Strip. This is Vegas and I feel fine! As many times as I've been here, I still get excited! We parked the vehicle and walked inside the casino. The Rio's pretty nice. It's colorful, but not too overly done. It's a fun, festive environment. We reached the lounge, sat down and ordered a round. The performer's name was Nat Turner. I don't know if that was his real name, but either way I'm glad he was staging a show and not a revolt. He came on stage wearing a shiny double-breasted coat and pants, which looked more like expensive silk pajamas. This guy had the voice, the moves and the band to back him up. He had a unique style and could do no wrong.

The audience was eating out of his hands. By the end of the night he had us all singing Commodores, Earth-Wind and Fire, and Marvin Gaye tunes. We finally turned in at about 1:00 A.M. (4:00 A.M. EST time).

November 26th

8:00 A.M.—The alarm went off. I rubbed my eyes and looked around. "Yeah, that's right. I'm in Vegas," I thought. Rich was already in the shower. I turned on the TV and opened the drapes. I skipped breakfast and practice, opting for a shower and a quick cup of coffee. We went down and found an open craps table. I bought in for $500. I was not able to get anything going, but didn't feel bad about my throw. Three hundred dollars later we decided to hoof it over to the Bellagio. Messing around with $5 units on other shooters and waiting to get the dice, I dropped $200 before deciding to take a walk. I was down $285 for the trip now and was feeling a little frustrated. Then I saw an open table on the other side of the pit . . . I'm there! Ten dollars on the Pass Line and two fast 7s on the come-out. I looked at my watch. It was about 9:30 A.M. Everything looked good. The dice were coming out together, going through identical motions, landing and stopping with minimal bounce. I established a point of 5, pressed up my odds and came right back with a 3-2 combo, making the point.

Somewhere along the way, the table filled up with excited players, but I hadn't noticed. At one point I remember hearing the boxman say to me, "Sir, you're making a believer out of me." Unfazed, I kept on with my routine; first the set, then the carefully balanced grip and then the soft delivery. Finally, because there were so many line bets at the other end of the table, the inevitable happened. One die hit an odds bet and turned off to the side. The 7 appeared and ended the party. I was brought out of my trance by a rousing round of applause. I looked down at the racks in front of me. They were filled with barber poles of red and green chips. I glanced at my watch . . . 10:12 A.M.! A 40- to 45-minute roll! I quickly took inventory . . . 65 units net! I wish I had pressed up a little more aggressively, but oh well, I'll take it.

"I must have made a dozen passes," I said as I pushed the stacks of red and green forward to be colored up. "You made ten points," the boss said, not sounding too enthusiastic. I picked up my purple and several blacks, placed a red chip on the line for the boys and started towards the cashier's counter. I saw Rich. "Where were you man? I just had a dinosaur roll!" showing off my assortment of colors. "Yeah," he said, sounding disappointed. "By the time I realized what was going on, it was too late. That table was so packed you couldn't fit a knife blade in there," he lamented. "Well, I probably had the roll of the weekend and was only betting $10 units," I said, sounding a little disappointed myself. By the time I sevened out, I had only pressed up to single green units. Usually, that is where I start.

10:35 A.M.—My adrenaline was still flowing so we took a walk. Heading over to New York, New York, we looked for a place to eat. Everything was crowded. We finally found a restaurant upstairs by the arcade. There weren't as many people so we bought some pizza slices and grabbed an open table. My nerves were back to normal and so was my blood sugar. At 12:45 we headed down to hit the tables. Without saying a word, Rich bee-lined for the blackjack pit and I for craps. Some of the tables at N.Y., N.Y. are too long. I avoided those. All of the tables at this casino have a hard layout bed. You can hear the dice clank as they touch down. All in all, a marginal casino for craps at best. I treaded lightly, picking up nine $5 units. I was up about $425 for the trip now. A slow start, but not to panic. We walked over to the MGM. Rich and I strolled through the entire casino to get to the monorail located near the main lobby. By the time we got back to Bally's, it was after 2:15 P.M. I went up to relax and jot down some notes for my journal.

3:35 P.M.—I was on my own for the next few hours so I went down to the Sports Book to catch my hockey team, the Red Wings. On the way over, though, I stopped to talk with Mark W., my casino host. "I don't see any problem with us picking up any expenses," he said. "You've got more than four hours a day in with slightly more than $100 average bet. Don't worry about anything. We'll take care of it," he assured me. "I just wanted to check on things, that's great," I replied. Ten minutes later, I was relaxing with my friend "Sam Adams" and watched as the Wings beat the Oilers, 4 to 2.

7:05 P.M.—Time for a bite to eat, and a then a hand or two at the dice tables. Playing with $25 units, I dribbled my way up another six or seven units, sporting one 12-minute roll and one 15-minute roll in the mix. I called it a day. Heading up to my room, number 2222, I discovered Rich there, lounging back. "Hey, you up for a pay-for-view?" I asked. "Yeah, how about *Phantom Menace*?" he posed. "Sounds good," I replied. This movie is a prequel to the *Star Wars* trilogy. Three hours later, we turned in. "$600 net . . . not a bad day for this Jedi knight," I thought as I drifted off to sleep.

November 27th

7:40 A.M.—Up before the alarm and first in the shower today. No practice, I went straight down for a quick coffee and bran muffin. On my way over to the craps pit, I ran into Rich. "Come on and play a few rounds with me," he encouraged. "Alright," I said. We sat down at a quarter table. I tossed over a C-note and received four green chips. That was all I was prepared to risk. Sitting at first base, I put $25 out in the betting circle. A 9 and an 8, I'll stand. Dealer has an 18 . . . darn! Five hands later, I was one and four with one tie. "This looks like my last hand Rich," I said pushing my last quarter out. I was right. The dealer pulled a five-card 21 to beat my pair of paints. "Hey, I'll be over at the craps tables. This is silly," I replied.

8:55 A.M.—I strolled right up to the first craps table I came upon thinking, "I can't do any worse than that blackjack game." Boy, was I wrong!?! Buying in for $500, I put $25 on the Pass Line. I picked up the dice and threw a hard 4. I quickly dropped $110 for the inside numbers and took $50 in odds. The next number thrown was a 10. "Damn, the only number I don't have," I thought. Next was a 3. I made some adjustments. Now I hit a 6. Before the dealer could pay me my $35, I threw down a $1 chip and instructed him to press both my 6 and 8 from $30 up to $48 each. I picked up the dice and let 'em go. "Seven-out, line away . . ." the stick called out. "A minor snafu," I thought. "I'm gonna come right back at these guys!" Another quick seven-out and I realized that I needed another table . . . and another $500 buy in! Well, so I thought, but the dice weren't even coming out of my hand together. They were totally out of sync. But I was determined to get my money back! "I want my $500 back! Yeah, and I want that lousy $100 I blew at blackjack as well!!" Now I was steaming. I threw down another $500 and set out to make my killing. I'll spare you the gory details, but it was me who got killed. The second buy in didn't even last as long as the first one. "You idiot! What did you just do?" I berated myself. "It takes all day to earn that kind money and you shot $1,100 in 30 minutes," I huffed as I bolted for the elevators. "I wish I had slept in!"

10:00 A.M.—Kicking off my shoes, I decided to forget about gambling for a while. I flipped on the TV. Indiana Jones was looking for the lost ark. A while later, the phone rang. It was my business partner back home. A big break in a business deal that we were working on had developed. Great news! After concluding the phone call, I noticed that my negative mindset disappeared altogether. I grabbed a pen and paper and started analyzing what happened earlier. "Let's see, no practice. Then after losing a quick $100 at blackjack I was in the wrong frame of mind. I bolted for the craps tables and hastily started betting full $25 units," I thought. "I was cold. The dice weren't landing together or tumbling together. Hell, they weren't even coming off my hand together!" Who was I kidding? I was chasing a falling piano. "I can get through this. I'll map out a strategy, keep my wits about me and work my way back." My attitude changed. I went down and ate a healthy-sized brunch. Then I came back up to the room for some serious practice. I had a great session in the practice rig and felt confident and calm.

1:05 P.M.—The craps pit was buzzing. All of the tables were full. All, but one. My position was available. Only two other people were playing. The dice were coming my way, so I put a quarter on the Pass Line. "Sir, this is a hundred dollar table," the stickman informed me. "A black table . . . well it was now or never," I thought. "Oh, no problem," I answered, quickly substituting a black for my green chip. I carefully set and threw them. Boy, they looked good. Both dice were going through identical motions, side by side. Seven was the come-out call, $100 up. The dice felt really good on the release . . . point of 6. I had $100 on the line with $100 odds and $120 placed on the 8. Next throw, an 8! +$140. "We're on our way," I thought. Next I threw a 5, a 10, and a 12. I made a slight adjustment and threw a hard 6 for the point! That's another $220. I shot an ace-deuce on the come out, but came right back with a 7 on the next roll. Eight was my next point. I had $100 with single odds and moved my $120 Place bet to the 6. Taking my time, I hit a 9, then back-to-back 4s. Feeling I was honing in on the 8, I put $5 up for the crew on the hard 8. Next throw was an 11. Then a minor set change and "Eight the call. It came hard. Pay the line and take the Don'ts," the stick yelled out. "Fifty and down for the boys." Then he turned to me adding "Thank you for that hard 8 sir!" Another $220 for me!

Coming out again I established the 8. With single odds and the 6 Placed, I threw $5 out and announced "The boys need a hard 8." "Sir, why don't you ride along with us this time?" the stick suggested. "Yeah, okay," I said tossing over another nickel. "He knows how to make this one," the stick barked to the rest of the table. I set and tossed the dice . . . a 5. That's an inside number, but I was too stingy to pick up the 5 and 9 for a hundred each. Next call was a 6, another $140! Then came a 5, a 10, and an 11. With 4-4 set on top, I picked them up and sent them on their way . . . hard 8 the call! That was $50 more for the crew and $220 plus $45 for me! Now the dealers were getting into the game. I put $5 on the line for the boys. The stick was leaning back, making sure to stay out of my way. "You look like you know what you're doing. Take your time, we got all day," he encouraged me. "Wow," I thought. "Usually these guys are giving me the business right about now! And this guy is telling me to take my time!" I carefully set and threw the dice . . . a 6. "I can shoot this," I proclaimed. I took $125 odds behind my Pass Line bet and dropped two nickels, announcing, "The boys got a pair of shoes." The dealers gave a nod of approval. I opted not to bet the hard 6 this time. First, I threw a 5, and then a 6! I don't remember if it was hard or not.

The next come-out roll produced a 9. I decided to pull back my $120 eight and just go with Pass Line and single odds. The next call was a hard 8. "Damn, I just took it down," I said, pointing to the Place bet. "Yeah, but your hard 8 from before was working," offered the stickman. "That's right. I forgot about that!" I replied. I pulled the $5 bet down and took the $45 winnings to press my odds bet up to $150. As I let the next throw come off, I felt one die stick just a little. "Oh no! Give me a good bounce." I thought, but like all good things must do . . . it was a 7. This time *the crew* gave me a round of applause. It was 28 throws and 35 minutes later. I had been betting like a Scrooge; never more than 1-1/2 times odds and essentially covering only the 6 and 8. That's alright, I still cleared over $1,100. Almost the exact amount I had lost earlier!

As I began to push my chips forward to be colored up, an Asian man at the other end piped up, "You stay! We give dice back to you!" The others agreed with him, but I felt too excited. My focus had been drained. I promised them I'd come back soon, but I went up to the room to catch a little CNN and a light nap.

4:00 P.M.—I awoke from my nap, had a little more practice up in the room, then I went down for an early dinner.

5:20 P.M.—After a quick sandwich at the Sidewalk Café, I walked over to the craps pit. I noticed that the same table from before was empty. I walked over thinking, "I don't know if I want to play $100 units right now." As I approached, I noticed that a yellow placard was in place and a different crew was there. It was only a $10 table. "What happened to everyone?" I inquired of the stick. "Table was running a little cold," he answered. "Well, maybe I can warm it up," I replied as I threw down $100. Adding "$10 on the Pass Line." The dice were offered to me. In my first attempt, I established and made a 5 and a few numbers before I sevened out. I looked down at my rack. No harm done, I was up $5.

The second try was much better. Two come-out 7s, then a 6. A few numbers later I popped the 6. The next come-out roll, I set 7s all around and gently tossed them. The dice landed and turned together. It looked like a 4-3 but the right die just turned off the 3 and ended up with the 5 on top, so the point was a 9. I hit and collected on three inside numbers. Because I always set the dice a certain way and I watch how they react, I noticed that the last few throws resulted in the left top face and the right front face of what I was presetting. This is what happened on the last come-out roll also. I threw $2 out toward the boxman and announced "6-3 hopping for the boys." Using "Set Transposition," I set the hard 6 on top (3-3) with a 2-6 on the front. The dice came off nice and landed together. The right die turned over an extra face and the result was a 3 and a 6! I hit a 17-to-1 long shot (only pays 15-to-1) for the crew and made my point.

The next come-out produced a 6. I threw a buck out on the hard 6 for the boys. I was making slight adjustments in my grip and a few throws later . . . bam! A hard 6! I was up to $25 units now. The next throw was a 7 for the come-out, then an 8 for the point. The next numbers were a 5, a 9, and then a 6. I turned the set over, cast them off and the 8 appeared! Another supervisor was watching me from the left side but they gave me no heat. I had the boys on the Pass Line. The next come-out was a 5. I dropped four-times odds behind my bet and gave the boys "a pair of shoes" as well. After a half dozen throws, the 5 finally came! The stickman was celebrating and the other dealers were having fun, too. The next point was an 8. I threw about three more numbers, but alas, my roll came to an end. I looked down at my watch. Not quite a half-hour roll. My $100 buy-in looked like $540. I was up somewhere between a grand and eleven hundred for the trip.

6:30 P.M.—Rich waved me over from a blackjack table. "Are you doing anything here?" I asked. "No, not really," he replied. "Let's take a walk and get some air," I suggested. "Sure," he said while pushing his chips forward to be colored. "Let's take a look over at the Flamingo," he offered. I nodded in agreement. After we crossed the street, I looked over in the direction of the Maxim, but it was dark. I had some good memories there. "Wow, I can't believe the Maxim is closed down. I wonder what's going to happen to it," I pondered. "Come on, let's go," Rich countered. So we headed up toward the strip. As we were walking along the Barbary Coast, a cacophony of sirens was drawing closer. A yellow hook and ladder was barreling west down the eastbound side of Flamingo Road. A second "big boy" was a couple of hundred yards behind him, riding the same path he had blazed. After that, a squad car and a rescue unit were in close pursuit. The convoy turned left on Las Vegas Boulevard in the direction of the Luxor. It was dark out, but I couldn't see any flames as I glanced down the south end of the Strip. The trucks were out of view now.

7:25 P.M.—We walked into the Flamingo and headed for the back of the casino floor, past all the slots. We looked around for a while, spotted an empty $25 double deck game. As we sat down, they brought in new cards. "Oh, no, you know how I feel about new cards," I said looking at Rich.

"You get a pair of Aces, split 'em, and draw two 2s. I'm out of here. Don't be surprised . . . " He cut me off, "Yeah, yeah, we'll see." First she fanned the cards out. Yep, they were all there. Then she flipped them over in one sweeping motion and swirled them with both hands. She broke them down into four half-decks, performed a couple of quick faro shuffles, one more break down, and a quick shuffle. That was it. "I can't watch. I'm going to walk around," I said. "See you around," he replied.

All of the craps tables were packed full. These tables are bowling alleys, 14 footers at least. Every once in a while a collective cheer would be heard at one of the tables. I passed by one as the shooter made his point. The cheer went up and startled me. Gamblers with beers in one hand and cigarettes in the other were trying to high-five each other. Beer was dripping and ashes were flying. I chuckled and kept walking. After the craps area there were a couple of roulette tables. I bought in for a stack of singles. The dealer was hitting a lot of second dozen numbers so I only bet on a handful of numbers at a time between 13 and 24. Three spins later, I needed another stack. I tossed down another twenty. The next throw . . . in and out of my 15. "Are these wheels gaffed?" I asked myself. "I sincerely doubt it," I answered my own query. "Not for a few five or ten dollar bets!" Another ten dollars later I decided that was all I was going to donate. I looked over in the direction of the blackjack tables, but I didn't see Rich. As I turned to walk around the roulette table, there was Rich. "Did you do any damage?" he asked. "No, I toasted half a buck here at roulette." I answered. "Oh is that all?" he came back. "Come on little brother, let's head back," I said.

9:50 P.M.—We made it back to Bally's. Saturday night —everything was packed and noisy. Great conditions for camaraderie, but not ideal for advantage players. We went up to the room and packed most of our things for the morning checkout. "You want to head back down?" I asked him. "No, I'm done for now," he answered. I flipped on the TV and we watched a little Commando with "Ah-nold" (the big man).

11:00 P.M.—Lights out, we called it a day. The lights from the new Paris casino were filtering through the crack in the drapes. I drifted off to sleep.

November 28th

8:20 A.M.—I woke up feeling well rested. Rich had beaten me into the shower again. I jotted down some notes for my journal and then showered. We finished packing and grabbed some breakfast. We checked out at 10:15 A.M. Bally's picked up all the room, food, and beverage charges. It looked like we had an hour to kill. A transport bus was to pick us up at 11:15 A.M. I wandered over to the craps pit and found an empty table in back, near the cashier's cage. I usually don't do well on the last leg of a gambling junket, so I rationed off one C-note for the final go around. I threw my $100 down on the table and was offered five dice. I came out with a 4, took double odds and Placed the inside numbers. Six was the call. I pressed up both the 6 and 8. Next throw was a 9. This time I pressed up the 5 and 9. The dice felt a little unstable. They had a smooth polished finish (which was nothing unusual) with some patches of perspiration. I felt one die slip slightly as I released them . . . an ace-deuce appeared. I wiped my hand on the table layout and took a little more time with my grip. I carefully lined up my targeted landing area just in front of the Pass Line and let them go. Again, one die came out with a wobble. I watched in dismay as it landed on its corner (instead of flat) and spun off to the side. The result was a 6-1. My roll had met with an untimely demise.

10:50 A.M.—Rich and I grabbed a cup of coffee and relaxed for a few minutes near the video poker machines. The transport would be by soon to take us to the airport for our 11:15 AM. flight. Which was really 2:15 P.M. our time. A pit boss stopped by on his way to a break. Knowing I liked to play at empty craps tables, he said "Hey there's two empty tables just waiting for you and your brother." I smiled and answered, "No, we got a flight to catch in a few minutes." He responded, "Well, I hope you had fun, then, and we'll see you again soon." I nodded, "Yeah, we had a great time."

I pulled out my pad to write down a few final comments. I was up for the trip $900 plus some change. With the exception of Saturday morning's meltdown, things went according to plan. Using my well-practiced throw and employing an average $25 unit size, I usually expect to clear about $500 per day. That would be a total of about $1,500 for this trip. I should have known after blowing the first two or three hundred dollars Saturday morning that it was time to stop. I could have skated with a nice $1,600 or $1,700 win. Well, it wasn't a bad trip. That $900 will buy a lot of Christmas gifts. Besides, I'll be back soon enough and . . . oh, hey the transport is here!

Chapter 15

Crap Stats and Calculations

Our game is grounded in rigid body mechanics. The math works in conjunction with the physical phenomenon to describe and measure what is happening. Blackjack and baccarat are games of mathematics. As cards are removed from play, the mathematical edge will sway back and forth like a pendulum. In games where the *motion* of a little white ball or a pair of three-quarter inch cubes determines the outcome of that independent trial, you have to look at the rudimentary physics involved. Once you realize that this is a dynamics problem first, then the math *does* fall into place. For random shooters, a frequency histogram averaged over tens of thousands of throws would converge to look like this:

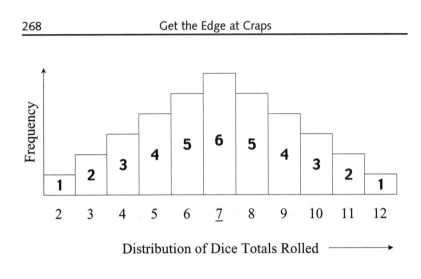

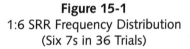

Distribution of Dice Totals Rolled ⟶

Figure 15-1
1:6 SRR Frequency Distribution
(Six 7s in 36 Trials)

For every 36 tosses, on average six 7s would occur, five 6s or 8s, four 5s or 9s, etc. This is about as far as the mathematical experts of the game will take it. Our comprehensive method of dice play can create a mathematical advantage over casino craps by altering the physical phenomena. That advantage is based on the controlled thrower's skill level in avoiding the seven-out after the point has been established. As we discussed in Chapter 8, the advantage can be measured and calculated for each shooter. It is unique and based on the *Sevens-to-Rolls Ratio (or SRR) for a shooter wishing to avoid* the 7. This is simply an average number of tosses it takes for one 7 to appear. For the above histogram (random) the SRR is 1:6, or for every six rolls on average, one will be a 7. In practice, the SRR can be calculated by simply dividing your total rolls by the frequency of 7s that occurred in those rolls. It can also be very useful to calculate your SRR for your casino sessions, but to do this, you should work with a partner who can record the data for you during your rolls with the dice.

Because there are two distinctly different directives in the game of craps, we need two SRRs. On the come-out roll, we set and shoot for the 7. Hopefully this SRR is less than 1:6 producing a higher frequency of 7s. During the point cycle, where we try to elude the sinister 7, we have an SRR that is greater than 1:6 for a lower 7s frequency. This second SRR is the chief SRR that we are interested in as Pass Line players. Remember not to include your come-out rolls when calculating this SRR value, unless you are setting against the 7 during this time. This may be the case if you have Come bets working. For a well-practiced precision shooter this SRR may be as high as 1:8. My personal SRR has seemed to plateau around 7.8 to 7.9 for the past year. Let's look at the frequency histogram, in Figure 15-2, for a shooter with an SRR of 1:7. For every 35 tosses, five 7s will occur (1:7). The remaining 30 throws have been normalized to pick up the slack.

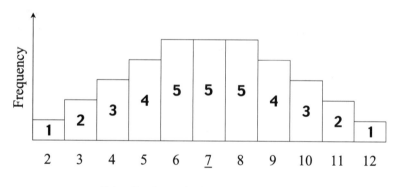

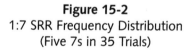

Figure 15-2
1:7 SRR Frequency Distribution
(Five 7s in 35 Trials)

Some interesting things happen here. One thing worth noticing is the frequency of 6s or 8s is now equal to the number of 7s occurring. That means we would actually have an even chance of hitting a 6 or 8 Place bet even though it pays 7 to 6. The advantage for a one in seven SRR shooter, placing the 6 or 8 can be easily calculated as follows:

(Actual payoff – Correct payoff) x probability x 100% = Percent edge

The actual payoff is 7 to 6. The fair or correct payoff should be 5 to 5 or even money, because the frequency of 6s and 8s now equals the frequency of 7s. This is due to our level of skill (1:7 SRR). The probability of hitting our 6 or 8 before the 7 is 5 in 10, or exactly one-half. The percent advantage for an SRR of 7 shooter, placing the 6 or 8 is thusly calculated:

(7/6 – 5/5) x 5/10 x 100% = +8.333% player's edge

Essentially, seven-sixths minus one equals one-sixth, divided by two then equals one-twelfth. This is our edge. Chris Pawlicki has calculated the controlled shooter's advantage for most bets when considering different SRR levels. Many of these calculations are included in the following appendices:

Appendix A: Pass Line (and Come bets) with Odds for Various SRRs
Appendix B: Crap Stats for Sharpshooter's Don't
Appendix C: Break-even and Advantage Calculations for the Place bets
Appendix D: Advantage Calculations for Hard Way bets
Appendix E: Advantage Calculations for Crapless Craps

If you are so inclined, you can use the sample calculations to plug and check out your own advantage, based on your SRR. If not, you can use the tables with various SRRs to look up your advantage. Just select the SRR closest to yours and determine your advantage for that particular wager. Also, you can use your SRR to estimate your advantage for all Place and Hard Way bets by using the graphs provided. Simply follow a straight line up from your SRR (marked on the horizontal axis) until it intersects the curve. Next, make a turn, following a straight line from the curve across to the vertical axis at the left to read off your advantage. It is not necessary to be concerned with your exact advantage. This will vary in the short term. There will be times when you can do no wrong and other times when you are struggling. However, a good understanding of where you are is helpful. These calculations are included to give you an idea of where you stand over the long haul and to give you confidence in your skills and ability. You can use the tables and calculations to select your own betting tactic from Chapter 9 or perhaps tailor one of your own tactics. The betting tactics discussed in Chapter 9 are keyed in to the SRR. The advantages calculated in the appendices are expressed as percentages. A simple explanation of a 10 percent shooter advantage is: out of every 100 units bet, the controlled shooter will win 55 and lose 45 units; (55 – 45) divided by the total units wagered equals 10 divided by 100, which is 10 percent.

The Normal Distribution

Once you have mastered a controlled delivery and can demonstrate a higher than random SRR, you will want to know what it is and have a high level of confidence in it. To properly verify your Sevens-to-Rolls Ratio you must observe your throw for an appropriate length of time and record the results. These results will make up your *sample space*. The larger the number of samples, *n*, that you have obtained, the more confident you are that your results are due to skill, not luck. You can gain confidence by employing some elementary statistics. Now is a good time to discuss something called the *normal curve*. The normal distribution, the bounded area under the normal curve and above the horizontal axis, describes countless sets of data in nature, industry and research. It can be used to describe a series of outcomes one would observe from a random game of craps if our sample size were large enough. The normal curve is shown in Figure 15-3. We will compare our observed data with the area under the normal curve to see if it is random or physically altered, and to what extent. The normal distribution is a *continuous* probability distribution, and the outcomes from a series of dice tosses are actually a *discrete* binomial distribution. We can, however, very accurately approximate a discrete binomial distribution with a continuous normal distribution if n (the number of recorded trials) is very large and p (the probability of an event's success) is *not* extremely close to either zero or one (0 percent or 100 percent).

If p is reasonably close to 0.50 (which is ideal), then n need not be as large to develop confidence in our throw. At 30 ways to throw a non-seven in 36 outcomes, the probability, or p of throwing a non-seven is simply 30 divided 36, or 5/6. The events described as throwing a 7, or throwing a non-seven cannot happen concurrently. They are mutually exclusive events, whose probabilities of occurring add up to 1.00, or 100 percent. Because the chances of throwing a 7 are mutually exclusive to throwing a non-seven, the chances of throwing a 7 are then 1 – 5/6, or 1/6. Another way to look at it is six ways in 36 to throw a 7 equals 1/6. Our probability for throwing the 7 is 16.67 percent, which is one-third away from 0 and two-thirds away from 50 percent. This is reasonable, but will still require several thousand recorded throws to validate. You know that p represents the probability that a particular event will occur. You also know that n represents the number of trials in our sample space. You now know that we will need to compare our observed sample data with the area or distribution of random data under a normal curve, sometimes referred to as a *bell-shaped curve*. If we are setting against the 7 and our frequency of hitting it is lower than expected for a random shooter over a significant number of trials, then indeed, we have the ability to influence the outcome.

The Mean

The *mean* or expected value of a randomly based distribution is of special importance. It not only describes the expected average of occurrence, but it also defines where the normal probability distribution is centered. For example, if we looked at the expected frequency of 7s occurring over 360 throws, we would expect 60 occurrences, or one hit every six tosses. Sixty is the expected average or mean, for the number of 7s resulting for a random shooter over 360 throws. Our bell-shaped curve will find its vertical axis of symmetry centered at our calculated mean of 60. The recorded number of 7s will probably be a little higher or lower for a random shooter with such a small number of trials, but its average will begin to converge on the expected average of one in six as you collect more and more data. For a random thrower, the chances that we will be proportionally closer to the expected mean after 3,600 throws is far greater than it would be for just 360 tosses. The same fact holds true when comparing 36,000 tosses to just 3,600 throws.

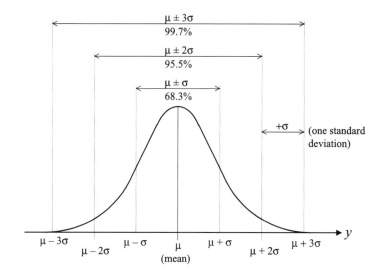

Figure 15-3

Chances are also good that we may never "land" on the exact mean or expected average, but we will get proportionally closer to this average as we record more throws—that is, unless the shooter truly is able to influence the dice. Then we will converge on some other average that reflects the shooter's level of skill. The trick is to determine whether we have created a new mean, based on a bona fide ability to do so, or just have not yet converged on the random average yet. If it appears that we are beginning to converge on an altered average for our recorded data, we will need some level of confidence to know that the dice are truly being influenced and it is not just some statistical fluctuation. We will need to calculate how much our data deviates from the random mean. This can be done by measuring the standard deviation, symbolized by "σ."

Standard Deviation

Standard deviations measure how far we are from the random, or expected mean, and what are the chances that our data is based solely on luck versus a genuine ability. One standard deviation is calculated as follows: $\sigma = \sqrt{npq}$, where the standard deviation is equal to the square root of the number of throws n times the random probability p of avoiding the 7 times the random probability, q of tossing a 7 (which is $1 - p$). The probability of avoiding the 7 is 5/6, while the probability of hitting it is 1/6. If we happened to record 4,680 throws, which would be 39 completed practice forms of 120 throws each, $\sigma = \sqrt{(4{,}680 \times 5/6 \times 1/6)}$ or simply the $\sqrt{(650)}$, which is 25.50. Our expected average for throwing a 7 is 4,680 divided by 6, or 780. Hence, our expected mean or average number of 7s is 780 for 4,680 rolls. For any normal distribution, 68.26 percent of the data under the curve is contained between the mean -1σ up to the mean $+1\sigma$ range. That would indicate that if we arbitrarily recorded 4,680 random rolls at the craps table, 780 – 26, or 754 up to 806 (780 + 26) of those rolls would result in a 7, 68.26 percent of the time. One hundred percent – 68.26 percent = 31.74 percent. Half of that, or 15.87 percent of the data, would be in the 806 or higher range, while the other 15.87 percent would be in the 754 or lower range. It is the lower frequency of 7s (754 or lower) that we are interested in.

If we threw only 754 sevens in 4,680 rolls, then there would be a 68.26 + 15.87, or 84.13 percent chance that this is due to ability and not luck. Our Sevens-to-Rolls Ratio would be 4,680 divided by 754, or 6.21. For our example, 780 is the mean and 25.5 is our standard deviation. If we desire a much greater factor of confidence, we can look at three standard deviations below the mean. For our example with 4,680 throws while trying to avoid the 7, we would need to be 3 x 25.5, or about 77 occurrences below the average of 780. The area under the curve between 780 – 77 and 780 + 77 (mean – 3σ and mean + 3σ) represents 99.73 percent of the total data. Again, we are only interested in the lower frequency of 7s (703 or lower). If we can throw only 703 or lower 7s in 4,680 throws, then there is a 99.73 + 0.135, or 99.865 percent chance that this average is due to skill. Our SRR for 4,680 throws with 703, 7s is 1:6.65. Let's assume that after 4,680 rolls, we could not secure an SRR of 6.65, giving us a 99.87 percent rate of confidence, so we record another 1,800 throws. For 6,480 total throws (57 practice sheets), the average number of 7s would be 6,480/6 or 1,080. $\sigma = \sqrt{(6{,}480 \times 5/6 \times 1/6)}$ which is $\sqrt{(900)}$ or simply 30. If your recorded number of 7s is equal to or lower than 1080 – (3 x 30) or 990, then you are three standard deviations under the mean and have a 99.865 percent confidence ranking. Your SRR would then be 6,480/990, which is 6.55.

If your SRR is lower than this, you will need to record even more trials. If you are content with two standard deviations (97.73 percent confidence), then you will need to average 1,080 – (2 x 30) or 1,020 sevens thrown in 6,480 total rolls. Your Sevens-to-Rolls Ratio would be 6,480/1,020 or 6.35. To complete the exercise, one standard deviation below the average (at an 84.13 percent ranking) would be 1,080 – 30 = 1,050 sevens thrown in 6,480 rolls. You are throwing with an SRR of 6.17 at a confidence factor of a little more 84 percent for one "σ" under average. Chances are, if our number of 7s is only one standard deviation under the mean, we will want to collect more data. Our lower frequency of 7s may be due to ability (84.13 percent confidence), but we will probably want at least two standard deviations to be more certain. Start off by recording at least 3,600 throws, then look for two standard deviations. One standard deviation would be $\sqrt{(3,600 \times 5/6 \times 1/6)}$ or about 22.4. Two standard deviations would be about 45. Our expected average is 600 sevens in 3,600 rolls. If you can roll 555 or fewer 7s in 3,600 tosses, then you will have a 97.73 percent or higher chance of possessing an SRR of 1: 6.49. If you cannot secure two standard deviations, then your SRR may be lower and require more throws to confirm. Record another 1,080 rolls and use the 4,680 model above to check your results. You can also check back with the chart in Chapter 8 to determine how many trials it takes to confirm different SRRs. Of course this all assumes that you have a well-developed delivery and can influence the dice's range of motion to begin with.

Appendix A
Pass Line with Odds for Various SRRs

First, I will take you through the calculations for a random, or 1:6 SRR game so you can see where these figures come from. These numbers, calculated for a random game, match up with the percent edges published in most craps books. The calculation summaries for a random game with various odds are included below in Table A-1. The mathematical model I use here contains 990 total rolls. That is because I economized on rolls by combining the mating points, the come-out craps numbers and the come-out naturals. Technically speaking, the number of point wins with zero odds when the point is 4, for example, is 27.5, but because the 4 and 10 function the same way, we are lumping 4 and 10 together at 55 wins. One-third of the 990 total rolls (330) will be come-out rolls. Of those rolls, 110 are come-out losers and 220 are natural winners. Two-thirds of 990 rolls (660) will establish points. The 4 or 10 will be established 25 percent of the time, or 0.25 x 660 rolls = 165 rolls. For a random game, two 7s will be thrown for each 4 or 10. That means one-third of 165, or 55 will be point repeats (wins) and two-thirds, or 110 rolls will produce seven-outs (losers) when the point is a 4 or 10. The 5 or 9 will be the point 33.33 percent of the time, so 220 rolls will establish a 5 or 9. Of those 220 rolls, 40 percent (88 rolls) will be winners and 60 percent (132 rolls) will be losers. This is because there are four ways to make a 5 or 9 (whichever is the point) versus six ways to a 7 in a random game.

Table A-1
Pass Line Player Advantages—SRR 1:6

Odds Amt.	Dice Totals	Craps 2, 3, 12	Ntrls. 7, 11	Points Established 4, 10	5, 9	6, 8	Totals
0 x	Wins:	0	220	55	88	125	488
Odds	Loses:	110	0	110	132	150	502
	% Edge:	(488 – 502)/(990 + 0) =					–1.414%
1 x	Wins:	0	220	165	220	275	880
Odds	Loses:	110	0	220	264	300	894
	% Edge:	(880 – 894)/(990 + 660) =					–0.848%
2 x	Wins:	0	220	275	352	425	1,272
Odds	Loses:	110	0	330	396	450	1,286
	% Edge:	(1,272 – 1,286)/(990 + 1,320) =					–0.606%
3 x	Wins:	0	220	385	484	575	1,664
Odds	Loses:	110	0	440	528	600	1,678
	% Edge:	(1,664 – 1,678)/(990 + 1,980) =					–0.471%
5 x	Wins:	0	220	605	748	875	2,448
Odds	Loses:	110	0	660	792	900	2,462
	% Edge:	(2,448 – 2,462)/(990 + 3,300) =					–0.326%
10 x	Wins:	0	220	1,155	1,408	1,625	4,408
Odds	Loses:	110	0	1,210	1,452	1,650	4,422
	% Edge:	(4,408 – 4,422)/(990 + 6,600) =					–0.184%
100 x	Wins:	0	220	11,055	13,288	15,125	39,688
Odds	Loses:	110	0	11,110	13,332	15,150	39,702
	% Edge:	(39,688 – 39,702)/(990 + 66,000) =					–0.021%

The 6 or 8 can be established 5/12 times 660 point rolls, or 275 ways. 5/11 times 275 (125 rolls) represents point winners for the 6 or 8 and 6/11 times 660 (or 150 rolls) are seven-outs. When you tally up all the come-out and point wins and subtract away the come-out and point losses, you arrive at the player's net gain or loss in units. For this case with zero odds taken, that equates to 488 wins – 502 losses, for a net loss of 14 units. This figure divided by the total number of units wagered will reveal the percent edge when making that bet. For a random game with no odds taken, we have 14 units lost over 990 units wagered (one unit for each of 990 rolls). This is where the –1.414 percent edge comes from that you read about. When you take odds behind your Pass Line wager, the net loss is still 14 units; however, you are losing this same amount with much more action or total money wagered. For example, at single odds, you are placing one more unit at risk when a point is established. That means you will have one unit out already for 990 rolls, but for 660 of those rolls, you will have an additional unit out for single odds. This creates a total of 1,650 units wagered. As a result, the denominator increases while the numerator remains constant. The percent edge gets watered down as more of the winnings are paid fairly. As additional odds are taken, the house edge is further diluted. It approaches zero, but never gets there when the game is random (SRR equals 6).

Now that you understand how the calculations are made and that they agree with the reported figures for a random game, let's look at what happens for a skilled shooter, throwing from the Pass Line. We will calculate our percent edges in the exact same manner. Table A-2 depicts Pass Line bets with various odds amounts for a shooter throwing randomly on the come-out, but then sporting a Sevens-to-Rolls Ratio of 1:7 when trying to avoid the 7 after the point has been established. The mathematical model I am working with will have 1,296 possibilities. I am again economizing by combining mating point numbers, craps and natural come-out numbers together in like groups. Otherwise, I would need to use

2,592 total rolls. For a random come-out roll, one-third (432 rolls) will present an instant winner or loser. Of those rolls, 144 are come-out losers and 288 are natural winners. Two-thirds of 1,296 (864) rolls will establish points. The 4 or 10 will be established 25 percent of these 864 rolls, which equates to 216 rolls. For a 1: 7 SRR game, five 7s will be thrown for three 4s or 10s. That means three-eighths of 216 (81) rolls will be point repeats (wins) and five-eighths or 135 rolls will produce 7s (losers) when the point is a 4 or 10.

The 5 or 9 will be set as the point 33.33 percent of the time on the random come-out roll, so 288 rolls will establish a 5 or 9. Of those 288 rolls, four-ninths (128 rolls) will be winners and five-ninths (160 rolls) will be losers. This is because there are four ways to make a 5 or 9 (whichever is the point) versus five ways to throw a 7 in a 1: 7 SRR game. The 6 or 8 can be established 5/12 times 1,296 point rolls, or 360 ways. 5/10 times 360 (180 rolls) represents point winners and 5/10 times 360 (also 180 rolls) are seven-outs. When you tally up all the wins and subtract away the loses, you arrive at the player's net gain in units. The net gain divided by the total number of units wagered will reveal the percent edge when making that bet. For an SRR of 7 with no odds taken, we have 58 units won over 1,296 units wagered. This is a +4.475 percent edge. As we add and take additional odds, this percent advantage leaps higher at first, but loses more momentum with each increasing odds amount.

Table A-2
Pass Line Player Advantages—SRR 1:7

Odds Amt.	Dice Totals	Craps 2, 3, 12	Ntrls 7, 11	Points Established 4, 10	5, 9	6, 8	Totals
0 x	Wins:	0	288	81	128	180	677
Odds	Loses:	144	0	135	160	180	619
	% Edge:	(677 – 619)/(1296 + 0) =					+4.475%
1 x	Wins:	0	288	243	320	396	1,247
Odds	Loses:	144	0	270	320	360	1,094
	% Edge:	(1,247 – 1,094)/(1,296 + 864) =					+7.083%
2 x	Wins:	0	288	405	512	612	1,817
Odds	Loses:	144	0	405	480	540	1,569
	% Edge:	(1,817 – 1,569)/(1,296 + 1,728) =					+8.201%
3 x	Wins:	0	288	567	704	828	2,387
Odds	Loses:	144	0	540	640	720	2,044
	% Edge:	(2,387 – 2,044)/(1,296 + 2,592) =					+8.822%
5 x	Wins:	0	288	891	1,088	1,260	3,527
Odds	Loses:	144	0	810	960	1,080	2,994
	% Edge:	(3,527 – 2,994)/(1,296 + 4,320) =					+9.491%
10 x	Wins:	0	288	1,701	2,048	2,340	6,377
Odds	Loses:	144	0	1,485	1,760	1,980	5,369
	% Edge:	(6,377 – 5,369)/(1,296 + 8,640) =					+10.145%
100 x	Wins:	0	288	16,281	19,328	21,780	57,677
Odds	Loses:	144	0	13,635	16,160	18,180	48,119
	% Edge:	(57,677 – 48,119)/(1,296 + 86,400) =					+10.899%

The following table is a consolidation of all the percent edges calculated for various Sevens-to-Rolls Ratios with different odds taken. Please keep in mind that the figures in Table A-3 assume a random come-out roll (SRR 1: 6) where a 7 or 11 is desired. The designated SRR reported will apply during the point cycle portion of the game where the shooter tries to avoid the sinister 7. For example, if a shooter throws an 11, then a 6, 5, 10, 3, 8, 5, 12, 9, 2, 4 and sevens-out, then his SRR for that roll will be 1:10. The 11 and 6 were thrown on the come-out rolls and do not count. The 5, 10 . . . 4, and 7 add up to ten rolls and were thrown when the shooter set against and tried to avoid the 7. One of these ten point cycle throws produced a 7. To gain a high level of confidence in your SRR, you will need to record many rolls. After you have perfected your throw and have recorded a few thousand rolls to figure your Sevens-to-Rolls Ratio, you can use this table as a reference guide. Most of you will have SRRs between 6 and 7, so I have included a column with 6.5 to give you a more accurate idea of where you stand.

Table A-3
Pass Line Advantages—for Various SRRs

Pass Line Odds			SRR Skill Level				
	1: 6	1: 6.5	1: 7	1: 8	1: 9	1: 10	1: 11
0 x Odds	−1.414%	1.646%	4.475%	9.540%	13.944%	17.810%	21.230%
1 x Odds	−0.848%	3.271%	7.083%	13.913%	19.857%	25.078%	29.702%
2 x Odds	−0.606%	3.968%	8.201%	15.787%	22.390%	28.193%	33.333%
3 x Odds	−0.471%	4.355%	8.822%	16.828%	23.798%	29.924%	35.351%
5 x Odds	−0.326%	4.772%	9.491%	17.949%	25.314%	31.788%	37.523%
10 x Odds	−0.184%	5.180%	10.145%	19.045%	26.797%	33.611%	39.648%
100 x Odds	−0.021%	5.650%	10.899%	20.310%	28.507%	35.712%	42.098%

Most of my serious students are playing in the plus two to plus five percent range, but a seven to eight percent advantage is not out of the question for the most skilled and dedicated shooters.

Appendix B
Crap Stats for Sharpshooter's Don't

Here is a sample percent advantage calculation for the Don't system presented in Chapter 12. Because Craps is a dichotomy of two games—the come-out game and the point game—the objectives of both games are different. Hence, we will assume different Sevens-to-Roll Ratios for calculating our percent edge. On the come-out roll, where the Don't shooter attempts to avoid the 7 (and 11) we will assume an SRR of 1:7. We have worked hard to develop an ability to avoid the 7 during the point cycle as a Pass Line player. Now we will definitely need it here to help reduce the huge come-out deficient we face for the Don't side of the game. In addition, once the point is established, we will assume that our shooter can set and throw 7s at the higher frequency of 1:5. This is when the Don't shooter is actually trying to seven-out. For the come-out roll, here is what the normalized frequency distribution for an SRR of 1:7 looks like:

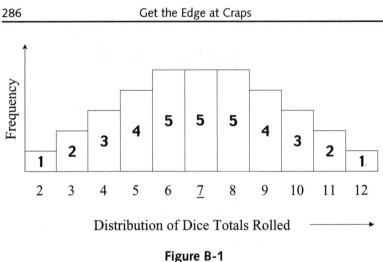

Figure B-1
1:7 SRR Frequency Distribution
(Five 7s in 35 Trials)

During the point roll, where we attempt to seven-out, we will use an SRR of 1:5 for our calculations. Figure B-2 shows how this normalized frequency distribution looks:

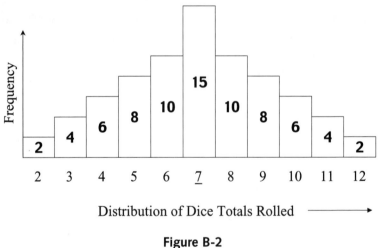

Figure B-2
1:5 SRR Frequency Distribution
(Fifteen 7s in 75 Trials)

Now that we have established our distributions, we can move on to our Don't Stats Table. Ordinarily 1,980 is the lowest common multiple used for a random game calculation. Because we are using a modified frequency distribution for both the come-out and point cycle, our population set will use 5,474 individual outcomes. This is the smallest total that will yield all whole number values for our Don't Stats Table. I did not combine groups of numbers like I did for the Pass Line calculations. First, we will look at the 1:7 SRR for the come-out. The come-out 12 will neither harm nor help us so we can bar the 12 as a no decision. As a result, we will see seven ways out of 34 possibilities to throw a natural pass, three ways to arrive at a craps decision and 24 ways to establish a point. This corresponds to 1,127 natural passes (losses for us), 483 craps (immediate winners) and 3,864 points established in 5,474 trials. The complete stats table follows:

Figure B-3
Don't Stats Table (Bar 12)

	Craps		Naturals		Points Established						Totals:
Dice Totals:	2	3	11	7	4	5	6	8	9	10	
Passes	0	0	322	805	138	224	322	322	224	138	2,495
Don't Pass:	161	322	0	0	345	420	483	483	420	345	2,979
Totals:	483		1,127		483	644	805	805	644	483	5,474
% Edge:	−11.76 on come-out				3.78	3.58	2.94	2.94	3.58	3.78	+8.84

If you sum up the columns for percent edges, you will see that we have a combined positive 8.84 percent edge over the house for the assumed SRRs. This table gives us a lot of information. You can see that even with a 1:7 SRR on the come-out roll we still have close to a −12 percent edge to overcome. After we get past the come-out roll, we are in the catbird's seat. Another way to calculate the Don't shooter's edge from the table is as follows:

$$\frac{2{,}979 \text{ Don't Passes} - 2{,}495 \text{ Passes}}{5{,}474 \text{ Total Trials}} = \frac{484 \text{ Don't Passes} \times 100\%}{5{,}474 \text{ Trials}} = +8.8418\%$$

The SRRs assumed for the above example are reasonable, but you may do better!

Appendix C
Break-Even Analyses for the Place Bets

I will take you through a step-by-step method of deriving the break-even SRR for the 6, 8 Place bets. Then I will report the 5, 9 and 4, 10 SRRs, which were calculated in a similar fashion. First, we set the percent edge equation equal to zero percent, letting χ equal the number of 6s or 8s in our newly weighted frequency distribution.

$$[7/6 - 6/\chi] \times [\chi/(6+\chi)] \times 100\% = 0\%$$
$$\text{divide both sides by } 100\%$$
$$[7/6 - 6/\chi] \times [\chi/(6+\chi)] = 0$$
$$[7/6 \times (\chi/\chi) - 6/\chi \times (6/6)] \times [\chi/(6+\chi)] = 0$$
$$[(7\chi - 36)/6\chi] \times [\chi/(6+\chi)] = 0$$
$$(7\chi - 36)/(36 + 6\chi) = 0$$
$$7\chi/(36 + 6\chi) = 36/(36 + 6\chi)$$
$$7\chi = 36; \text{ then } \chi = 36/7 \text{ or } 5.143$$

You need to throw 5.143, 6s or 8s versus six 7s to break even. We can now calculate the weighting factor used to create the 6, 8 break-even frequency histogram below. The weighting factor equals 5.143 (required) divided by 5.000 (random) = 1.029. The resulting histogram looks like this:

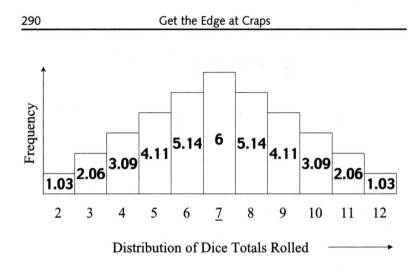

Distribution of Dice Totals Rolled $\longrightarrow$

Figure C-1
1:6.143 SRR Frequency Distribution
(Six 7s in 36.857 Trials)

1.029 x 30 = 30.857 non-7 numbers + six 7s = 36.857 total numbers in our histogram. Finally, we can calculate the SRR needed to break even for the 6 or 8 Place bet as follows:

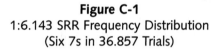

36.857/6 = 6.143

That's right, the SRR needed to break even with the 6 or 8 placed is only 1: 6.143. Another way to look at it is that seven 7s in 42 rolls is random, but seven 7s in 43 rolls is break-even. 7 x 6.143 = 43 rolls. 1/43rd (or 2.326 percent) influence is all that is needed to break even for the 6 or 8 Place bet. You do not need to *control* the dice to profit at craps. All that is needed is a minute amount of *influence*! Because the house vig is smaller on the Pass Line bet as compared to the 6, 8 Place bet, a shooter with an SRR of 6.143 will make modest sums if he makes a Pass Line bet with odds and Places the 6 and 8 (a wash) only. Imagine how much havoc a shooter with a 1: 8 or even a 1: 7 SRR can cause!

Incidentally, the break-even SRR for the 5 or 9 Place bet works out to be 1: 6.357 with 5/89 or 5.618 percent influence needed.

Similarly, the 4 or 10 Place bet requires an SRR of 1: 6.556, requiring a lofty 8.475 percent (5/59) of influence.

For this reason I usually employ the Place bet pyramid strategy described in Chapter 9, starting with two units on the 6 and 8, one unit on the 5 and 9, and no units on the 4 or 10.

6 or 8 Place Bet: Random, Skilled, and Infinite SRRs

I have calculated percent edges for different Place bets at various SRR levels. Here is a subset to show what some of these look like for the 6, 8 Place bet.

SRR 1:6 (random): six 7s versus five 6s or 8s =
6/5 correct payoff
[7/6 actual payoff – 6/5 correct payoff] x 5/11 probability x 100% =
-1.515% edge

SRR 1:7 (skilled): five 7s versus five 6s or 8s =
5/5 correct payoff
[7/6 actual payoff – 5/5 correct payoff] x 5/10 probability x 100% =
+8.333% edge

SRR 1:∞ (infinite): zero 7s versus five 6s or 8s =
0/5 correct payoff
[7/6 actual payoff – 0/5 correct payoff] x ∞/(∞ + B) x 100% =
↑   ↑   ↑
0   limit approaches 1   some finite constant
+116.667% max. edge

Appendix D

Advantage Calculations for Hard Way Bets

The advantage calculations for the Hard Way bets are made in the manner as they are for the Place bets. The actual payoff minus the fair payoff times the probability of hitting the hard way combination times 100 percent. The fair payoff is altered because of the skill level. Calculations are included for an SRR of 6, 7, 8, and 9. Frequency histograms are included for SRRs 8 and 9.

1:6 SRR

Hard 6, 8: Pays 9 to 1 instead of 10 to 1 for a random distribution.

$$(9/1 - 10/1) \times 1/11 \times 100\% = -9.091\%$$

Hard 4,10: Pays 7 to 1 instead of 8 to 1 for random distribution.

$$(7/1 - 8/1) \times 1/9 \times 100\% = -11.111\%$$

1:7 SRR

With a 1:7 SRR, there are now five 7s plus four easy 6s or 8s versus one hard 6 or 8. For the hard 4 or 10 scenario, there are five 7s plus two easy 4s or 10s, or seven versus one hard 4 or 10. So the calculations look like this:

Hard 6, 8: Pays 9 to 1 instead of 9 to 1 (actually a fair payoff) for a 1:7 distribution.

$$(9/1 - 9/1) \times 1/10 \times 100\% = 0.000\%$$

Hard 4,10: Pays 7 to 1 instead of 7 to 1 (this is a fair payoff also) for a 1:7 distribution.

$$(7/1 - 7/1) \times 1/8 \times 100\% = 0.000\%$$

1:8 SRR

The 1 to 8 frequency distribution chart was not included previously, so I am including it here. Notice that there are 48 total outcomes with six 7s. The non-7 numbers are proportionally weighted to fill the 42 remaining occurrences:

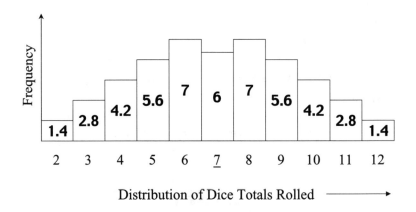

Figure D-1
1:8 SRR Frequency Distribution
(Six 7s in 48 Trials)

The numbers can get to be large, so I am using fractional values. With an SRR of 8, there are six 7s plus 5.6 easy 6s or 8s, for a total of 11.6 versus 1.4 ways to a hard 6 or 8. For the hard 4 or 10 scenario, there are also six 7s plus 2.8 easy 4s or 10s, which is 8.8 versus 1.4 hard 4s or 10s. So the calculations will look like this:

Hard 6, 8: Pays 9 to 1 instead of 11.6 to 1.4 for a 1:8 distribution.

$$(9/1 - 11.6/1.4) \times 1.4/13 \times 100\% = +7.692\%$$

Hard 4,10: Pays 7 to 1 instead of 8.8 to 1.4 for a 1:8 distribution.

$$(7/1 - 8.8/1.4) \times 1.4/10.2 \times 100\% = +9.804\%$$

1:9 SRR

Because it was not included previously, the 1 to 9 frequency distribution is being shown here, below. There are 54 total results with six 7s. The 48 non-7 numbers are weighted to fill the remaining occurrences proportionally:

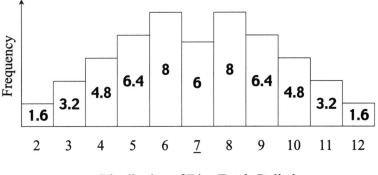

Distribution of Dice Totals Rolled ⟶

Figure D-2
1:9 SRR Frequency Distribution
(Six 7s in 54 Trials)

With a 1:9 SRR, there are six 7s plus 6.4 easy 6s or 8s, for a total of 12.4 ways to lose versus 1.6 hard 6s or 8s to win. The hard 4 or 10 scenario has six 7s plus 3.2 easy 4s or 10s, which is 9.2 ways to lose versus 1.6 ways to a hard 4 or hard 10. The calculations follow:

Hard 6, 8: Pays 9 to 1 instead of 12.4 to 1.6 for a 1:9 distribution.

$$(9/1 - 12.4/1.6) \times 1.6/14 \times 100\% = +14.286\%$$

Hard 4,10: Pays 7 to 1 instead of 9.2 to 1.6 for a 1:9 distribution.

$$(7/1 - 9.2/1.6) \times 1.6/10.8 \times 100\% = +18.519\%$$

Appendix E
Crapless Craps

A newer twist on craps tries to put the squeeze on your bankroll. Several players have asked me about a different version of craps that they have seen in some Vegas and Southern casinos. It is referred to as Crapless Craps or Never-ever Craps. Anytime the casinos present a new game to the public, you can bet your bankroll that it is to their benefit to do so. Well, this is certainly true for the random shooter, but if you take a closer look at my analysis, you might be surprised. At first glance, this version of craps is alluring—even seductive. You cannot lose on the come-out roll! The 2, 3 and 12 are no longer natural losers; they become points with big odds payoffs. However, that is where the excitement ends. While it is true that the 2, 3, and 12 cannot hurt you on the come-out roll, they more than make up for it by becoming tough points to repeat. In addition, the 11 is no longer a natural winner on the come-out roll. It also becomes a tough point to make. Let us see how this works against us:

Table E-1
Making the Tough Points

For a Random (1:6) Sevens-to-Rolls Ratio

Point # Est.	Traditional Craps Win	Traditional Craps Lose	Crapless Craps Win	Crapless Craps Lose	% Gain over Regular Craps
2	0%	100%	1/7 = 14.29%	6/7 = 85.71%	+14.29%
3	0%	100%	1/4 = 25.00%	3/4 = 75.00%	+25.00%
12	0%	100%	1/7 = 14.29%	6/7 = 85.71%	+14.29%
11	100%	0%	1/4 = 25.00%	3/4 = 75.00%	−75.00%
Net Gain (or Loss) for Tough Points:					**−21.42%**

When a 2 or 12 is thrown on the come-out roll, we will repeat the point one-seventh of the time (one 2 or 12 versus six 7s) and seven-out six-sevenths for a random game. Because we traditionally lost 100 percent of the time when a 2 or 12 was thrown, we are gaining 14.29 percent more wins on our Pass Line bets. After the 3 is established, it will win one-quarter of the time (two 3s versus six 7s), for a net gain of 25 percent. However what they give you with one hand, they more than take away with the other. The 11, which previously won 100 percent of the time on the traditional come-out roll will, like the 3, now only win 25 percent of the time. This results in a loss of 75 percent for your Pass Line bet when an 11 is thrown. If you sum up the total net gains and losses for crapless craps versus traditional craps, you will see an average net loss of 21.42 percent for situations where any of these four numbers become your point.

On the come-out roll, you will either throw a 7 and win, or throw a non-7 and establish that number as your point. Now, just as you would in traditional craps, you must repeat that number before the 7 appears, in order to win. Come bets work similarly. You won't find any place on the layout for Don't bettors. That action is reserved for the house, and why not? It is enjoying a 5.382 percent overall edge versus the ordinary 1.414 percent edge against the Pass Line player with no odds. As the Pass Line bettor in this particular game, taking odds becomes important. A Pass Line player taking single odds knocks the edge down to 2.936 percent (versus 0.848 percent in traditional craps). Taking double odds will reduce the edge to 2.018 percent versus the traditional 0.606 percent. Other bets available will pay the same as in the regular version of the game. At only 1.515 percent vigorish, the 6, 8 Place bets are the best bets on the table, unless you are willing to take at least four times odds behind your Pass Line bet. The house's edge is about three and half times larger for this new twist on an old game for the random shooter. The following calculations show how this 5.382 percent casino advantage is arrived at. I included more of the longhand calculations than normal, for the odds bet calculations.

Table E-2
1:6 SRR Crapless Crap Stats

	Natural			Established Points							Totals
Dice Totals	7	2	3	4	5	6	8	9	10	11	12
Roll Totals:	2,310	385	770	1,155	1,540	1,925	1,925	1,540	1,155	770	385	13,860
Pass Wins:	2,310	55	193	385	616	875	875	616	385	193	55	6,557
Pass Loses:	0	330	578	770	924	1,050	1,050	924	770	578	330	7,303
Prob. of Win:	1/6	1/7	1/4	1/3	2/5	5/11	5/11	2/5	1/3	1/4	1/7	47.3%

The total number of rolls for this mathematical model:
13,860
The total number of Pass Line wins (naturals + point wins):
6,557
The total number of Pass Line losses (0 craps + point losses):
7,303

Pass Line Net = 6,557 wins − 7,303 losses = −746 units

Odds Net = odds won (6 & 8) + odds won (5 & 9) + odds won (4 & 10) + odds won (3 & 11) + odds won (2 & 12) − 7,303 units (number of total point losses)

Odds won on each point number =
Payoff x Number of Rolls x Probability of a Win

Odds won (6 or 8) = 6/5 x 1925 x 5/11 = 1050 for each, x 2 for both: 2,100

Odds won (5 or 9) = 3/2 x 1540 x 2/5 = 924 for each, x 2 for both: 1,848

Odds won (4 or 10) = 2/1 x 1155 x 1/3 = 770 for each, x 2 for both: 1,540

Odds won (3 or 11) = 3/1 x 770 x 1/4 = 577.5 for each, x 2 for both: 1,155

Odds won (2 or 12) = 6/1 x 385 x 1/7 = 330 for each, x 2 for both: 660

Total Odds Won: **7,303**

Odds Net = total odds won – total Pass Line losses = 7,303 – 7,303 = 0 (which is expected for random). 13,860 total rolls minus 2,310 natural wins on the come-out leaves 11,550 point rolls. We can now calculate the house advantage for different odd bet situations:

Zero Odds:

Pass Line Units Wagered   = 13,860 rolls x 1 unit   =13,860 units

Odds Amount Wagered   = 11,550 rolls x 0 units   = 0 units

Total Wagered = P.L. + Odds   = 13,860 units + 0 units =13,860 units

Player's Win = P.L. Net + Odds Net = –746 units + 0 units   =–746 units

Player's Advantage = Player's Win/ Total Wagered = –746 units/13,860 units = – 5.382 percent

1 x Odds:

Pass Line Units Wagered   = 13,860 rolls x 1 unit   = 13,860 units

Odds Amount Wagered   = 11,550 rolls x 1 unit   = 11,550 units

Total Wagered = P.L. + Odds   =13,860 + 11,550 units   = 25,410 units

Player's Win = P.L. Net + Odds Net = –746 units + 0 units   =–746 units

Player's Advantage = Player's Win/ Total Wagered = –746 units/25,410 units = –2.936 percent

2 x Odds:

Pass Line Units Wagered   = 13,860 rolls x 1 unit   = 13,860 units

Odds Amount Wagered   = 11,550 rolls x 2 units   = 23,100 units

Total Wagered = P.L. + Odds   = 13,860 + 23100 units   = 36,960 units

Player's Win = P.L. Net + Odds Net = –746 units + 0 units   =–746 units

Player's Advantage = Player's Win/ Total Wagered = –746 units/36,960 units = –2.018 percent

3 x Odds:

Pass Line Units Wagered	= 13,860 rolls x 1 unit	=13,860 units
Odds Amount Wagered	= 11,550 rolls x 3 units	=34650 units
Total Wagered = P.L. + Odds	= 13,860 + 34,650 units	=48,510 units
Player's Win = P.L. Net + Odds Net	= –746 units + 0 units	=–746 units

Player's Advantage = Player's Win/ Total Wagered = –746 units/48510 units = –1.538 percent

5 x Odds:

Pass Line Units Wagered	= 13,860 rolls x 1 unit	= 13,860 units
Odds Amount Wagered	= 11,550 rolls x 5 units	= 57,750 units
Total Wagered = P.L. + Odds	= 13,860 + 57,750 units	= 71,610 units
Player's Win = P.L. Net + Odds Net	= –746 units + 0 units	= –746 units

Player's Advantage = Player's Win/ Total Wagered = –746 units/71,610 units = – 1.042 percent

10 x Odds:

Pass Line Units Wagered	= 13,860 rolls x 1 unit	= 13,860 units
Odds Amount Wagered	= 11,550 rolls x 10 units	=11,5500 units
Total Wagered = P.L. + Odds	= 13,860 + 115,500 units	=129,360 units
Player's Win = P.L. Net + Odds Net	= –746 units + 0 units	=–746 units

Player's Advantage = Player's Win/ Total Wagered = –746 units/129,360 units = – 0.577 percent

100 x Odds:

Pass Line Units Wagered	= 13,860 rolls x 1 unit	=13,860 units
Odds Amount Wagered	=11,550 rolls x 100 units	=1,155,000 units
Total Wagered = P.L. + Odds	=13,860 + 1,155,000 units	=1,168,860 units
Player's Win = P.L. Net + Odds Net	= –746 units + 0 units	=–746 units

Player's Advantage = Player's Win/ Total Wagered = –746 units/1,168,860 units = –0.064 percent

The random craps player gets pummeled pretty badly in this version, but what about an accomplished controlled thrower? Can he overcome the negative edge? Can he per-haps enjoy an even greater edge than he would see in the traditional game of craps? The answer to all of the above is yes, and I will show you why!

The following table summarizes about ten or 12 pages worth of probabilistic calculations for several skilled throw scenarios regarding the Pass Line wager. The Sevens-to-Rolls Ratio of 1:6, or random, uses the standard 36 possible dice outcomes with six 7s for its frequency distribution. An SRR of 1:7 uses a modified frequency distribution where five 7s in 35 outcomes are possible and the SRR of 1:8 uses a frequency table of 48 outcomes with six 7s (see an earlier portion of this chapter).

Table E-3
Pass Line Edges for Various SRRs

Game:	Crapless Craps			Traditional Craps		
SRR	1 in 6	1 in 7	1 in 8	1 in 6	1 in 7	1 in 8
No Odds	-5.38%	1.52%	7.60%	-1.41%	4.48%	5.02%
1 x Odds	-2.94%	6.20%	14.23%	-0.85%	7.08%	11.38%
2 x Odds	-2.02%	7.95%	16.71%	-0.61%	8.20%	14.03%
3 x Odds	-1.54%	8.87%	18.01%	-0.47%	8.82%	15.49%
5 x Odds	-1.04%	9.82%	19.36%	-0.33%	9.49%	17.04%
10 x Odds	-0.58%	10.71%	20.61%	-0.19%	10.15%	18.54%

Look at the 1:6 column (random) for crapless craps. Note how large the house vigorish is as compared to the 1:6 column (random) for plain old craps. This was the original intent of the game's creation. It appears to be a wolf in sheep's clothing. Now look what happens as we examine the edge for a player with a 1:7 SRR. He is now playing with a positive edge of 1.515 percent when no odds are taken. Follow the column down. Something interesting happens once you reach three times odds. Compare this value to the 1:7 SRR player at three times odds playing regular craps and you will note the same skilled thrower actually fares better with crapless craps! From here on down the column, and into the next column (1:8 SRR) the same controlled thrower will continue to command a greater advantage. What has happened? Well, essentially the frequency distribution for the 2, 3, 11, and 12 have sufficiently increased enough (because of the shooter's level of skill) to leverage these numbers against the casino. In other words, at random or 1:6 SRR, you are shortchanged on your winning payoff, but an expert shooter (say 1:8 SRR) is hitting the non-7s at a rate that is 40 percent higher. He effectively has created a double-edged sword that enables him to leverage the payoffs and create overages. Look at the table below for the 1:8 SRR shooter. Compare this data to that found in the Table E-1 for a random thrower.

Table E-4
Making the Tough Points

For a Skilled (1:8) Sevens-to-Rolls Ratio

Point # Est.	Traditional Craps		Crapless Craps		% Gain over Regular Craps
	Win	Lose	Win	Lose	
2	0%	100%	7/37 = 18.92%	30/37 = 81.08%	+18.92%
3	0%	100%	7/22 = 31.82%	15/22 = 68.18%	+31.82%
12	0%	100%	7/37 = 18.92%	30/37 = 81.08%	+18.92%
11	100%	0%	7/22 = 31.82%	15/22 = 68.18%	−68.18%
Net Gain (or Loss) for Tough Points:					**+1.48%**

So, what does all this mean? In a nutshell, Crapless Craps is an expert level game that has distinct advantages for 1:8 SRR players. It is marginally better for 1:7 SRR players taking triple odds or 1:7.5 SRR players with double odds behind their Pass Line wagers.

Additional points to remember:

- Place bet the 5, 6, 8, and 9 the same way you would in traditional craps.
- Buy the 2, 3, 11, or 12 just like you would buy the 4 or 10.

- Regarding random throwers—Place the 6, 8, or Come bet if you are taking at least four times odds. However, realize that Come betting in traditional craps is much easier on the bankroll.
- There is no Don't betting available in this game.
- As always, tread lightly with the hard ways and proposition bets.

Wrapping It Up

Well, there you have it! By analyzing the optimal dice sets when considering all possible ranges of relative dice motion, creating the best control grip, discovering the most efficient method to deliver the dice and putting a scientific background behind it all, I hope that I helped to set aside some of the myths concerning dice control. Don't get me wrong. It is not something that you pick up in a week or two of casual practice. Like anything worthwhile, it will take a concerted effort. But, you now hold the blueprint for success in your hands. I believe that anyone sufficiently motivated can learn these skills. I have held no information back; everything is included in this primer. You have the instructional experience of over 600 (and still counting) serious students, whom I have personally instructed and worked with on actual craps tables. There are over ten man-years of work and experience in this book—experience that I originally never intended to share. What you do from this point on is up to you. It is what you make of it. I wish each one of you the best of success. For those of you who are interested in further study and personal lessons and form critique from the Sharpshooter, read on.

Sharpshooter's Course on Dice Setting and Precision Shooting

There are some books that you can read and web sites that you can visit where you can pick up different aspects about setting and controlling the dice. Many gamblers have read a book that I co-authored with Jerry Patterson, *Casino Gambling*, where we dedicated an entire section to controlled throwing. Some of the readers were able to develop their own rhythm rolls. This book you are reading is dedicated entirely to controlled throwing and encompasses all of the up-to-date techniques developed. However, the serious precision shooter, the one who wants to correctly learn the methods and develop the proper muscle memory habits, will consider taking the course on precision dice shooting that I have developed. The two most important reasons for this are *time* and *money*.

It could take you several months to figure everything out and apply it to your throw. Along the way, you could incur many unnecessary losses. My course is your short-cut and will expedite your learning process, saving you time in getting up to speed with your precision shooting and saving you money on unnecessary losses which may occur if you are not really influencing the dice but only think you are. You can elevate your game into the profit arena and generate winnings much quicker.

How will my course accomplish this?

To start, we break the learning process into five elements, or linchpins, of dice control: the set, grip, and throw are the *mechanical linchpins*, the physical ones that tip the house odds to your side of the table; the "zone" is the *mental linchpin* which involves focus and concentration; betting/money management is the *financial linchpin*. All five of these are crucial to permanently and consistently creating and profiting from your advantage.

My dice setting and precision shooting course addresses each of these five linchpins in a unique and all encompassing learning program featuring home study and practice, classroom instruction, videotape instruction, dealer school workshop, and one-on-one instruction to assess your grip and controlled throw. This is followed up with Internet support and e-mail networking with other students for joint casino play. This course has graduated over 600 dice shooters since I developed it in 1996.

For a detailed newsletter describing the course, contact me using the coupon at the back of this book or visit my Web site at *www.Sharpshootercraps.com.*

Index

Contact Sharpshooter

Phone: (800) 211-9666
E-mail: Sharpshooter@Sharpshootercraps.com
Web Site: www.Sharpshootercraps.com
Or mail this form to: Sharpshooter; P.O. Box 236; Gardnerville, NV 89410-0236

Dear Sharpshooter,

    I want more information about how to become a Precision Dice Shooter and command an advantage over the casino. Please send a detailed newsletter about your Study Program which includes: Home Study and Practice, Classroom Lectures and Dealer School Workshops hosted in casino cities, an E-mail network of other controlled dice throwers for posing questions, comments and connecting in the casino for joint play and critique.

    I understand that your program is fully guaranteed and that there is no obligation to purchase.

    Also send me the free information I have checked below:

[ ]   Your free Precision Dice Shooting Newsletter

[ ]   A list of your recommended Web Sites featuring precision dice shooting

[ ]   Please send information about updates or other items noted in this book; specifically I am interested in the following: _____

_____

_____

Name:_____
Street Address:_____
City/State/Zip:_____
Telephone (optional):_____
E-mail:_____

FRANK SCOBLETE BEST-SELLERS

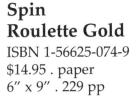